Painting European FOLK ART

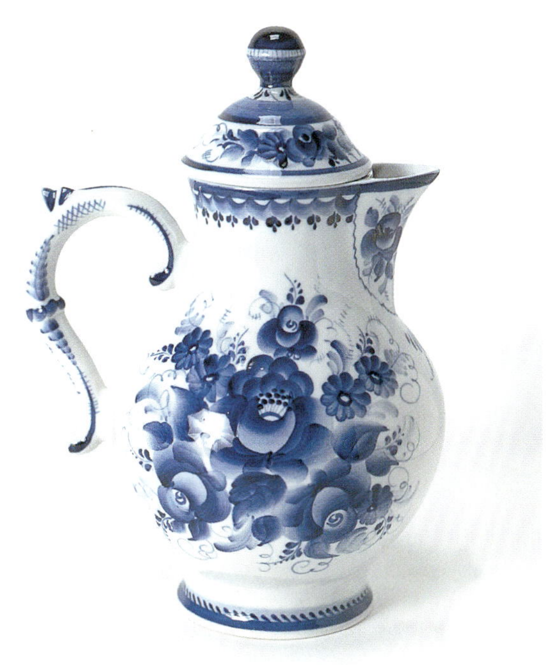

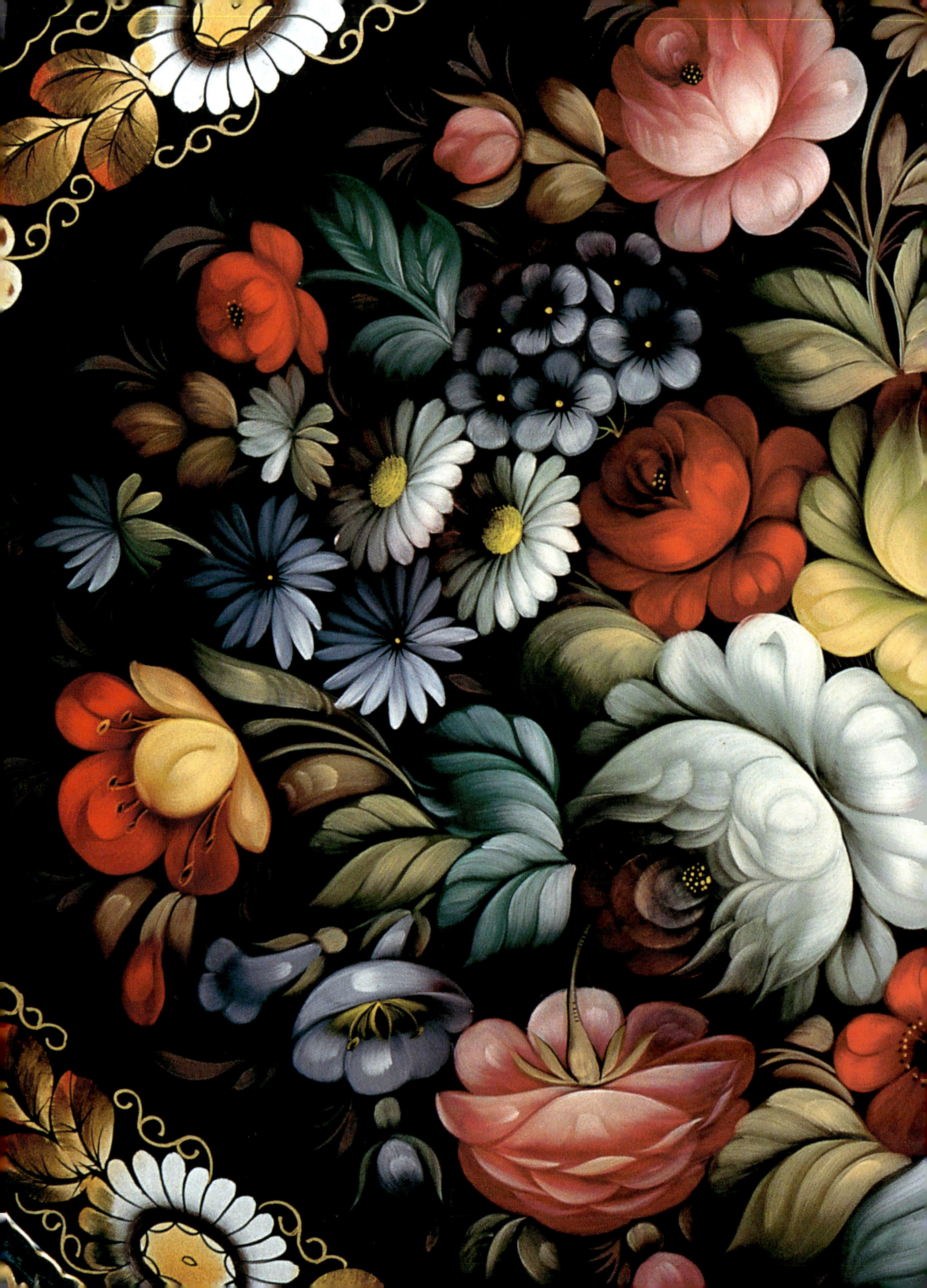

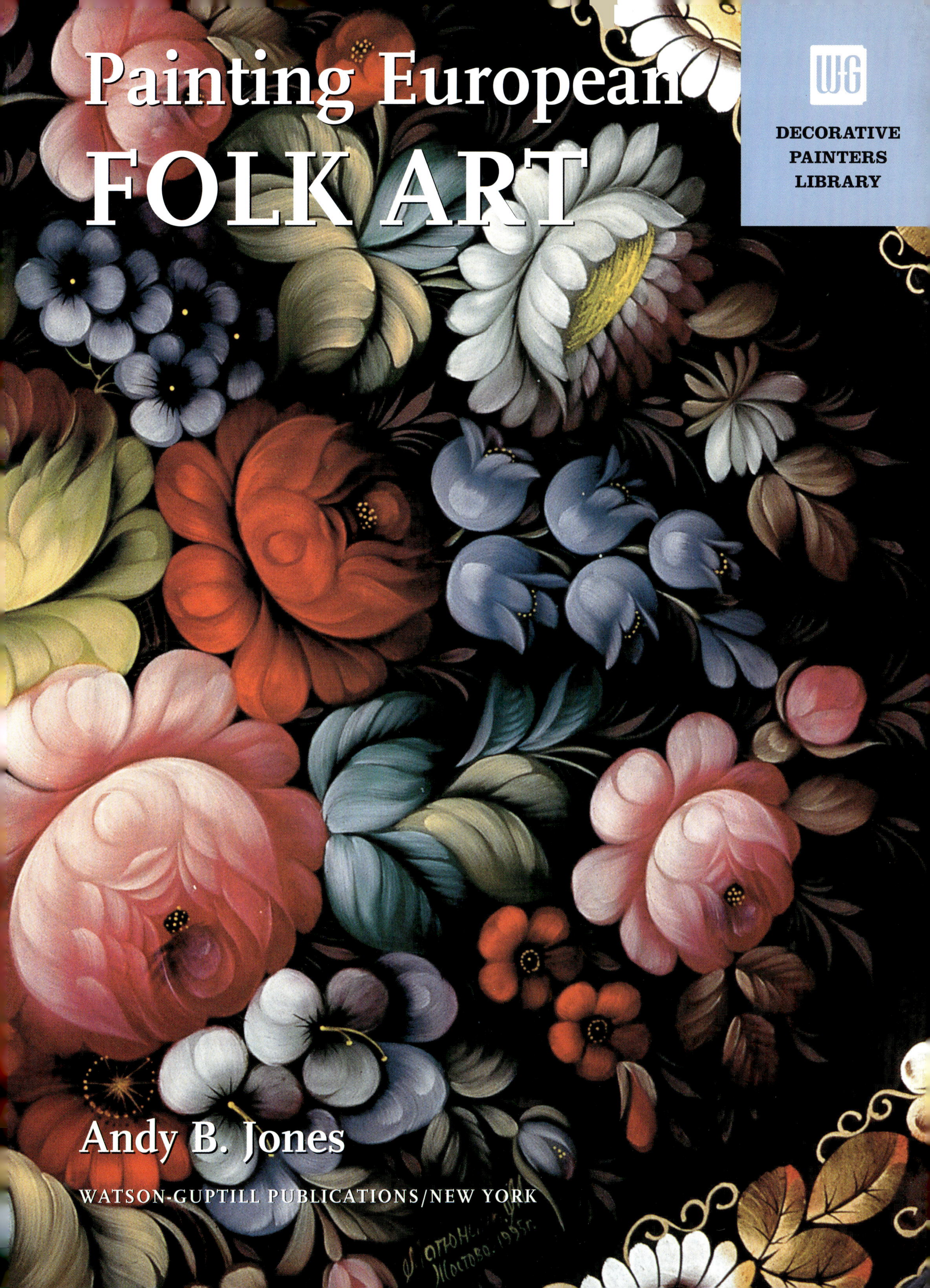

Painting European FOLK ART

DECORATIVE PAINTERS LIBRARY

Andy B. Jones

WATSON-GUPTILL PUBLICATIONS/NEW YORK

Half-title page: Gzhel coffeepot. Courtesy of Marybeth Ray.
Title page: Zhostovo tray. Courtesy of Phillip C. Myer.

Senior Acquisitions Editor: Candace Raney
Senior Developmental Editor: Joy Aquilino
Edited by Sarah Fass
Designed by Areta Buk
Graphic production by Ellen Greene

First published in 2001 by Watson-Guptill Publications,
a division of BPI Communications, Inc.,
770 Broadway, New York, NY 10003
www.watsonguptill.com

Library of Congress Cataloging-in-Publication Data
Jones, Andy (Andy B.)
Painting European folk art : Andy B. Jones.
p. cm. -- (Decorative painter's library)
Includes index.
ISBN 0-8230-1283-2
1. Acrylic painting--Technique. 2. Folk art--Europe. 3. Decoration and ornament--Europe. I. Title. II. Series.

TT385 .J66 2001
745.7'23--dc21 00-061462

Printed in Malaysia

First printing, 2001

1 2 3 4 5 6 7 8 9 / 09 08 07 06 05 04 03 02 01

Contents

Introduction

The types and styles of European folk art are as varied as the cultures that populate the continent. European folk artists exhibit joy and vibrancy in all of their art forms, from woodcarving to embroidery to painting to the multitude of others that have flourished in Europe over the centuries. To trace the development of all of these forms would be a lifelong task, and I am a painter, not a historian. However, I would like to share with you some of the characteristics of the different decorative painting styles presented in this book.

ENGLISH FOLK ART

English folk art is generally related to textiles, but there is one noteworthy exception: narrow boat painting. Beginning in the 1800s, narrow boats were used to move goods through England's extensive canal system, and the transit companies that owned the boats frequently employed artists to decorate them. The artists working for each company developed a unique style, including a distinctive "rose," which was the most common motif. Rose motifs were also frequently used on the *buckby cans* (water cans) that were prominently displayed on the boats. The charming floral and geometrical designs used by narrow boat painters were applied with enamel paint augmented with artists' oil colors. The traditional colors were green, white, red, and yellow, but pink was also occasionally used for rose forms.

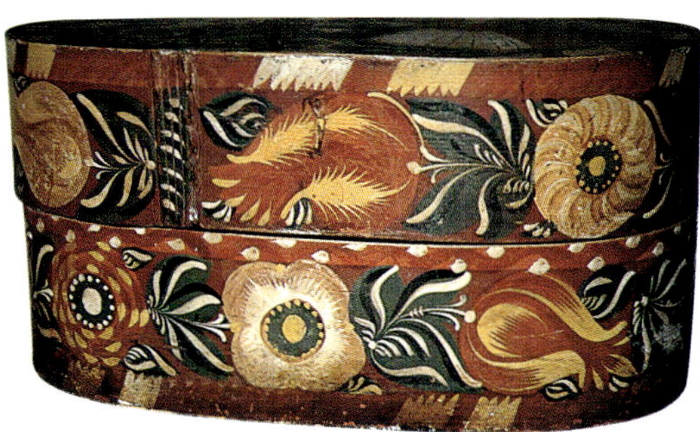

The happy couple pictured on the lid of this bride's box is surrounded by floral motifs, including blossoms and tulips. Note that the sides of the box are also decorated in the Bauernmalerei style.

GERMAN FOLK ART

By the late 1700s, German folk artists had developed a delightful painting style called Bauernmalerei, which translates roughly to "farmer painting." From the beginning, there were as many different styles of Bauernmalerei as there were practitioners of the art form. While many of the pieces included simple, lovely flower forms—including tulips, roses, and small blossoms—and, less frequently, birds, each artist developed a distinctive way of presenting the different forms. Some of the painting styles were very crude, while others showed a high level of skill. One thing the pieces had in common was their bright coloration. Popular colors included blues, reds, whites, and yellows. The passage of time has led to a mellowing of the appearance of older pieces, which now have a beautiful patina. The Bauernmalerei style was used to decorate many different types of household objects, including boxes, trunks, and *shranks* (armoires).

DUTCH FOLK ART

In the 17th and 18th centuries, the Netherlands was a major maritime power with a booming shipping industry. Dutch sailors produced beautiful woodcarvings to adorn their ships and homes. During the winter, when the canals and ports were frozen, they also painted household items to liven their interiors. Early folk paintings were generally attempts to imitate the appearance of carved wood, so they were done in one color on a natural wooden background. Later, the addition of color brought about a dramatic change in Dutch folk painting. Another factor in the development of Dutch folk art was the influence of Scandinavian painting and carving, which was introduced to Holland via trade.

The Hindeloopen style of painting developed in the northern port town of the same name in the late 1700s. There are two distinct "schools" of Hindeloopen painting, each named after the original practitioner of the style. The older school is Roosje, founded by Arend Roosje; later, Gerard Huttinga founded a second school. Both schools produce beautiful folk art. The Huttinga style is painted with bright colors. Its most recognizable technique mimics the look of Dutch Delft porcelain by using shades of only one color. The Roosje style is typically painted with darker colors, and the designs are primarily symmetrical.

Completely different in appearance is the Assendelfter style of painting, which originated in the northern town of Assendelft in the 17th century. This style is more refined and more elaborate than the Roosje and Huttinga styles. While most folk painting stylizes a few motifs, the Assendelfter style incorporates literally dozens of natural motifs, including flowers, fruits, and birds. The development of Assendelfter painting is a good illustration of how a country's economic situation can affect its folk art. At first, peasants painted dowry chests, candlesticks, and other household items in this style both to brighten up their homes during the winter months and as a secondary source of income. Later, as the Netherlands became a maritime superpower and its citizens grew wealthier, the folk art they produced became more elaborate, and the more affluent homes often had elaborately painted walls and furniture in addition to the smaller domestic objects.

RUSSIAN FOLK ART

The Russian folk arts are varied and demonstrate the ingenuity of the Russian people; each region has a special type of folk art for which it is known. One of the most admired Russian folk art forms is miniature lacquerware, which comes from the towns and villages surrounding Moscow. Early Russian lacquer paintings were copies of Chinese lacquer that had made its way to Russia through trade. The manufacture of lacquerware in Russia dates at least as far back as 1720, when artists were commissioned to paint panels in the Chinese style for Peter the Great. Over time, the Russian artists became extremely adept at lacquer painting, and miniature painting in particular. They began to decorate papier-mâché boxes with floral motifs and scenes from Russian fairy tales. Before the Revolution of 1917, most of the artists in the four miniature-painting centers—the villages of Fedoskino, Palekh, Kholui, and Mstera—engaged in the painting of icons. However, after the revolution, a new art form of miniature painting developed because the church was no longer able to support the painting of icons. Since the breakdown of the Communist system of government in Russia, icon-painting has returned as an art form. Fortunately, secular miniature-painting also continues.

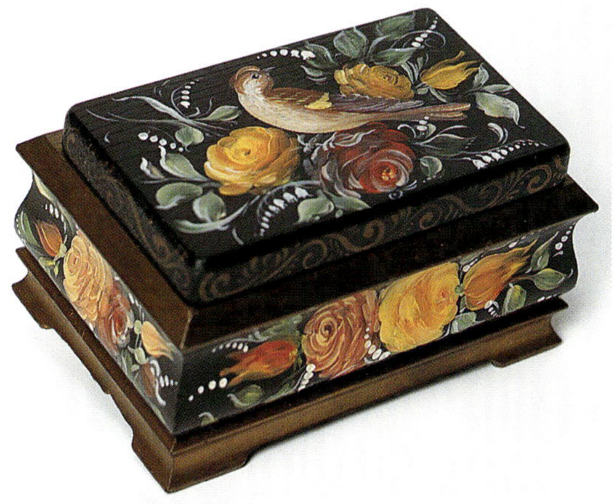

A contemporary example of authentic Assendelfter painting, this box was painted by Dutch National Flower Painter Jacques Zuidema.

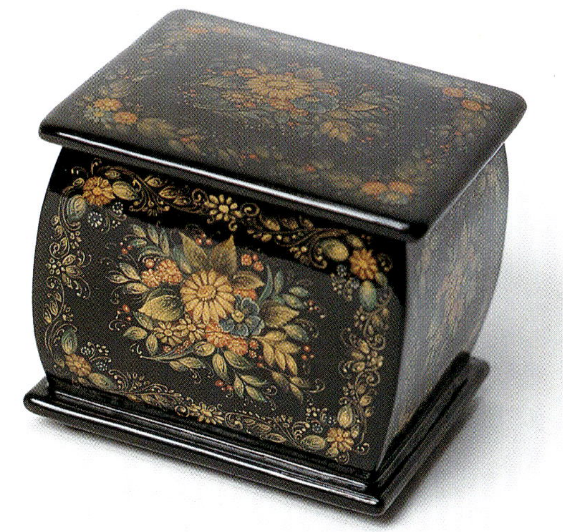

This box from Mstera shows elaborate floral decoration. The delicate painting and the minute detail are typical of the Russian craftsmen who paint these tiny pieces—usually without magnification.

Gzhel is a traditional Russian white porcelain painted with shades of deep, intense blue. It is a monochromatic art form, which in this case means that the tints and shades of blue that appear on the pieces are actually several levels of transparency of just one color. The porcelain pieces often have extremely elaborate forms, and the decoration matches them. The Russian craftspeople who originated Gzhel porcelain were inspired by blue-and-white Chinese porcelain and Dutch Delftware, both of which entered the courts of the Russian Czars through trade. Gzhel is still being produced in Russia. It is extremely beautiful and collectible.

One of the most beautiful forms of Russian folk art originated in Zhostovo, a magical village about forty miles outside of Moscow. The magnificent floral painters who live and work there have created a vocabulary of graceful, stylized floral and fruit motifs that are simply breathtaking. Their use of color is stunning and

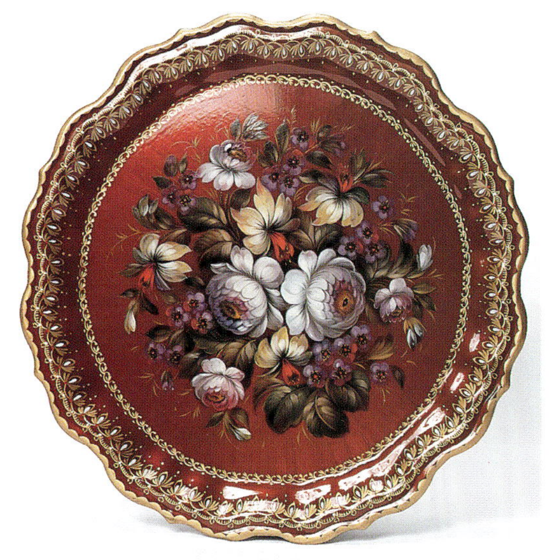

This tray was painted by a Zhostovo Master Artist, Nina Goncharova, whose trays are in museum collections around the world. It is painted on a metallic red background. Notice the elaborate border design on the tray. Contemporary Zhostovo artists paint on a variety of different surfaces, including boxes and wooden eggs.

the variety of motifs and designs is seemingly endless. These artists work in oils and dry their pieces in large ovens after each layer of paint has been applied.

NORWEGIAN FOLK ART

Norway is known for its embroidery and its rosemaling, or rose painting, which was traditionally painted in oil colors. Each region has a distinctive style of painting. Over the years, as an area became prosperous, its artists were able to travel to other parts of the country to see the kind of painting being done there. This travel brought external influences to the rosemaling of one area, yet each region's style remained unique. It would be virtually impossible to describe every type of rosemaling, and of course, each artist develops a unique way of painting each style. A variety of books about rosemaling is available; some are devoted to the history of the art form, while others teach different techniques.

Rogaland rosemaling is one of Norwegian folk art's most recognizable forms. Its designs contain graceful C or S scrolls; leaves with

This trunk was painted in Rogaland in 1847. It has a typically Norwegian deep blue background. Notice the symmetry, both of each individual design and of the trunk as a whole.

Photo: Vesterheim Norwegian-American Museum, Decorah, Iowa.

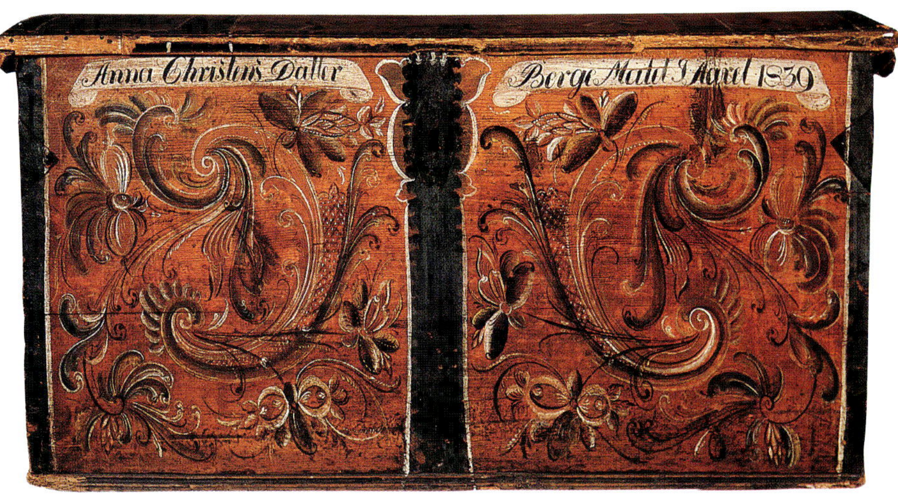

Painted in the Telemark style in 1839, this dowry chest is a quintessential piece of rosemaling. The free-flowing, asymmetric C and S scrolls and the elaborate floral forms are what we have come to expect from the Norwegian painting style. Notice how each design is different from the opposite design.

Photo: Vesterheim Norwegian-American Museum, Decorah, Iowa.

gently rounded ends; and a variety of flower forms, including tulips, blossoms, bonnet lilies, and roses. It is also characterized by symmetry and the use of cross-hatching.

Expressive, flowing scrollwork and asymmetrical designs characterize the Telemark style of rosemaling. It is the only style of rosemaling that may be painted with either an opaque or transparent technique. The designs are built around a "root" or central point of the design, from which scrolls and flowers are formed. Typical Telemark scrolls are formed in either S or C shapes; the flowers are asymmetrical and it is rare for two to be painted alike.

Valdres is one of the more stylized forms of rosemaling. Traditionally painted on blue, green, or black backgrounds, pieces in this style are characterized by pointed S-shaped leaves and rather complex flower forms. The designs are often asymmetrical and tend to have more overlapping elements and fewer scrolls than other rosemaling styles.

ABOUT THIS BOOK

My goal in writing *Painting European Folk Art* is to expose you to a variety of European folk art styles. To this end, I have included actual or historical pieces to whet your appetite for more, as well as presenting my own interpretations of these art forms, all painted with acrylics. I do not profess to have mastered all of these types of folk art; it would take several lifetimes to be able to achieve a high level of proficiency at all of these art forms. What I have done is given you some stylistic pointers and information so that you can continue to study the styles you decide you like best.

The collections of many fine art, folk art, craft, and historical museums throughout the United States include fine examples of European decorative painting. Take the time to seek these institutions out and study the treasures they house. Read books. Be open.

Try the different styles presented here, and then decide for yourself what you want to study further. The most important thoughts I can leave you with are to practice until you have good brush control (this will make painting anything you choose much easier) and to paint with a joyous heart. Exact replication of the projects is not important; what is important is that you have tried. With trying there is no failure. I urge you to use this book as the starting point on a journey that can last a lifetime and be filled with splendid discovery of both your own talents and the beauty created by the folk artists of the world.

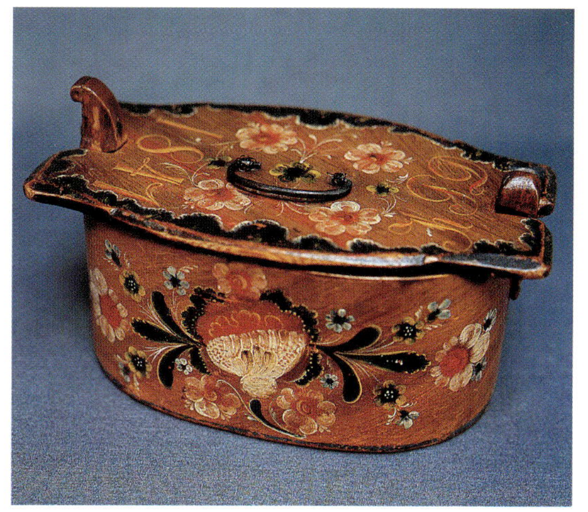

The tine box at left—used for storage—is from the Valdres region and was painted in 1847. The floral forms are more elaborate and complex than those painted in the other rosemaling styles.

Photo: Vesterheim Norwegian-American Museum, Decorah, Iowa.

THE DECORATIVE PAINTERS LIBRARY

The books in the Decorative Painters Library are designed to fulfill two goals. The first is to instruct beginning painters in the fundamentals of the craft. This essential information, which is covered in depth over three chapters, is then applied to achieve the second goal of the series: to give readers the means to create inspiring projects that feature patterns in a specific subject area. The instructions can be followed exactly as they appear, or adapted to accommodate the artist's personal tastes. A painter can choose a project that corresponds to his or her skill and confidence level by noting the "degree of difficulty" rating:

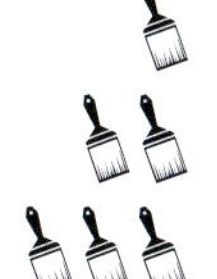

EASY

MODERATE

CHALLENGING

Whatever your interests and goals as an artist, I hope that this book encourages you to pursue your creative development. If your energies are focused on decorative painting, I urge you to join the Society of Decorative Painters, an international organization with hundreds of chapters across the United States. For more information, contact them at the following address:

Society of Decorative Painters
393 North McLean Boulevard
Wichita, Kansas 67203-5968
(316) 269-9300
http://www.decorativepainters.com/

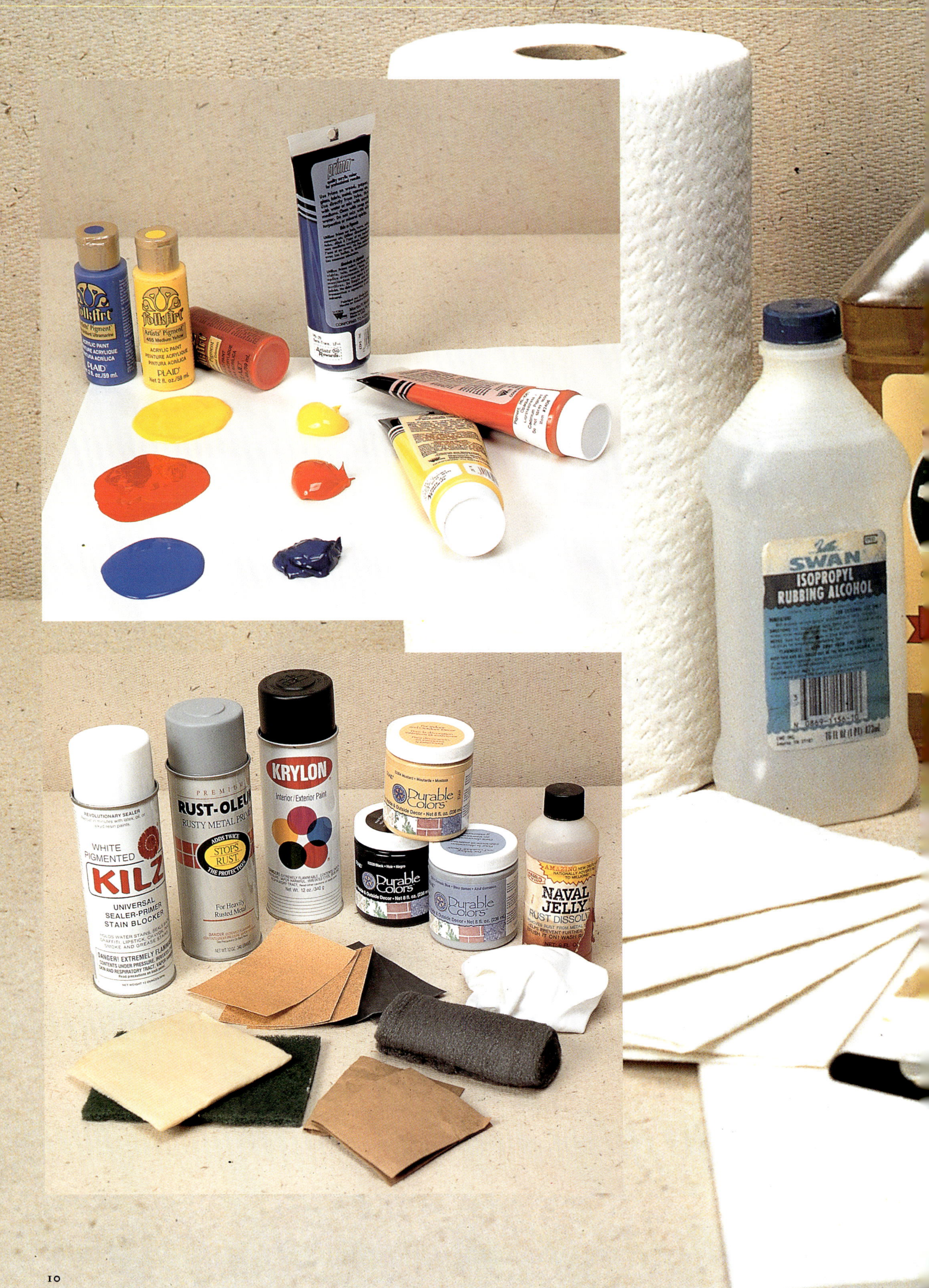

Artists' Pigment
ACRYLIC PAINT
PLAID
SWAN
ISOPROPYL
RUBBING ALCOHOL
KRYLON
Interior/Exterior Paint
WHITE
PIGMENTED
UNIVERSAL
SEALER-PRIMER
STAIN BLOCKER
STOPS RUST
For Heavily Rusted Metal
Durable Colors
NAVAL
JELLY

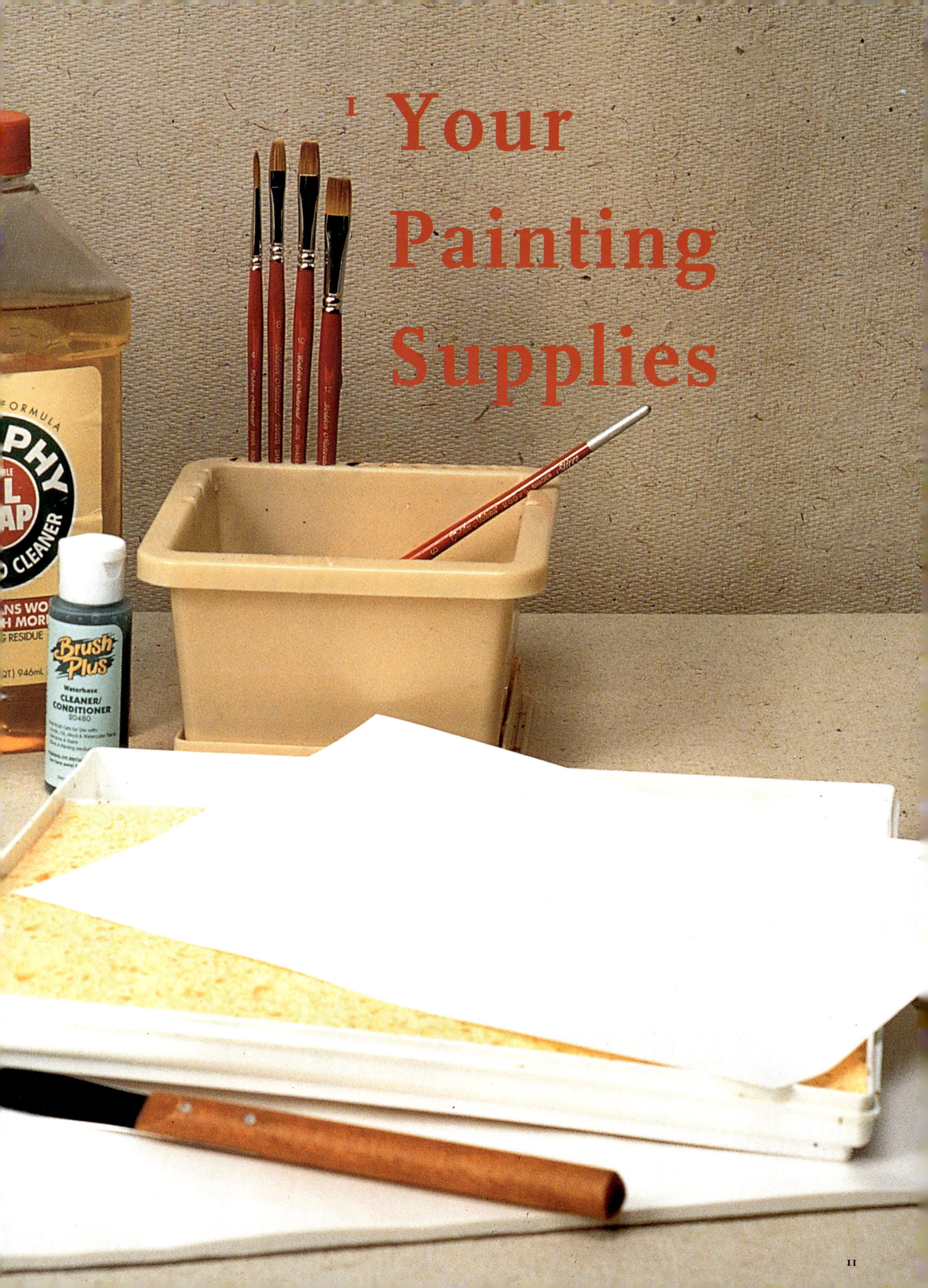

1 Your Painting Supplies

Working with Acrylic Paints

Originally introduced to the fine art and crafts markets during the 1950s, acrylic paints quickly gained popularity because of their bright, rich coloration, quick drying time, and ease of clean-up. Almost all of the painting techniques demonstrated in this book were originally done with oil paints, or with a type of modified oil-based paint called japan paint. I learned to paint with oil paints, then began using acrylics when they became popular, and today I use acrylic paints for most of my decorative painting projects. Recent advances in paint technology have made it possible to recreate the look of the old techniques with acrylic paints, making the process much easier.

Acrylic paints come in two varieties: *craft acrylics* and *artists' acrylics*. The colors of craft acrylics, which are labeled with descriptive color names like "barn red," are often created by mixing several pigments. Because the labels on these paints don't usually indicate which pigments were used to make a color, many times mixing two colors together can yield an unpleasant or unexpected result. Despite these limitations, using craft acrylics straight out of the bottle is fine for many applications, such as base-coating a project prior to painting a design.

Shown here are the two types of artists' acrylic paints. Squeeze-bottle acrylics *(left)* have a fluid consistency, while tube acrylics *(right)* are more gel-like.

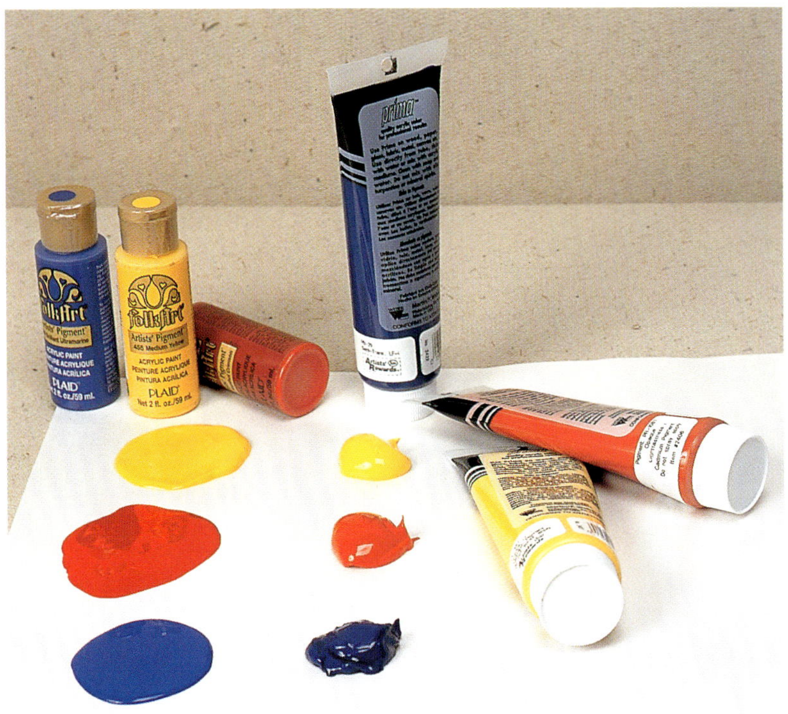

For painting designs, though, I prefer to use artists' acrylics. Sold in tubes or in 2-ounce plastic bottles, artists' acrylics contain pure pigments, and each color is identified by the name of the pigment that was actually used to impart color to the paint, such as burnt umber or naphthol crimson. This information is particularly important when mixing colors, since you always know which pigments you're using as well as the result you're likely to get.

WORKING PROPERTIES

Acrylic paints consist of pigments suspended in a polymer emulsion (a mixture of an acrylic resin binder and water). They dry in only 15 to 30 minutes; once dry, the paint film is waterproof. Acrylics allow an artist to execute a step, then let it dry completely (with no chance of smearing) before proceeding to the next step.

The most important reason for knowing about a paint's *working time*—the amount of time that you have to work with it before it begins to dry—is that it determines which methods you can use to blend colors during the painting process. When they're used straight from the bottle or tube, acrylics dry too rapidly to be applied one at a time and blended on the painting surface; if you attempt to do this you'll be fighting a losing battle with the intrinsic character of the paint. Instead, you must use techniques that take advantage of their rapid drying time. One option is to blend colors on the brush, then apply the already blended color to the surface and leave it alone to dry. You can do this in several different ways; see "Sideloading" (page 30) and "Doubleloading" (page 31) for more information.

It is possible to modify acrylic paints by adding *mediums,* which are compatible substances that allow artists to manipulate the character of paint. Sometimes a medium is added so that paint can be applied to a surface that isn't normally receptive to it (for example, glass). In this book, mediums are used primarily to extend the paint's working time for blending techniques such as working wet-in-wet (page 29), as well as to make beautifully translucent glazes for antiquing (page 41). See "Acrylic Mediums" (page 17) for more information.

BUYING PAINTS

When you shop for paints, don't feel you must buy every color that's on the shelf or in a specific product line. You can either purchase the colors on the materials lists that accompany each project, or you can learn to mix virtually any color using just a few bottles of paint. (See "Choosing and Using Color," page 27.) If you're new to color mixing, you may want to purchase some of the craft colors that are called for. Below is a complete list of colors that were used to paint the patterns in this book. (For some projects, it may be necessary to purchase or mix additional colors for basecoating.) I use FolkArt Artists' Pigments and FolkArt Acrylic Colors, which are manufactured by Plaid Enterprises and packaged in 2-ounce squeeze bottles. These paints are available at most art supply and craft stores.

PROJECTS PALETTE FOR *PAINTING EUROPEAN FOLK ART*

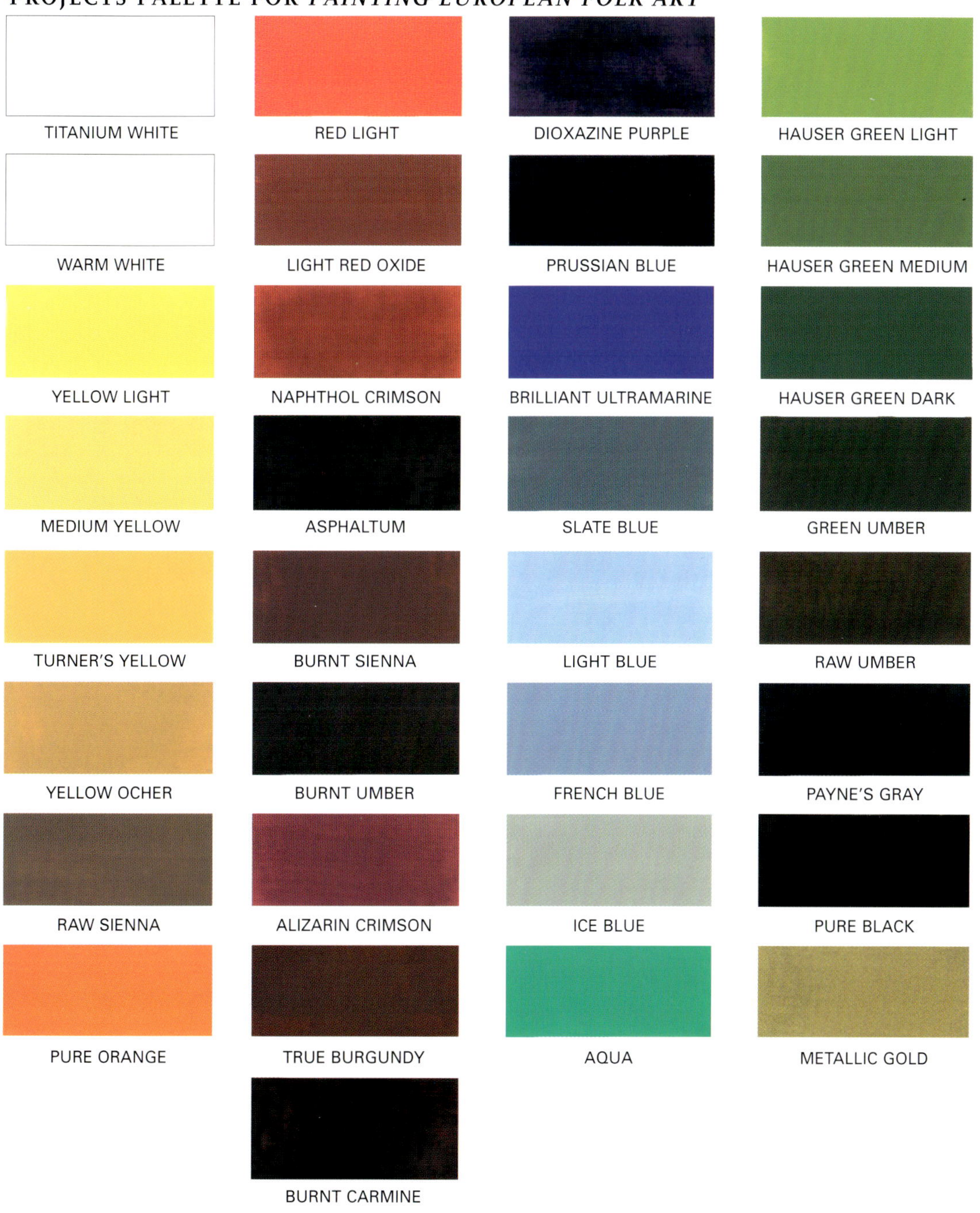

Selecting Your Brushes

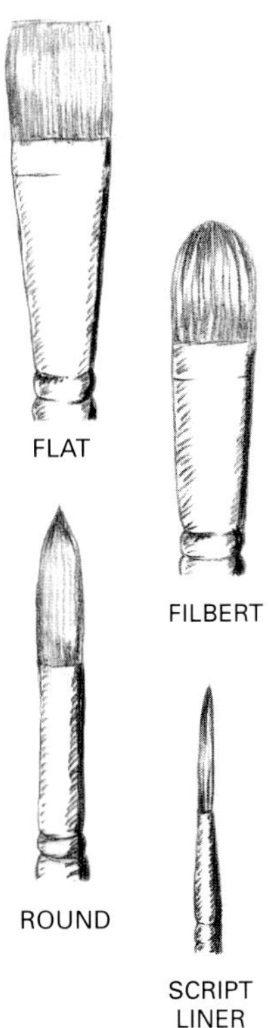

Basic brush shapes.

Without a doubt, brushes are your most important decorative painting tools. You should always use the best brushes that you can afford, as only good-quality brushes will allow you to achieve satisfactory results. Brushes of inferior quality will frustrate you because they won't perform properly. I find that my students' painting problems are often caused by inferior brushes, or by brushes that have been ruined by neglect. If you start with good-quality brushes and maintain them properly, they will perform well for many years.

BRUSH BASICS

HAIRS The word "hairs" is commonly used to refer to the part of the brush that holds and applies paint, though brushes can be made of animal hairs such as sable, squirrel, badger, and boar; synthetic fibers like nylon or polyester; or a combination of the two.

SHAPES The part of the brush in which the hairs are arranged is called a *ferrule*. Ordinarily made of metal, the ferrule also attaches the hairs to the handle. As explained below, the shape of the ferrule determines the shape of the hairs. The basic shapes of brushes used for decorative painting are flat, round, bright, and filbert. As the name suggests, the hairs of *flat* brushes are held in a flattened ferrule, and are all very close to the same length. *Brights* also have same-length hairs, but the hairs are shorter than regular flats. The hairs of *round* brushes are arranged in a cylindrical ferrule and taper to a soft point. *Liners* are small round brushes whose hairs taper to an extremely fine point. *Filberts* are also rounded at the end, but the hairs are held in a flat ferrule.

SIZES The sizes of most of the brushes you'll use for decorative painting are listed in catalogs by number—from 10/0 (the smallest) to 24. A size 2, for example, is about 1/8 inch; a size 10 is 3/8 inch. Sizes for larger brushes are often given in inches.

As you gather together a collection of brushes, buy every other size within a category, then fill in as needed. Of course, if you're going to paint primarily small things, purchase the smaller brushes first. If you're painting large things, don't forget to get a small brush for detail work.

DECORATIVE PAINTING BRUSH KIT

In addition to serving as an all-around basic decorative painting brush kit, the assortment of brushes listed below is used to create the European folk art projects in this book.

I use brushes manufactured by Silver Brush Limited for my decorative painting. Their brushes are superior in quality and available nationwide. Their Ruby Satin line is made with nylon hairs only, and their Golden Natural series is manufactured with a blend of synthetic filaments and animal hairs. I use the mixed-hair brushes for most of my work. The properties of the natural hair allow the brush to hold moisture and release it evenly, while the synthetic hair gives the brush "spring," or resiliency. Try several of each kind of brush to determine which work best for you.

- *Flats*. Golden Natural Series 2002S, nos. 4, 8, and 10. I use flat brushes for the majority of my decorative painting work because they are so versatile.
- *Rounds*. Golden Natural Series 2000S, nos. 4 and 6. Round brushes are necessary for creating beautiful brushstrokes, especially large comma strokes. Select brushes with fine points and full "bellies," or midsections, and make sure there are no stray hairs protruding from the ferrule. You'll have to "break in" your new brushes over three or four painting sessions before they will become more responsive to your hand.
- *Liners*. Golden Natural Series 2007S, no. 2 (script liner), Golden Natural Series 2005S, no. 2 (liner). Liners come in several different hair lengths; for example, spotters have very short hairs, and script liner, or scroll, brushes have very long hairs. Regular liners fall somewhere in the middle. Script liners are designed to hold a lot of paint. The one I recommend, which has very long hairs, can be used for most fine detail work. If you practice using this versatile brush, you will quickly become comfortable with the long hairs and appreciate its responsiveness. However, many painters find that the script liner's long hairs make it difficult to paint teardrop strokes with them. You will find it easier to use a regular liner brush when painting these strokes.
- *Filberts*. Ruby Satin Series 2503S, nos. 4, 6, and 8. Filberts are useful for highlighting.

Because their hairs have rounded corners, they don't leave the conspicuous marks that are sometimes left by flat brushes.

- *Wash brush.* Golden Natural Series 2008S, $^{3}/_{4}$ inch. This large flat brush is very useful for applying basecoats (see page 34) and for any decorative painting application where large areas must be covered with paint.
- *Mop brush.* Golden Natural Series C9090S, $^{3}/_{4}$ inch. This very soft brush, made from top-quality goat hair, is designed for very lightly blending and softening paints or glazes, and for softening background antiquing. It should *never* be used for paint application.
- *Glaze/varnish brush.* Series 9094S, 1 inch. This sturdy brush is far superior to a foam brush for the application of varnish in that it is much less likely to form air bubbles on the project surface. It can also be used to prime and basecoat small and medium-sized projects.

BRUSH CARE AND MAINTENANCE

The correct procedure for cleaning a brush must be mastered from the beginning, and your brushes must be cleaned after every painting session. Brushes will quickly be ruined if you allow paint to dry or harden in the bristles. No matter how skillful a painter you are, your work will suffer if you mistreat your brushes. With proper care and cleaning your brushes will perform as they were designed to, and should last for years.

Use water and a mild soap to clean brushes that have been used with acrylics. Rinse the brushes in cool, running water, working the bristles gently against the palm of your hand. As you rinse the brushes, add a small amount of brush cleaner or conditioner, or a mild vegetable oil–based liquid soap such as Murphy Oil Soap. Continue working the brush in your palm until no more color is released from the brush. Store the brushes bristle up in a glass or jar with nothing pressing on or bending the bristles.

Acrylic paint that has been allowed to dry in a brush can sometimes be removed by cleaning the brush in rubbing alcohol, which acts as a solvent, "melting" the paint so that you can loosen it from the hairs of the brush. Once you've loosened the paint, clean the brush with water and soap as described above. Alcohol is hard on brushes, so use this cleaning method only when absolutely necessary. The best strategy is to never allow paint to dry in your brush!

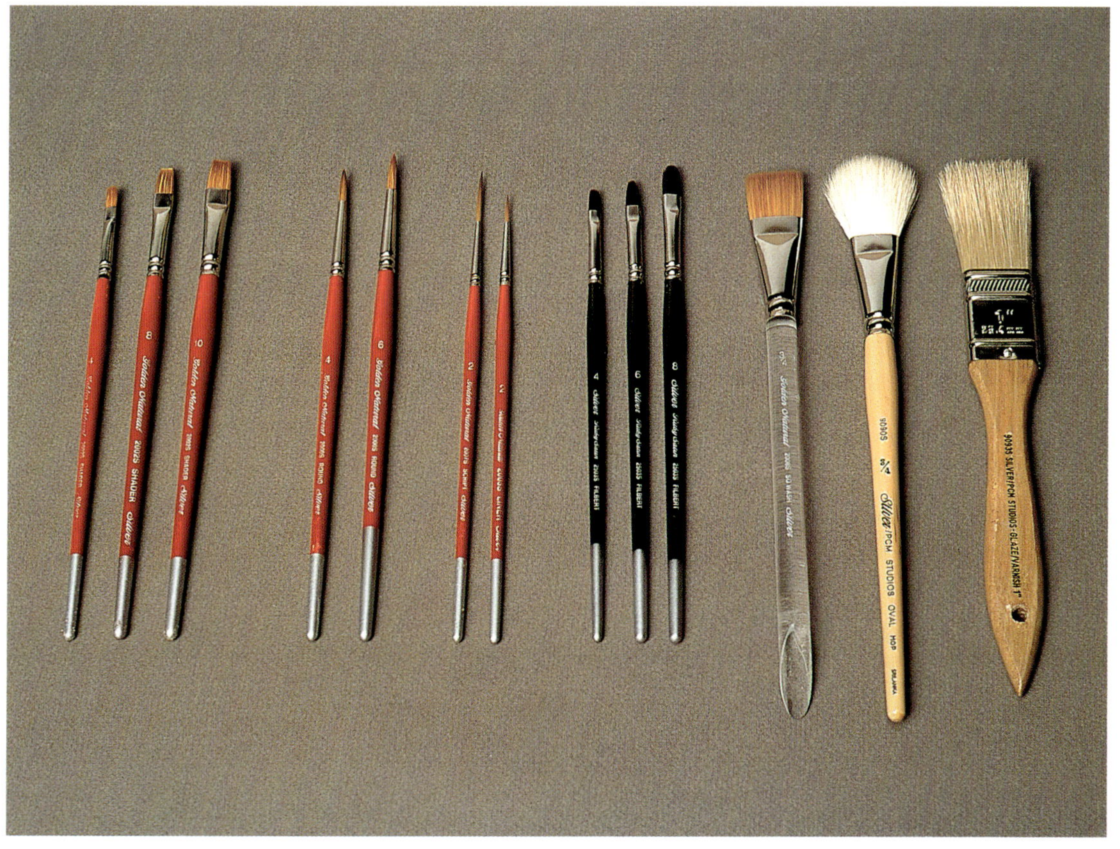

The brushes you'll need to create the projects in this book *(from left to right)*: nos. 4, 8, and 10 flats; nos. 4 and 6 rounds; a no. 2 script liner; a no. 2 liner; nos. 4, 6, and 8 filberts; a $^{3}/_{4}$-inch wash brush; a $^{3}/_{4}$-inch mop brush; and a 1-inch glaze/varnish brush.

Decorative Painting Necessities

In addition to your paints and brushes, you'll need a variety of supplies in order to create the projects in this book.

BASIC PAINTING SUPPLIES

PALETTES Acrylic painters need two palettes. For mixing color and loading your brushes, you'll need a wax-coated disposable paper palette designed for use with water media. (If you use a palette designed for oil painting, the surface will wrinkle and buckle and make it difficult to paint.) This type of palette is very convenient: Just tear off the used sheet and throw it away at the end of a painting session, or when the sheet is completely covered with paint. Purchase the largest size you can find so that you can use a single sheet for more than one session.

You'll also need a covered palette that will keep your acrylic paints moist. A good choice is the Sta-Wet Palette made by Masterson Industries. For a detailed description on how to set up your palettes, see "Getting Started," page 22.

PALETTE KNIFE You'll need a palette knife for mixing paints. Invest in a good-quality one with a long, flexible blade. If you purchase a good palette knife, you'll only have to make the purchase once. Don't buy a plastic palette knife or one with a stiff blade or you won't be able to "feel" the consistency of the paint as you mix it.

WATER CONTAINER You'll need a container of water for rinsing brushes during your painting sessions. You can purchase a container designed for this purpose, or use any sturdy, wide-mouth

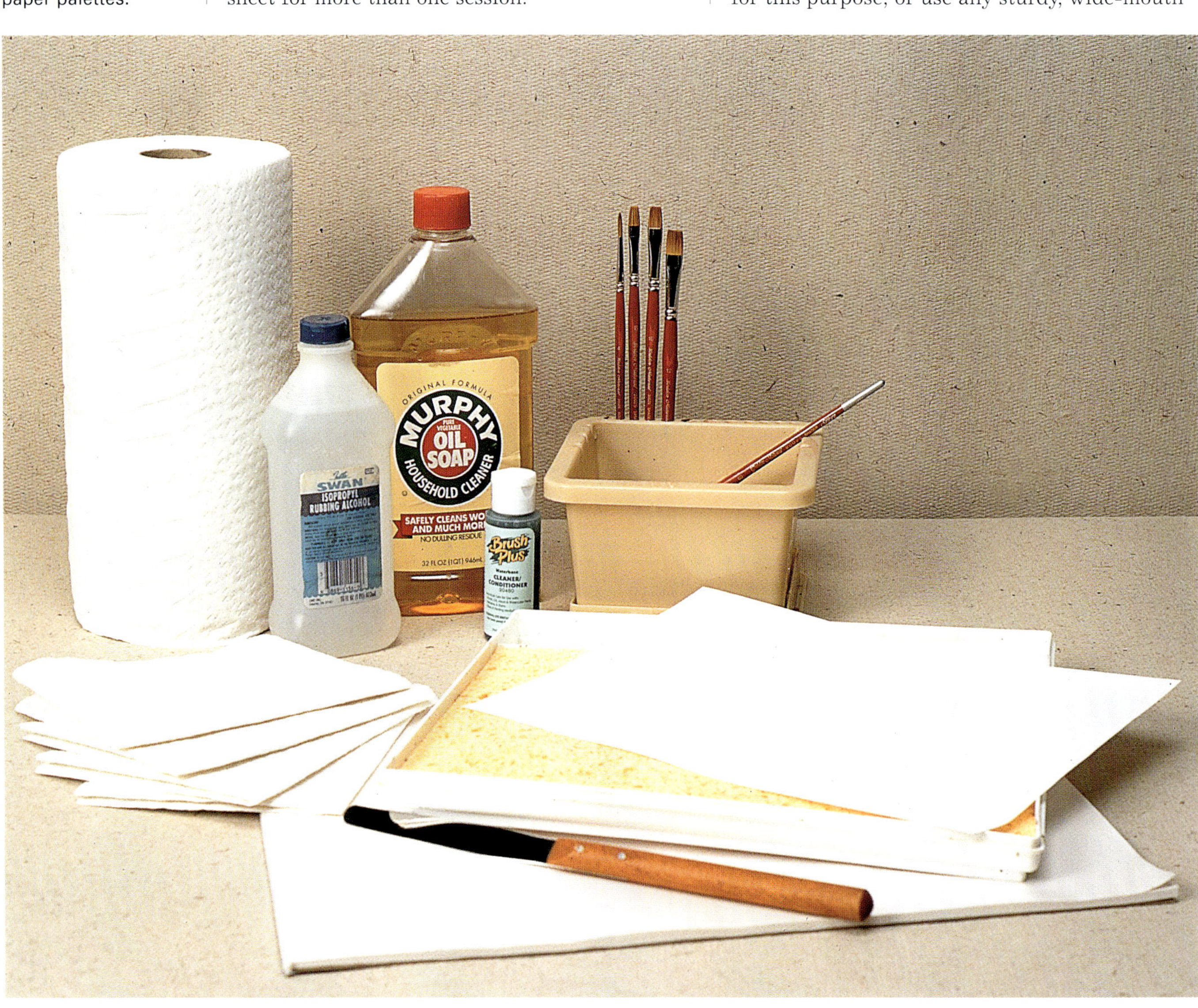

Basic painting supplies: paper towels, brush conditioner and Murphy Oil Soap (for cleaning brushes), a water container, palette knife, and Sta-Wet and disposable paper palettes.

container that won't tip over easily. The container shown in the photograph on page 16 has special slots designed to hold brushes and a ribbed area in the bottom of the well to help remove paint from the hairs.

PAPER TOWELS Always use high-quality paper towels that are soft as well as absorbent. You'll be wiping and blotting your brushes on paper towels often while you work, and rough, coarse ones can cause the hairs to curl or separate.

SOAP FOR CLEANING BRUSHES Use a commercial brush cleaner or a mild vegetable oil soap to clean dirty brushes without leaving any residue. Both can also be used to clean dirty hands.

RUBBING ALCOHOL Alcohol can be used to clean residue of dried paint from your brushes. You should always try to remove all the paint from a brush before it has a chance to dry, but if some paint does dry in the brush, dip it into alcohol, then work the hairs in the palm of your hand before cleaning it as described on page 15.

ACRYLIC MEDIUMS

Four mediums formulated especially for use with acrylic paints are required to complete the projects in this book. These mediums not only make the paints easier to work with, but they also yield some beautiful translucent effects. I use FolkArt acrylic mediums, which are made by Plaid Enterprises.

BLENDING GEL This revolutionary product, which is also called gel retarder, extends working time without thinning the paint's consistency—in other words, without making it watery—an important consideration for blending applications.

DIMENSIONAL BRUSH STROKE GLOSS MEDIUM When acrylic paint is applied to a surface it generally flattens out. This medium allows your brush strokes to retain their ridges or dimension. You can also use it to impart a bit of transparency to the brush stroke. Dimensional Brush Stroke Gloss Medium has enough body to maintain its shape even if very little color is added to it.

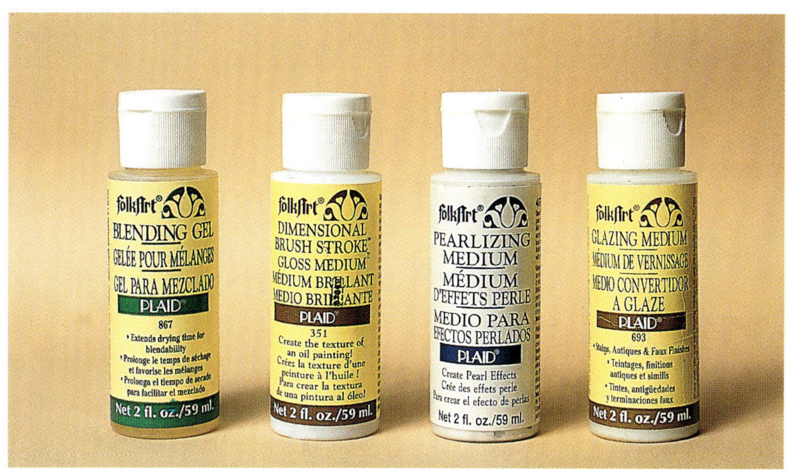

Acrylic mediums: Blending Gel (referred to generically as gel retarder), Dimensional Brush Stroke Gloss Medium, Pearlizing Medium, and Glazing Medium.

PEARLIZING MEDIUM This translucent medium imparts a pearly luster to paint. To add a shimmer to a color, you should mix it with the paint. A slightly different effect-an iridescent glow—is created by applying the medium over a color. See section on painting in the Assendelfter style (page 58).

GLAZING MEDIUM In addition to extending the working time of acrylic paint, this product also makes it beautifully translucent. In this book, Glazing Medium is used to create glazes for antiquing (see page 41).

SURFACE PREP SUPPLIES

Before you can actually begin painting a design, you'll need to prepare the surface of your project. The following are some standard supplies for preparing wood and metal surfaces.

SANDPAPER Sandpaper is available in hardware stores and home improvement centers. You'll need two grades: medium (#220-grit) for the initial rough sanding, and fine (#400-grit) for smoothing and finishing. Buy a package of each so you have them on hand.

TACK RAG OR CLOTH A tack rag is a piece of cheesecloth that has been treated with resin and varnish. Its extremely sticky surface is used to remove sanding residue, giving finished pieces a smoother, more professional look.

SCRUB PAD Use a scrub pad to "sand" a primed wooden surface prior to basecoating or to remove grime from metalware.

Decorative Painting Necessities

STEEL WOOL Like scrub pads, steel wool can be used to clean dirt and rust and from metalware before priming.

NAVAL JELLY Naval Jelly removes rust from metal. Use it on metal objects that have accumulated grime or show any signs of rust. Carefully follow the manufacturer's directions and wear rubber gloves when using it.

PRIMER Primer is required for metalware as well as for some wooden pieces. If your wooden pieces are small, you can use a spray primer. For metal objects, use a spray-on, flat-finish gray primer specially formulated to inhibit rust and provide a reliable surface for paint.

BASECOAT PAINT To impart color to the surface, you can use craft or artists' acrylics or latex house paints. I enjoy using Durable Colors by Plaid, acrylic paints that are specially formulated to deliver excellent wearing strength. They are available in a wide range of colors, are semigloss in sheen, and can be cleaned up with soap and water.

BROWN PAPER BAG An unprinted brown paper bag (like the ones at your local grocery store) can be used to smooth a final coat of basepaint or an interim coat of varnish.

COTTON RAGS Lint-free cotton rags, like those made from old T-shirts, are indispensible for wiping off antiquing glazes or stains.

VARNISH I varnish all of my decorative painting projects with a good quality water-based polyurethane. For small oprojects I like FolkArt Artists' Varnish, which is sold at many art supply and craft stores. If you plan to varnish many pieces, you can buy gallon-size cans of Varathane at home improvement stores. These

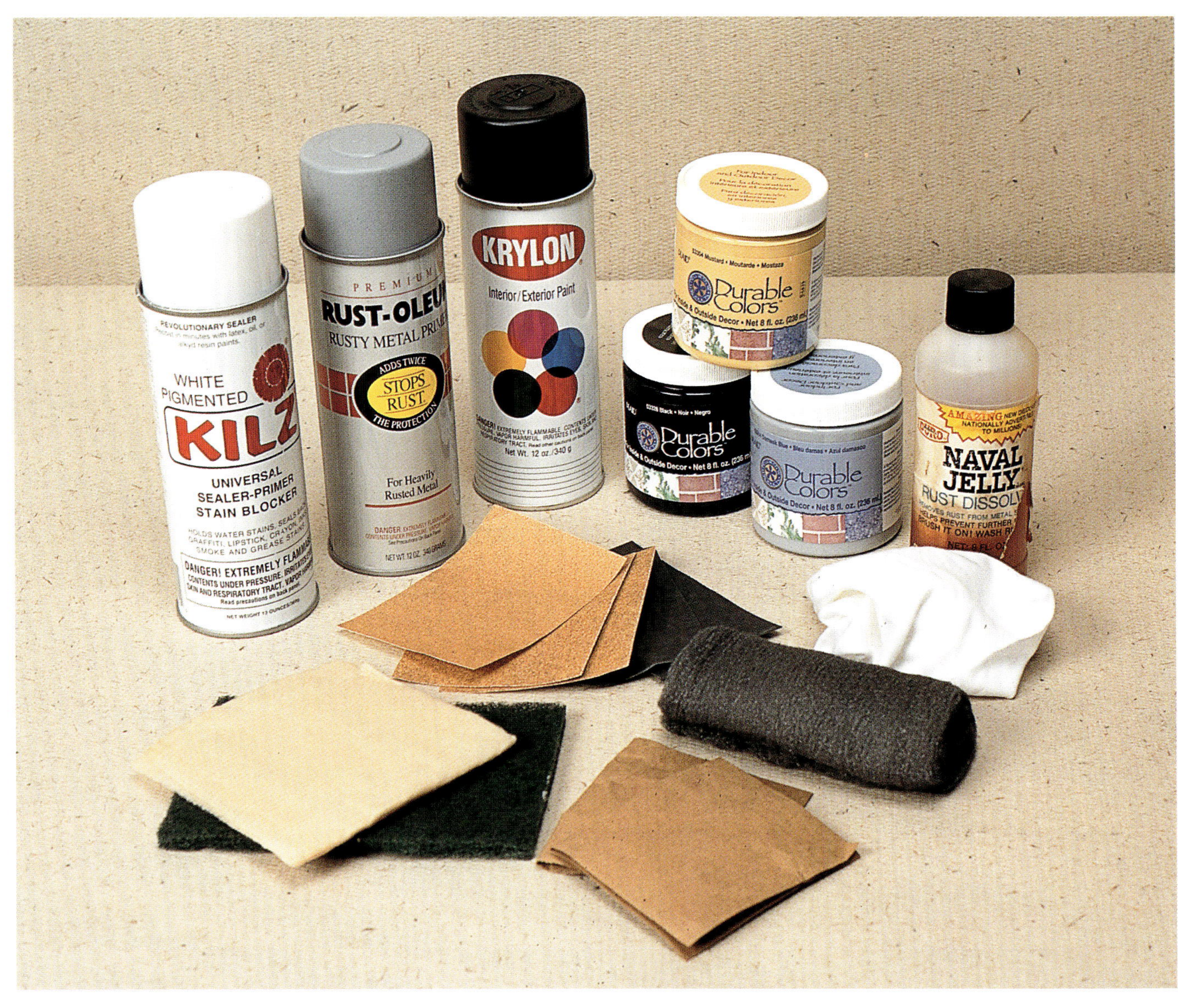

Surface prep supplies: primers for wood and metal, Durable Colors acrylic paints for basecoating, Naval Jelly, sandpapers in several grits, cotton rags, very fine steel wool, a tack rag, a scrub pad, and pieces of a brown paper bag.

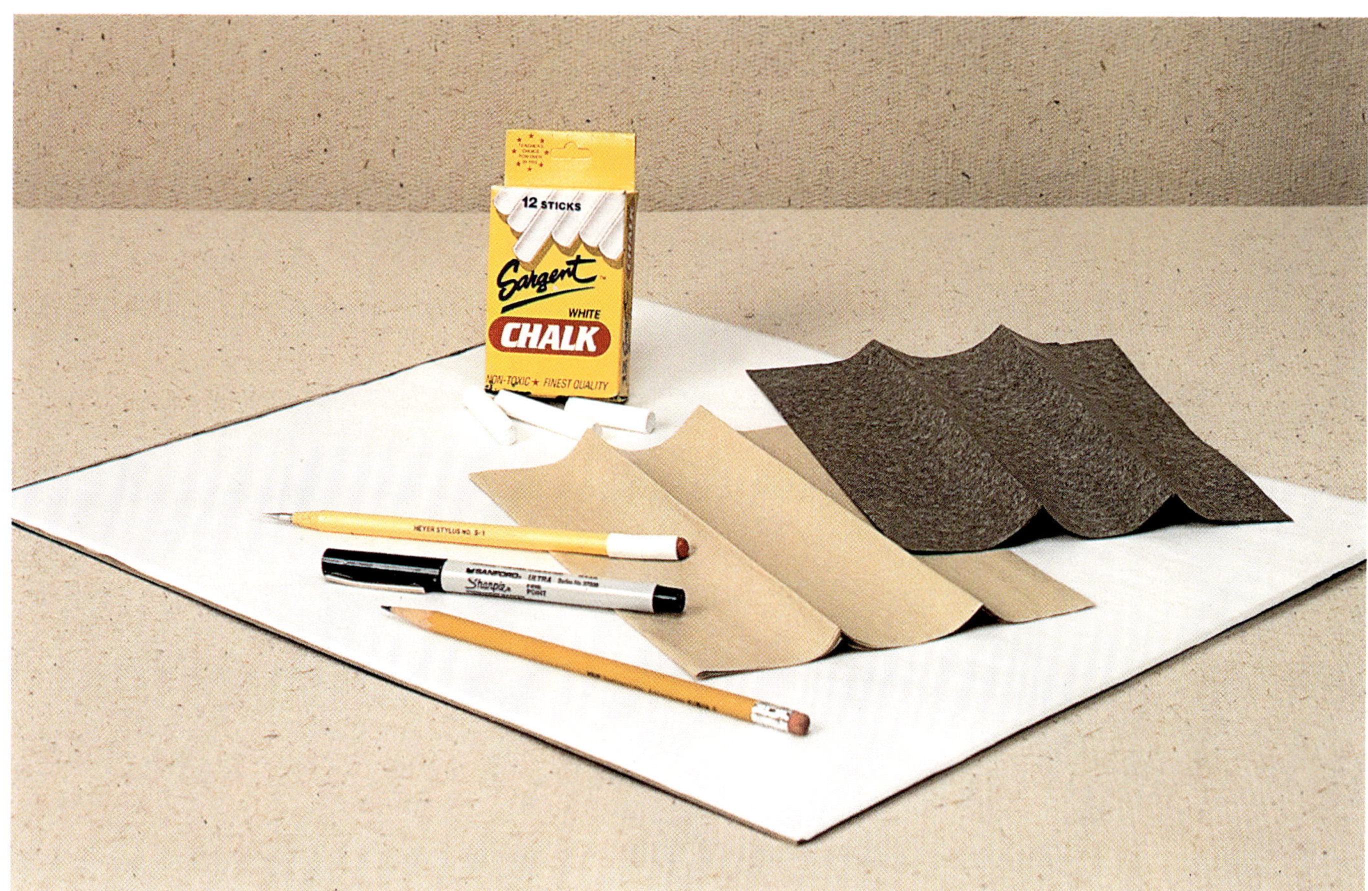

two brands are available in a range of sheens, from matte to high-gloss.

TRACING AND TRANSFERRING SUPPLIES

Once your surface is properly prepped and ready for decorative painting, you'll need to trace a pattern and transfer it to the surface. (See "Tracing, Sizing, and Transferring Patterns," pages 38–40, for detailed instructions.)

TRACING PAPER This transparent paper is specifically designed for tracing. Do not attempt to substitute tracing paper with tissue paper, which is not sturdy enough. Tracing paper can be purchased in art and craft stores and is sold in several sizes. Buy a package of at least medium-sized paper in order to avoid having to piece several smaller sheets together.

FINE-TIP BLACK MARKER Use a fine-tip marker to trace patterns onto tracing paper. Choose one that contains permanent ink so your tracings won't smear.

TRANSFER PAPER This special paper, which is designed for transferring decorative painting patterns to surfaces, will wash off with water. Do *not* use graphite or typewriter carbon paper, which will cause unsightly messes. Use white transfer paper on dark- to medium-value surfaces and gray transfer paper on light- to medium-value surfaces.

STYLUS Similar in shape to a pen, a stylus is used to trace the lines of a pattern in order to transfer them to a project's surface. Unlike a pencil, a fine-point stylus produces a consistent fine line, so use one whenever you transfer a pattern.

CHALK Purchase a box of ordinary blackboard chalk to transfer simple strokework designs. Do not buy dustless chalk or sewing or tailor's chalk—neither will work—and avoid colored chalk because its pigment might bleed through or otherwise affect the color of your paint.

PENCIL A pencil is invaluable for making marks that will need to be erased, such as the center point of a surface. Do not use a pencil to transfer patterns because it will make increasingly wide lines as its point dulls with use.

TAPE Use Scotch or painter's tape to keep tracings and transfer paper in place.

Tracing and transferring supplies: A large pad of tracing paper, chalk, transfer paper in white and gray, a stylus, a fine-tip black marker, and a pencil.

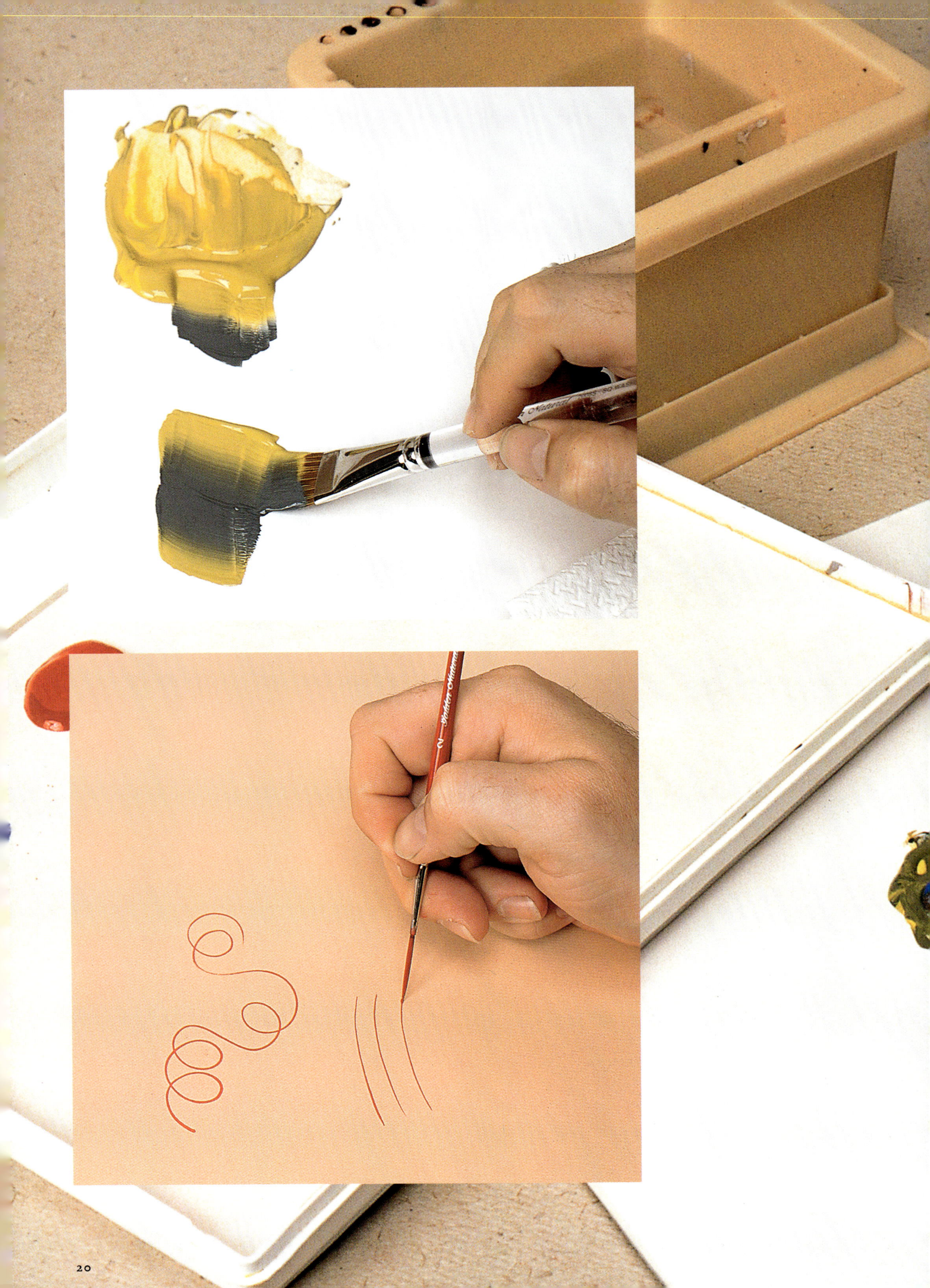

2 Decorative Painting Basics

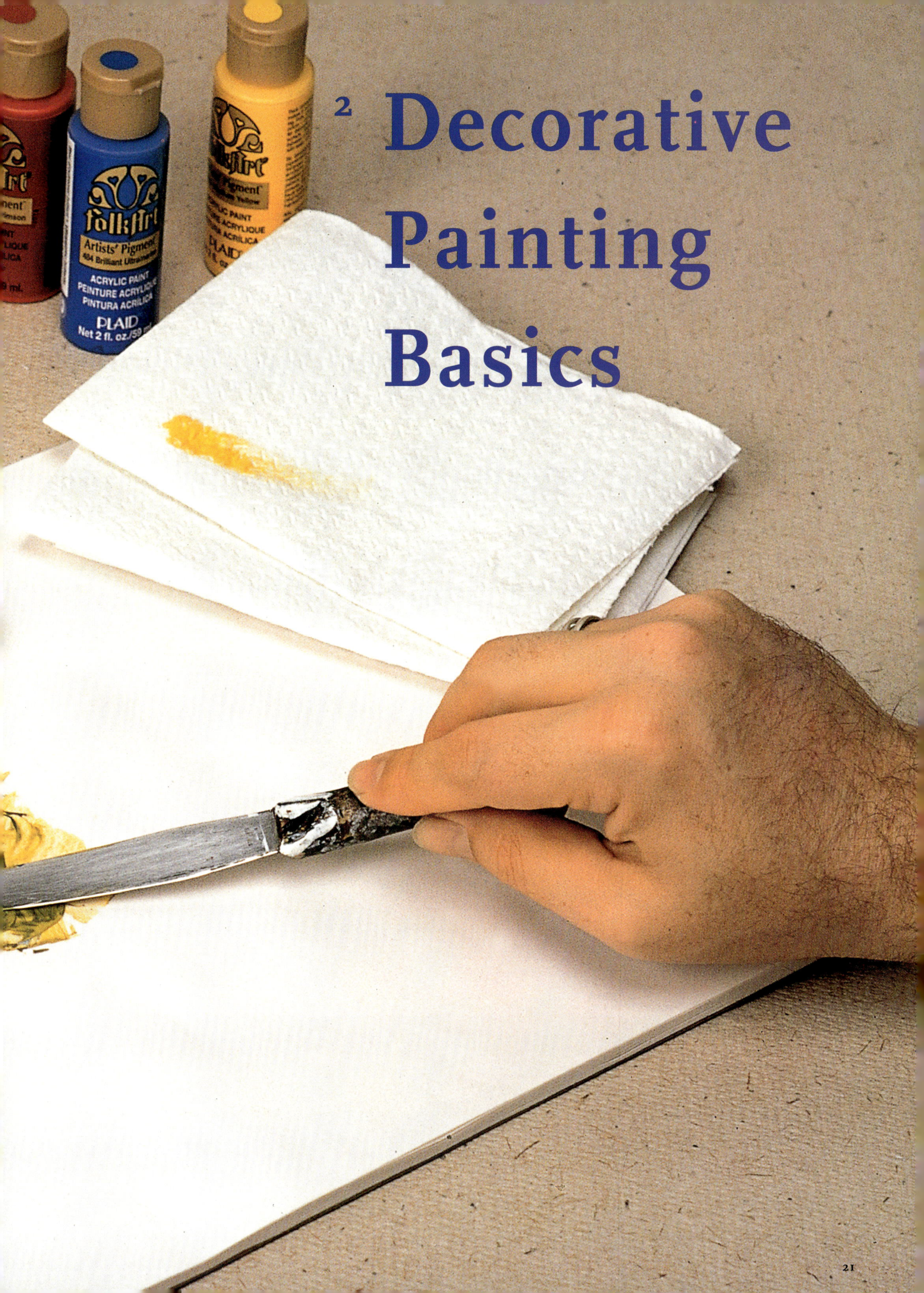

Getting Started

After you've gathered together the necessary supplies, the next step is to organize your palettes so that you can begin learning how to handle your paints and brushes.

SETTING UP

Over the years, I've developed a routine of working with two palettes: I store my paints in a Sta-Wet palette to keep them moist and workable, and I mix colors and load my brushes on a disposable paper palette. This may sound a bit complicated, but it really fits my working style. If you try my method, I think that the process of painting will be easier for you, which in turn will make you more likely to succeed.

To prepare the Sta-Wet palette for painting, immerse the special palette paper in water. It's best to soak the paper overnight, because if you don't soak it long enough it won't keep the paints moist. Once the paper has been soaked, wet the sponge thoroughly, place it in the plastic tray, then lay the special paper over the wet sponge. Blot the palette paper with a piece of paper towel to remove any standing water, and it's ready for your paints. The palette should remain moist for several hours, although you may need to mist it with water occasionally. When the palette is covered, the paint can remain usable for days or even weeks.

I almost never load my brush or mix colors on the wet palette because I want to keep the colors I store there clean and pure. When I'm ready to paint, I take the cover off the wet palette, use my palette knife to move some paint to a clean area of my disposable paper palette, then either load my brush or mix my new color with the knife.

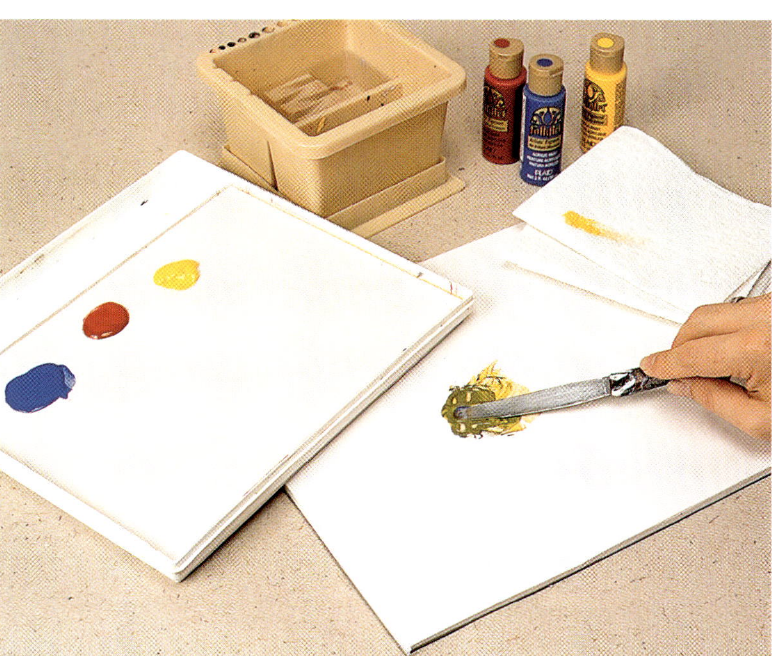

I use my palette knife to move paint from my wet palette to my paper palette for mixing colors and loading brushes. To keep the paints on my wet palette clean, I wipe the knife on a paper towel before picking up a new color.

THE "RIGHT" CONSISTENCY

The term *consistency* refers to how thick or thin the paint needs to be for a particular painting technique. For most of the techniques that are used in this book, you'll be able to use your paint straight from the bottle or tube, which has a thick, creamy consistency.

To do brushstroke work—the "Essential Brushstrokes" that are shown on pages 23–26—you'll need to thin the paint by adding a little water to it and mixing them together with a palette knife. While you're mixing, keep the paint from spreading all over the palette by continually pushing it into a single mass. The consistency should be loose: When you pick up some paint on the palette knife, it should slide and drip off the knife with ease. To do linework, which involves creating fine, detailed lines (see page 26), the paint will need to be even thinner—the consistency of thin soup—but not so thin that it hardly contains any color. You don't want to paint your projects with "dirty water"!

Learning to create different paint consistencies requires some patience and practice. The only way to become skilled at handling paints is to actually sit down and begin painting.

LOADING A BRUSH

Stroke the brush into the paint, then apply pressure as you pull some paint away from the puddle, which will cause the hairs to spread. When you release pressure, the hairs will draw together, pulling paint into the brush. Repeat this procedure several times on both sides of the brush until its hairs are completely filled with paint.

Essential Brushstrokes

Mastering the brushstrokes shown below and on the following pages will help you learn to handle your brushes and paints competently—an accomplishment that is essential to your painting success. Most traditional European folk art painting techniques require exceptional brush control, a fact that is evident in the work of its original practitioners. With practice, you too can master these fundamental skills, but don't let the thought of having to practice lead you to consider skipping this section. If you can't control your brushes, your painting experience will be filled with frustration. Although you won't need to master all of these brushstrokes in order to complete a specific project, giving each one a try can only increase your skill and give you confidence, which in turn will make your painting experience more enjoyable.

COMMA STROKE

This quintessential brushstroke is the foundation of all the strokework you'll need to master. Using basically the same technique, a comma stroke can be painted with either a flat brush or a round brush. Decorative painters should know how to paint both, which require a fluid motion and considerable practice in order to achieve a graceful-looking result.

FLAT BRUSH COMMA STROKE Before you begin, thin the paint with water until it flows effortlessly from the brush (see "The 'Right' Consistency," on the opposite page).

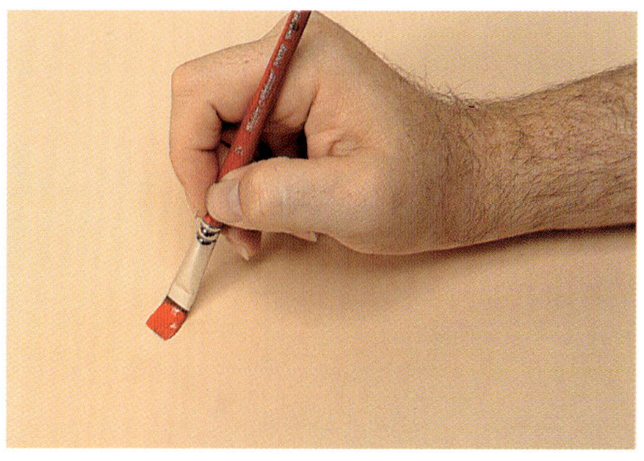

1 Angle the brush toward the corner of your surface, gently touch its hairs to it, then immediately apply pressure. The ferrule (the piece of metal that attaches the hairs to the brush) should *almost* touch the surface.

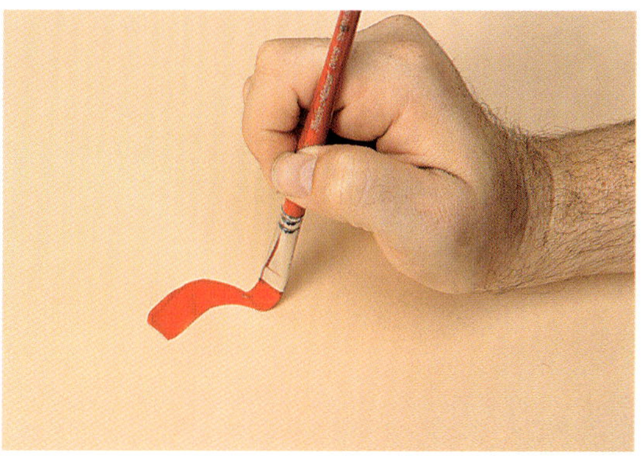

2 As you pull the brush hairs along the surface, gradually release the pressure . . .

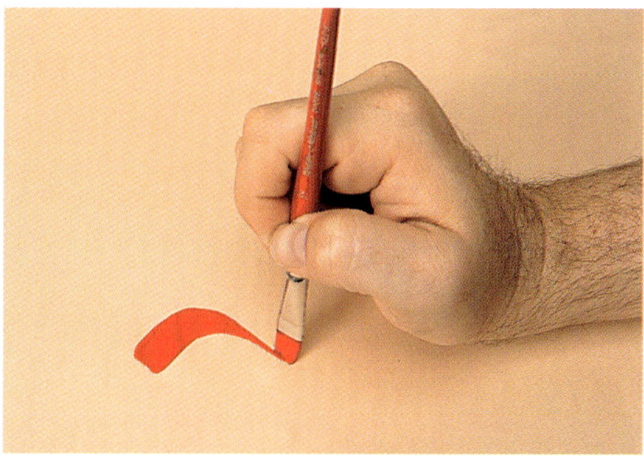

3 . . . while lifting the brush back to its chisel edge. This single, continuous motion will form the brushstroke. Do *not* turn or twist the brush. The brush will make the stroke simply by applying and releasing pressure while dragging it. If you're having trouble, attach a small piece of masking tape to the end of your brush handle. When you paint the stroke, the tape should *not* move—if it does, you're turning the brush.

Essential Brushstrokes

ROUND BRUSH COMMA STROKE To paint a comma stroke with a round brush, load the brush with loose-consistency paint (see "The 'Right' Consistency," page 22). Don't twirl the brush to a fine point after loading it; if the brush is too pointy, it will be difficult to make a nicely shaped head on the stroke.

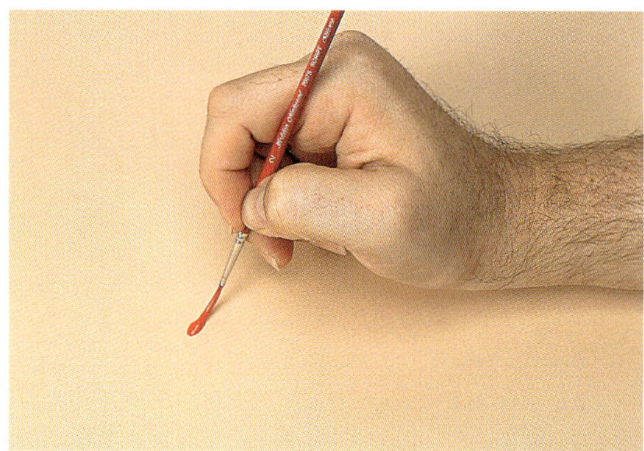

1 Angle the tip of the brush toward the corner of your surface. Touch the brush to the surface and apply pressure to it. The hairs will spread out, forming a nice rounded curve.

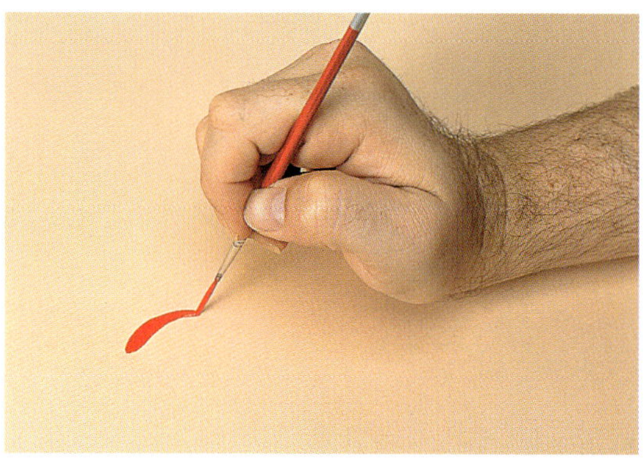

2 Gradually lift the brush as you drag it toward yourself, which will cause the hairs to spring back . . .

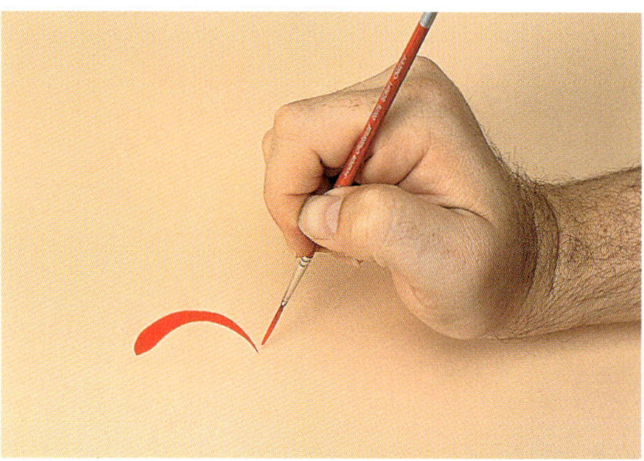

3 . . . and slowly taper to a fine line. You don't need to twist or turn the brush in order to do this. The release of pressure will cause the hairs to form the rest of the stroke.

TEARDROP STROKE

The teardrop is basically the opposite of a round brush comma stroke. It starts out thin and ends with a nicely rounded "head." Unlike the comma stroke, however, the teardrop stroke requires a pointy brush tip. You can move the brush toward you or away from you as you form this stroke. Decide which method is more comfortable for you as you practice.

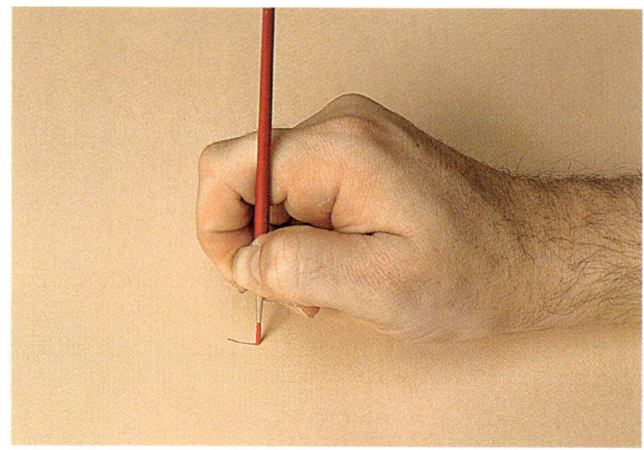

1 Load the brush and twirl it to form a pointed tip. As you begin to form the stroke, apply light pressure.

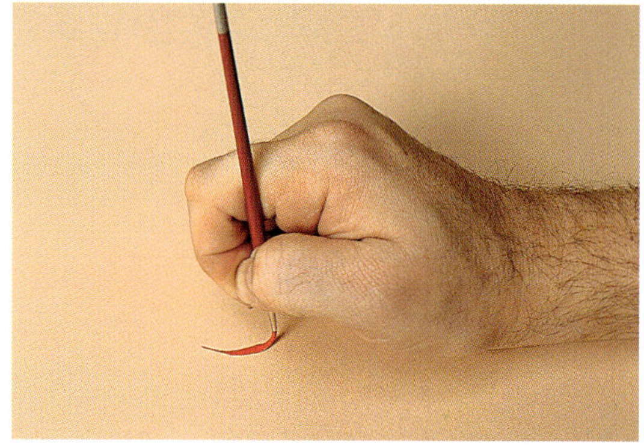

2 As you continue the stroke, gradually increase your pressure on the brush.

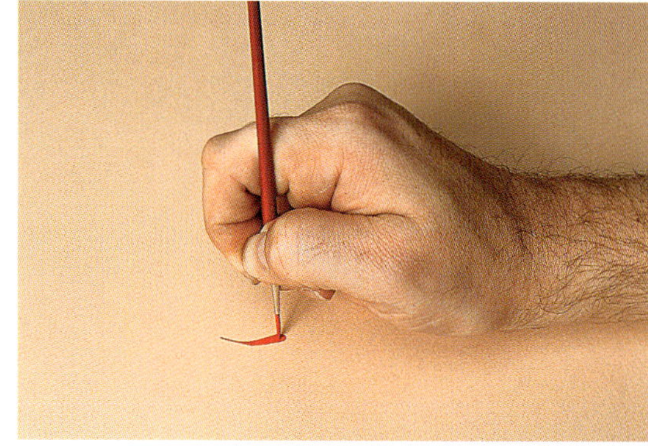

3 When you feel the stroke is fully formed, simply lift the brush from the surface. Be careful not to *pull* the brush as you lift it. (As a variation, you can add a scroll to the end of the stroke by pulling a line from the side or end of the stroke.)

S STROKE

This stroke is one of the most graceful in the decorative painter's repertoire. It's similar to the comma stroke in that it requires a single, continuous motion with a gradual application and release of pressure on the brush. You should learn to paint both left- and right-facing S strokes.

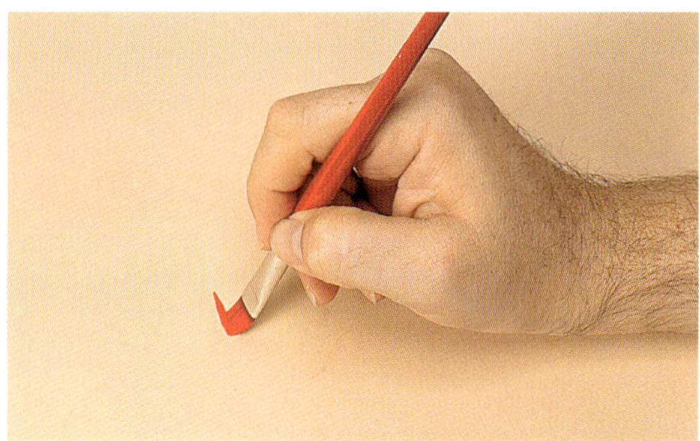

1 Angle a loaded flat brush toward the corner of your surface. Start the stroke by standing the brush on its chisel edge, then slide it toward yourself to create a short, thin line.

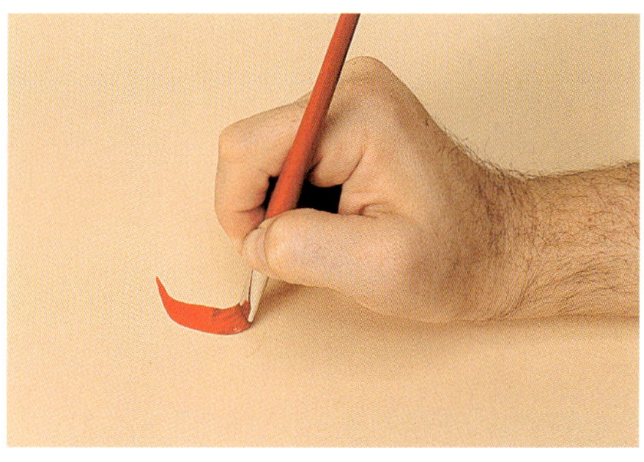

2 Begin to apply pressure as you slide the brush along the surface, gradually increasing pressure until you reach the middle of the stroke. Gradually release the pressure as you continue to slide the brush.

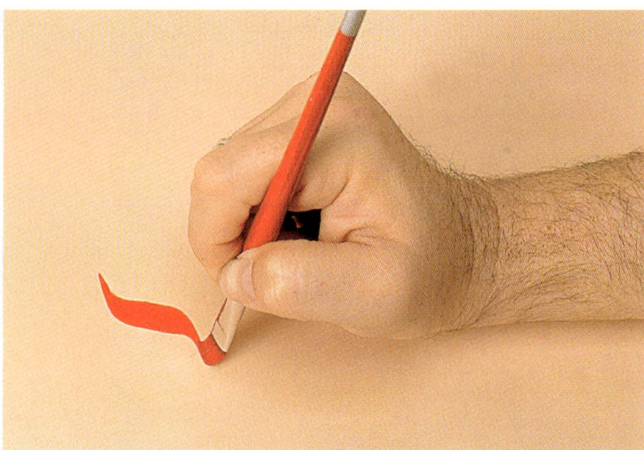

3 End the stroke with the brush on its chisel edge to create another short, thin line. The angle of the lines at the beginning and end of the stroke should be the same.

U STROKE

The procedure for making a U stroke is similar to that for the S stroke except that the shape of the stroke is different.

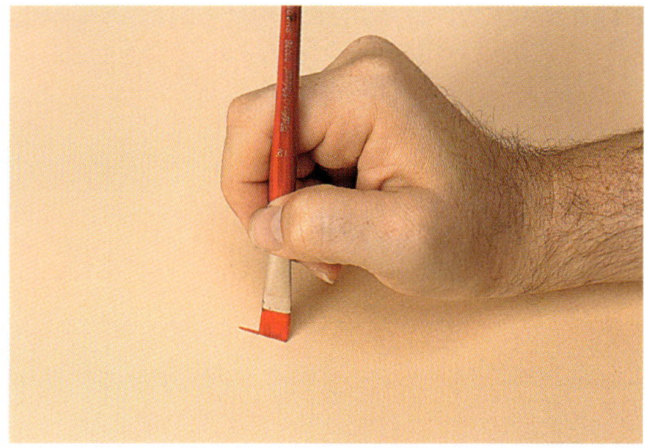

1 Stand a loaded flat brush on its chisel edge. Pull the brush toward yourself to make a fine line . . .

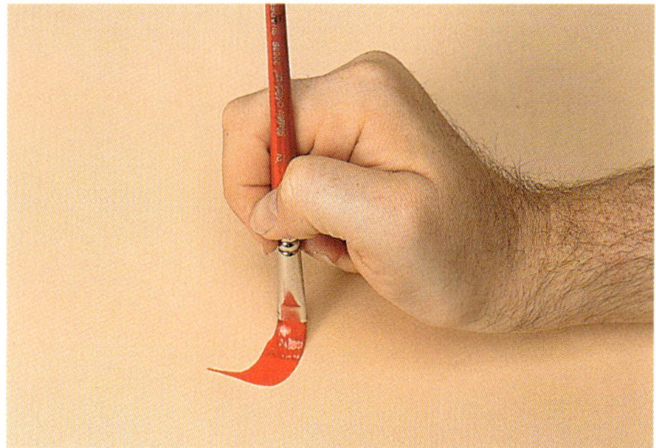

2 . . . then gradually apply pressure to form the wide part of the U. Don't turn the brush, just slide it to the right or left.

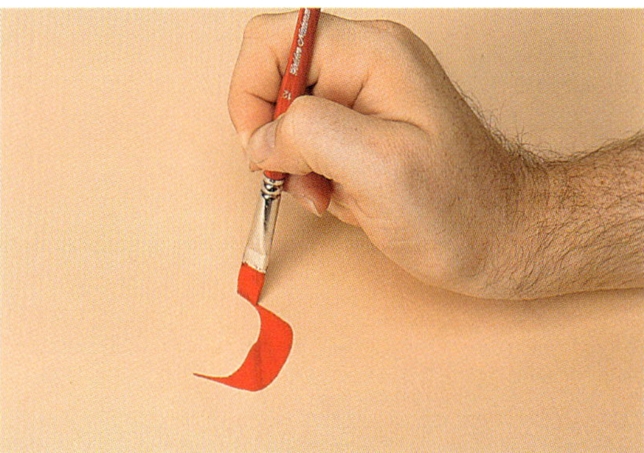

3 To complete the stroke, gradually release the pressure on the brush until it's standing on its chisel edge once again.

Essential Brushstrokes

LINEWORK

Linework is done with a script liner brush using paint that has been thinned to a consistency similar to that of drawing ink so that it flows freely from the brush. If the paint is too thick, it either won't flow from the brush or it will produce thick, unattractive lines. To load the brush, completely fill the hairs with paint (see page 22), then gently twirl them to a fine point as you remove them from the puddle of paint. You need to apply only the slightest pressure to create fine lines and squiggles, and it takes practice to develop the light touch you need.

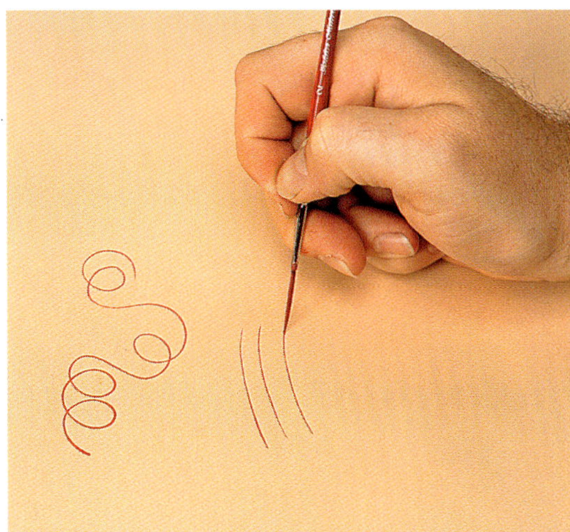

It's fun using one brush to create several different effects.

TIPPING

A stroke painted with a tipped brush contains two or more colors. In this book, tipping is primarily used in the Assendelfter style of painting.

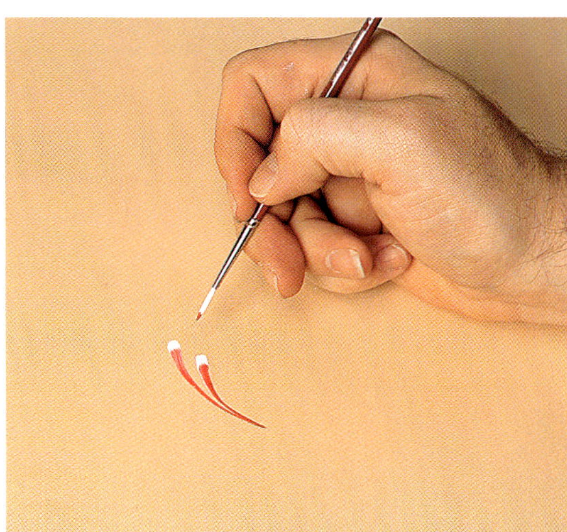

Load the brush with paint, then wipe the tip clean and dip it in another color. The strokes formed with a tipped brush should be two-toned.

HANDLE DOTS

Handle dots aren't brushstrokes per se, but they are made with a brush—the handle end! Simply dip the handle into a puddle of paint, then touch the handle to the surface to create a perfectly round dot.

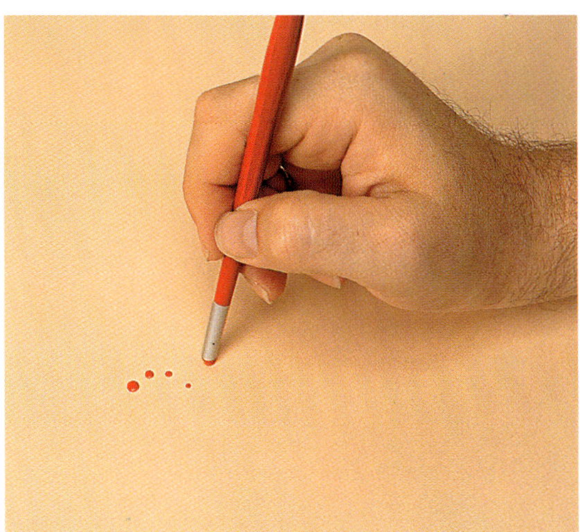

To make a series of uniform dots, reload the handle before making each one. To make a series of progressively smaller dots, just load the handle once.

Color and Value

CHOOSING AND USING COLOR

A *color wheel* makes it easy to understand relationships among colors, which can in turn help an artist create successful mixtures. The standard artist's color wheel includes twelve colors. The three *primary colors*—red, yellow, and blue—are the ones from which all others are mixed, but they can't be mixed from any others. Theoretically, you should be able to make any color using just red, yellow, and blue paint, but the realities of paint chemistry require that we use a few more.

The primary colors lie equidistant around the color wheel. By mixing two primaries you get a *secondary color.* The three secondaries—orange (red + yellow), green (blue + yellow), and violet (red + blue)—lie between the primaries on the wheel. Mix a primary and a secondary and you'll get a *tertiary color,* of which there are six: red-orange, yellow-orange, blue-violet, red-violet, yellow-green, and blue-green.

Colors that lie directly opposite one another are called *complements,* a word derived from the Latin word *complementum,* meaning "to complete," which in this case refers to a complete grouping of three primary colors. For example, yellow and violet are complements; yellow is one primary, and violet contains the other two (red and blue), which completes the primary triad. In theory, mixing two complements creates a neutral, grayish color, but the result is often a murky color known informally as "mud."

The following are some tips for creating successful color mixtures:

- Mix colors according to the sequence cited in the instructions. The first color called for is the dominant color in the mixture. For instance, if the instructions call for a mixture of titanium white + dioxazine purple, begin with a small puddle of white paint and add tiny amounts of purple until the desired color is reached.
- When creating a mixture, always add color in very small amounts. It's always easy to add color, but very difficult to reverse the effects of adding too much. At that point, it's usually easier to start over again than to fix it.
- So that each paint color will remain pure, get into the habit of wiping your palette knife before using it to pick up a new color or to add more color to a mixture.

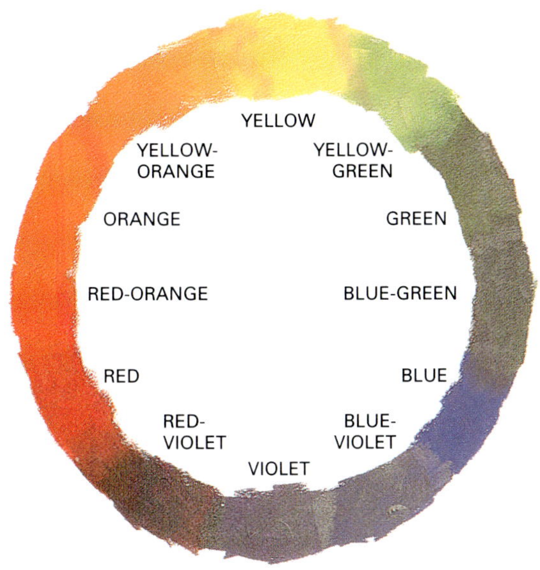

In addition to illustrating various mixtures, a color wheel shows that primary colors are the most intense because they are pure; the secondaries and tertiaries are less intense because they are mixtures. Cool colors fall on the blue-green side of the wheel, while warm colors are on the red-orange side.

HOW VALUE WORKS

The term *value* refers to how light or dark a color is. This concept is most clearly illustrated by a *value scale,* which consists of progressive gradations of gray, ranging from white to black. Although every step in the scale can be identified as "gray," each is a different value.

Every color can be lightened and darkened to create a range of values. This is important because by using a range of values in your painting, you can give an object dimension. As you can see below, a painted circle takes on a three-dimensional appearance when a wider range of values is used.

The most obvious way to change a color's value is to add white or black to it, but doing this often changes the color too drastically. Another option—which often yields better results—is to add other colors. For instance, if you add black to yellow you'll get a greenish hue. To get a dark yellow, try adding violet.

Don't let the occasional uncertainty of color mixing undermine your enthusiasm or your self-confidence. The project instructions will guide you and help you make good choices.

This ten-step scale illustrates the range of values that can be created by mixing white and black.

A circle painted with a single value is just a circle. Painted with several values, it becomes a sphere.

Blending Techniques

Blending techniques are not specifically necessary to paint in the decorative painting styles presented in this book. However, the ability to blend paint effectively is an essential skill that every decorative painter should possess. In order to successfully produce three-dimensional effects, you must be able to paint gradations of color and value so that they gradually—almost imperceptibly—melt one into the next. Before you begin a project, practice the blending techniques that are specified in the instructions. This will make the process of painting the pattern much easier.

Although blending techniques weren't typically used in most styles of European folk art painting, I've used them in a few of the projects because they can simulate the look of certain styles with a minimum of difficulty.

BEFORE BLENDING: APPLYING AN UNDERCOAT

An essential decorative painting skill, *undercoating* simply means to paint an element with a single solid color. There are two ways to undercoat a motif: by applying the paint smoothly, or by giving it a slight texture.

A smooth application is the more traditional method. To achieve a smooth undercoat, simply load a brush—usually a flat brush—with paint straight from the bottle or tube. Using the brushstrokes demonstrated on pages 23–26 (or variations of these), first apply the paint around the motif's outer edges, then smoothly stroke the paint toward its center until the motif is completely filled in. There shouldn't be a defined ridge around the motif's edge, and the paint shouldn't have a noticeable texture. If the color or texture of the background is still visible once the paint has dried, apply a second coat, but not before making sure that the first coat is dry.

If the project instructions call for a textured undercoat (the Narrow Boat Painting project requires one), start by applying the paint around the motif's edges. As you fill the interior of the motif with color, use the chisel edge of the brush to stipple the paint slightly. This method of application breaks the surface of the paint, so two coats may be needed. Apply the second coat using the same technique, making sure that the first coat is dry before you begin. Avoid creating a noticeable buildup of paint—the goal is simply to produce a slightly irregular texture.

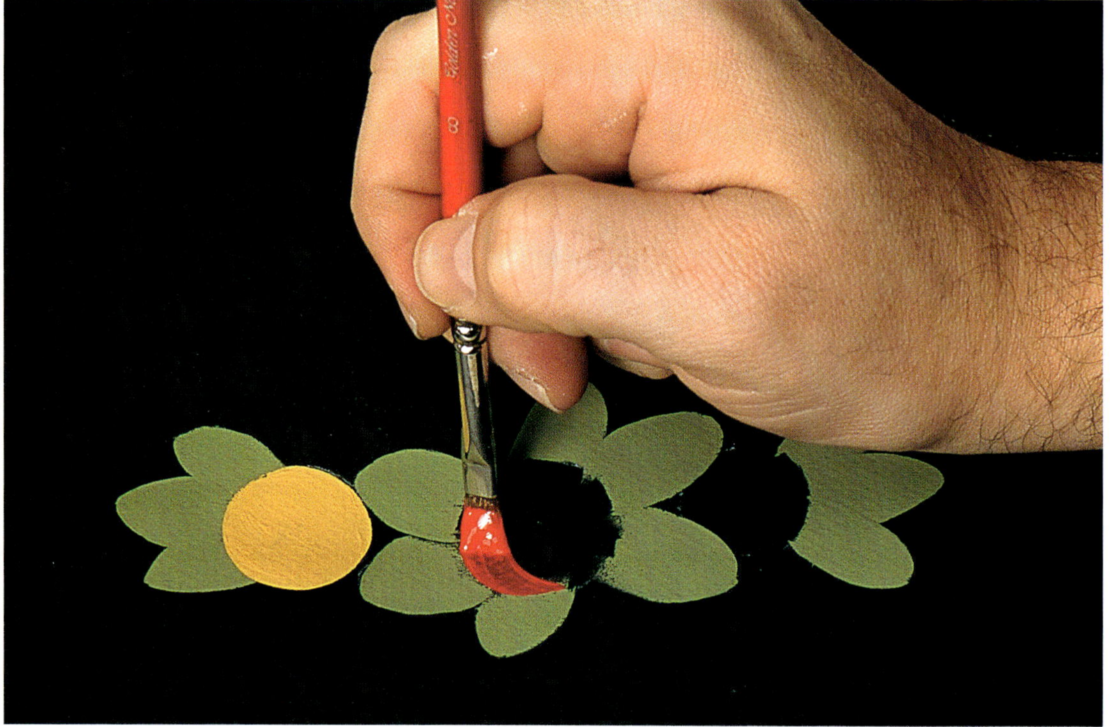

Begin undercoating by applying paint around the motif's outer edges, then smoothly stroke it toward the center.

WORKING WET-IN-WET

There is more than one way to work wet-in-wet. One is a true blending technique; by using it, you can create absolutely seamless gradations between several colors or values. Begin by applying a layer of gel retarder to the area to be painted. Then apply a generous amount of each color or value. Wipe the brush clean on a paper towel (*don't* rinse in water), then very lightly blend the colors together wherever there is a visible line of demarcation. When the colors are smoothly gradated but each individual color can still be identified, STOP blending; if you don't, you'll end up with only one color.

The second way of working wet-in-wet is particularly well suited to the creation of designs composed primarily of strokework. For this wet-in-wet technique, begin by applying a base of color. Then, while this layer is still wet, apply a second layer of strokes. The top strokes will pick up some of the first color, resulting in subtle color effects that are achievable no other way. The secret to painting this kind of wet-in-wet successfully is to work quickly and deliberately. If your brush picks up too much of the wet base color when you are applying overstrokes, simply wipe it on a paper towel, reload it, and keep painting.

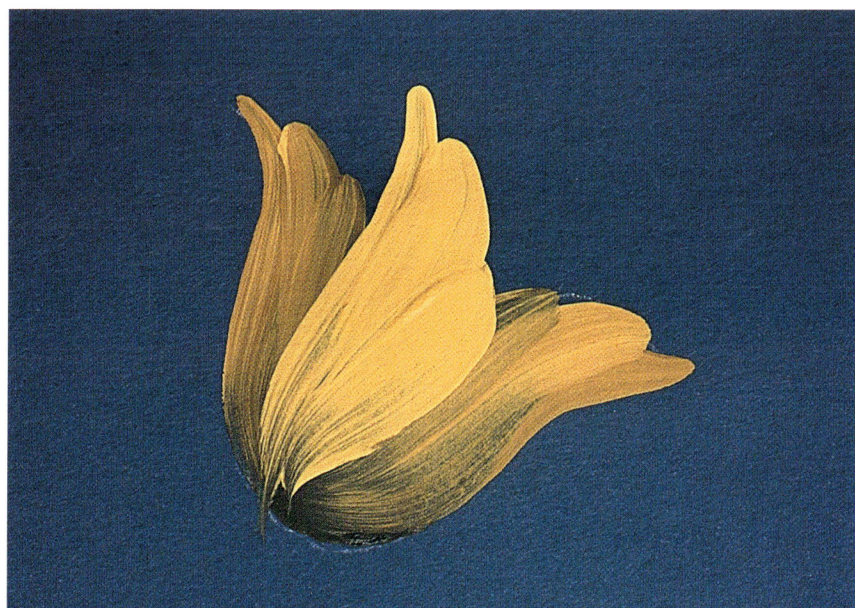

The subtle shading of the individual strokes on this tulip flower are achieved by painting on a base of gel retarder.

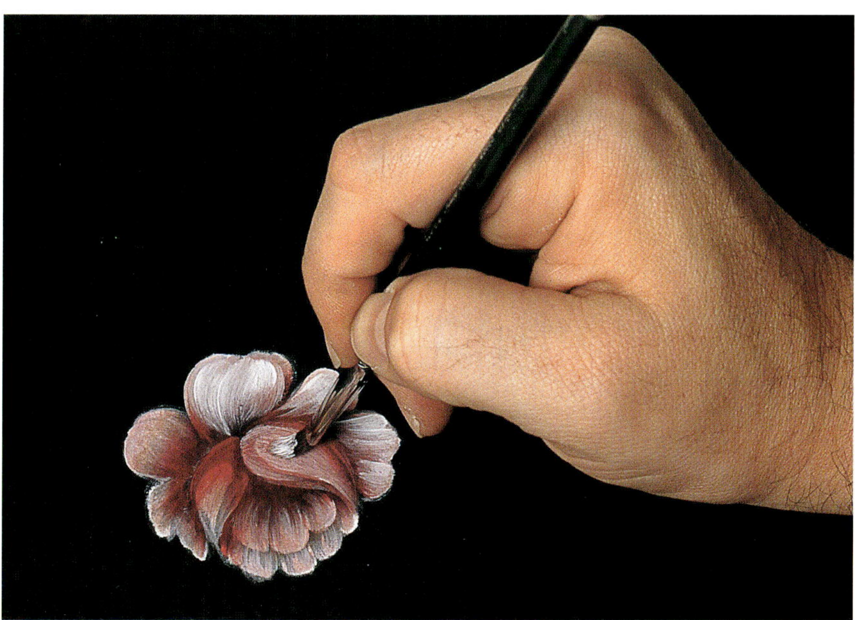

The strokes of white on the petals are tinged with the pink paint of the base color.

Blending Techniques

SIDELOADING

Sideloading is an invaluable blending technique that is used to create dimension within a motif. Instead of applying several layers of paint to create a gradual progression of color or value, a sideloaded brush is loaded with paint in such a way that its stroke gradually fades from full color on one side to little or no color on the other, an effect that is known as *floated*, or gradated, color.

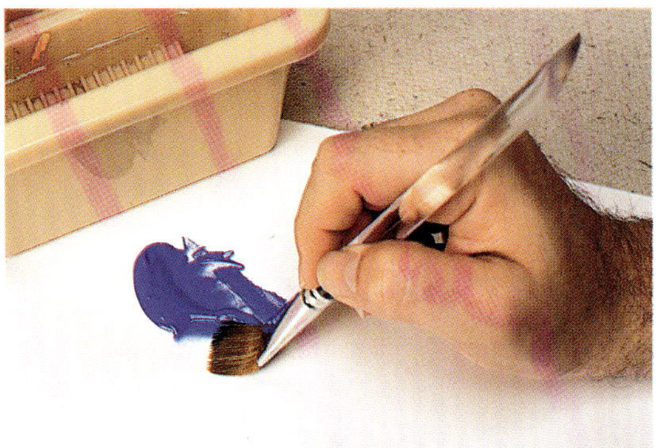

1 Moisten the brush in water, then blot it on a paper towel. So that you don't pick up too much color on the brush, slowly stroke one side of the brush next to the puddle of paint, almost as if you're "sneaking" the brush into the paint as you carefully work it into the hairs.

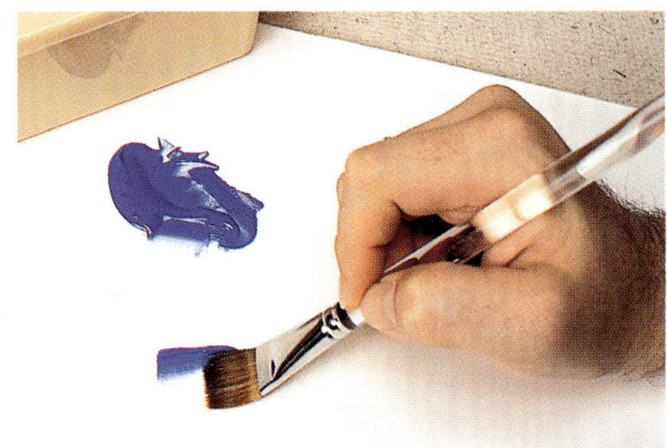

2 To distribute the paint across the brush, move to a clean area of the paper palette and stroke the brush over and over *in one spot*. The color in the stroke should *gradually* fade from full-strength on one side to clear water on the other. Be sure to make your strokes only about an inch long.

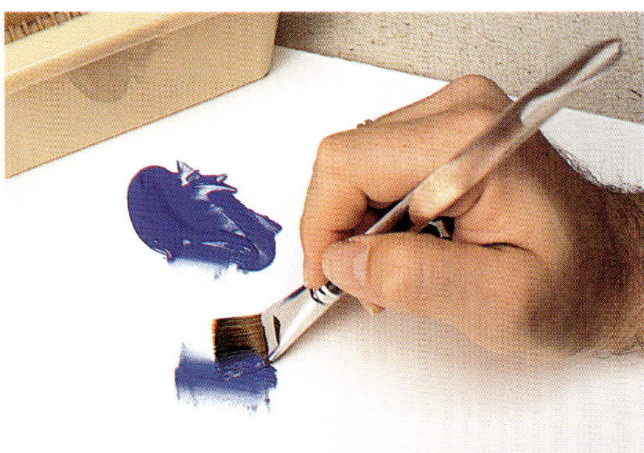

3 Working in the same spot, flip the brush over and repeatedly stroke the loaded side of the brush against the full-strength edge of the stroke.

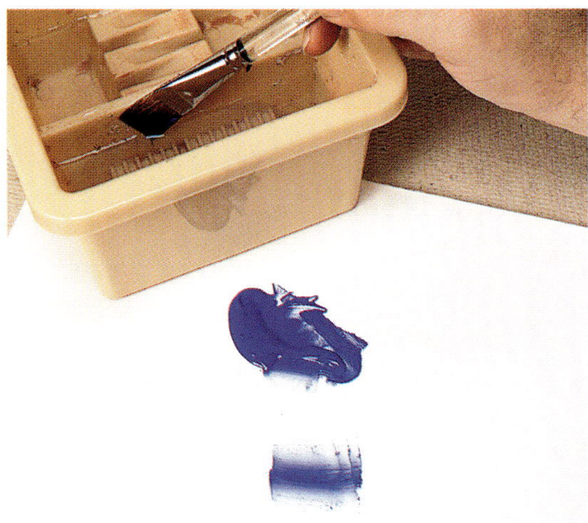

4 The brush should be properly sideloaded at this point; if it isn't, repeat steps 1 through 3. See the box at left for advice on how to correct and/or avoid other common sideloading problems.

TROUBLESHOOTING

- If you make your strokes longer than an inch (A), or if you make more than one set of strokes, you'll be painting the palette and removing paint from the brush instead of distributing it across the hairs. Keep stroking the brush in the same area, as long as the paint remains moist.
- If the paint beads up on the palette (B), or if the paint extends across the entire width of the brush, then the brush contains too much moisture. Gently blot the brush on a paper towel and try again.
- If the paint seems to drag (C), or if the brush doesn't have enough moisture in it, dip the corner of the more heavily loaded side into water. This area of the brush will absorb less moisture, giving you more control over how much water is in the brush. Be sure to blot the brush on a paper towel any time you add moisture to it.

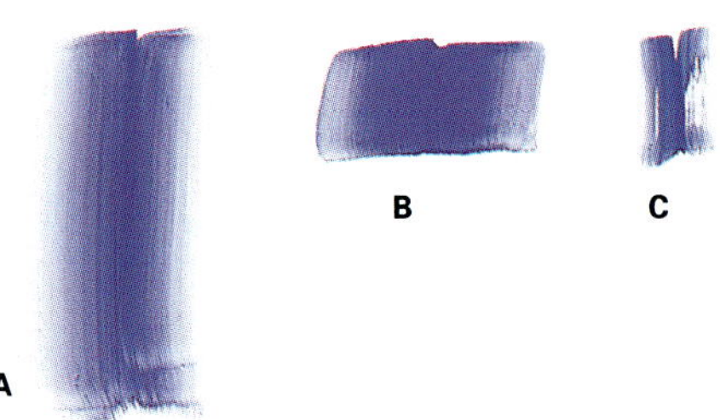

DOUBLELOADING

A variation on sideloading, *doubleloading* loads each side of a brush with two different colors or values of paint. In the stroke produced by this technique, the two colors or values on either edge gradually blend to create a third color or value in the center.

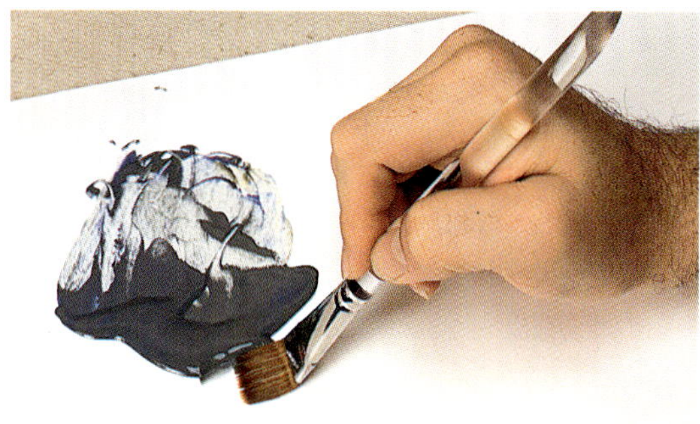

1 Moisten the brush with water, then blot it on a paper towel. Load one side of the brush with the first color by "sneaking" it into the paint as you stroke it along the edge of the pile.

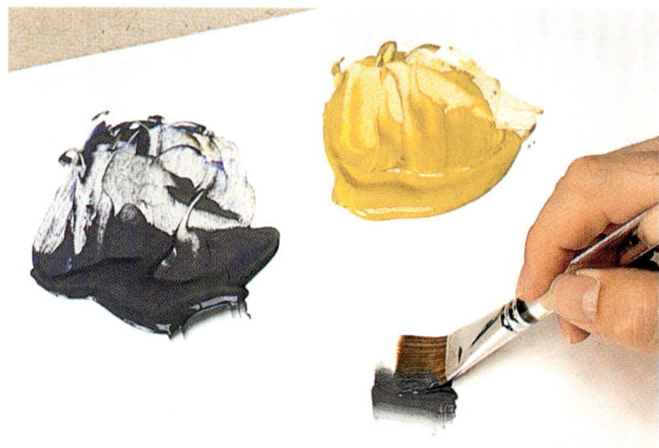

2 To distribute the paint halfway across the brush, stroke it *in one spot* on a clean area of the palette. Don't make your strokes more than about an inch long or the paint will begin to discharge from the brush. Flip the brush over, then stroke the more heavily loaded side against the full-strength edge of the stroke.

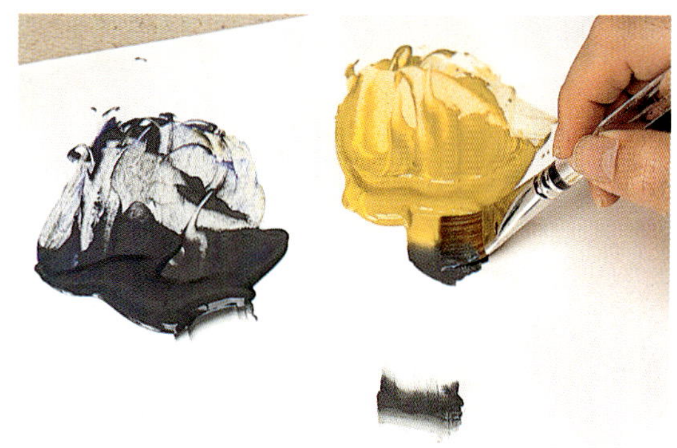

3 Repeat step 1 to load the empty side of the brush with the second color.

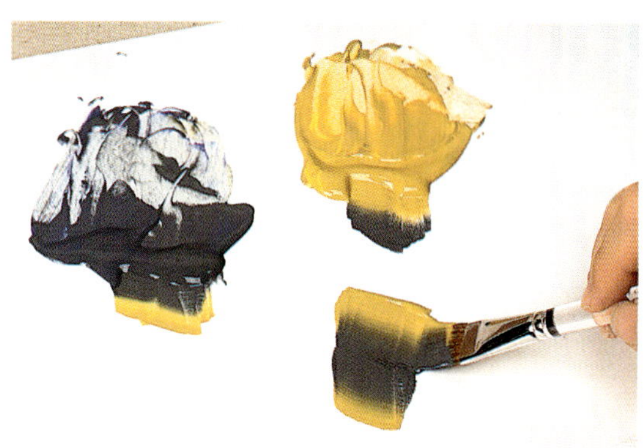

4 Stroke the side of the brush loaded with the first color against the same color on the stroke. Flip the brush and repeat on the other side of the stroke. Pay attention to what you're doing: Don't put the wrong edge of the brush into the wrong color. Load the brush with a little more of each color and continue stroking until the brush is full of paint.

TROUBLESHOOTING

- If the two colors aren't blended enough (A), pick up more paint and continue stroking in the same spot until the two gradually blend together.
- Sometimes the stroke becomes overblended, which muddies the colors on the palette as well as in the brush (B). To correct this, wipe the brush on a paper towel before starting again, but don't clean the brush completely or you'll undo all the good work you've done to fill it with paint.

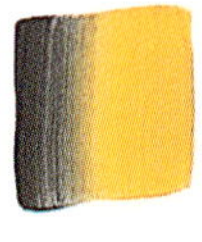

A

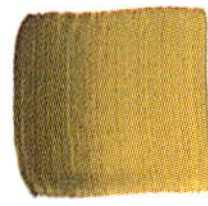

B

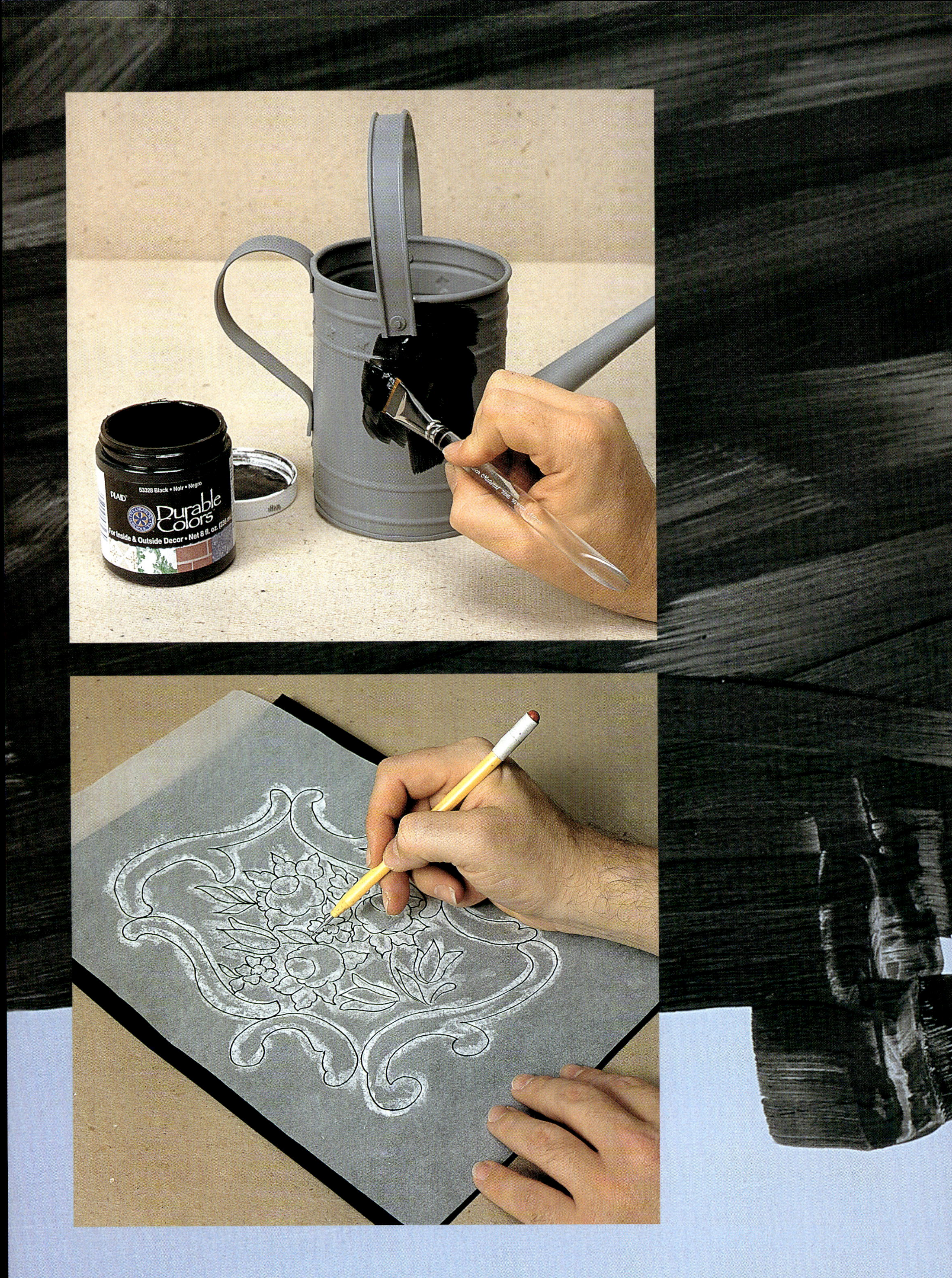
PLAID
53328 Black • Noir • Negro
Durable Colors
For Inside & Outside Decor • Net 8 fl. oz.

3 The Painting Surface

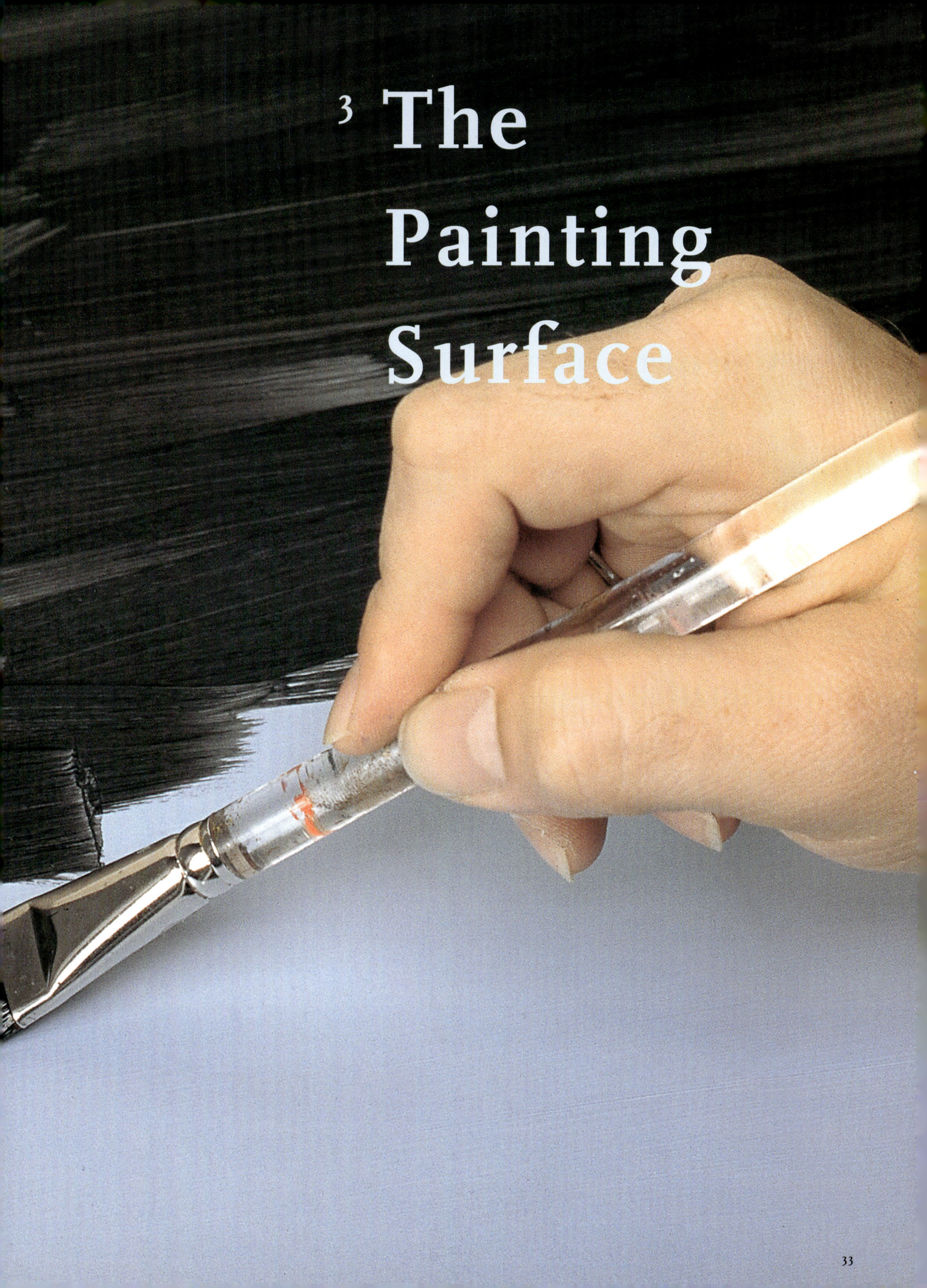

Preparing Wood

The guidelines below apply to the preparation of new, unfinished wood. If you would like to repaint an already finished piece, you can prime and basecoat it without stripping it first, as long as the wood is in good condition and the finish isn't flaking off or peeling away. If the piece is in poor condition, strip it with a commercial paint and varnish remover following the manufacturer's instructions. When the stripping process is complete, putty, prime, and sand the piece as needed, then proceed with the desired surface treatment.

APPLYING WOOD PUTTY

The first step in preparing a wood surface for painting is to fill in any nail holes, dents, or imperfections with wood putty. Pick up a small amount of putty with a clean palette knife and apply it to the affected area, smoothing out the surface and slightly overfilling any concave areas. Follow the manufacturer's directions with regard to drying times. At this point, the piece is ready for either priming or sanding.

PRIMING

This step generally isn't necessary unless a piece has many knots or you plan to basecoat it with a light color. If you do need to prime a piece, don't spend time sanding it before you prime it because the primer will "raise" the wood grain, or cause it to swell, which requires sanding anyway. Apply one coat of good-quality, white-pigmented primer with a wash brush or a glaze/varnish brush (the size of the piece will guide your choice of brush), then let it dry according to the manufacturer's directions.

SANDING

If you haven't primed your piece, sand it with medium-grade (#220-grit) sandpaper; if you have, sand it with a fine grade (#400-grit) or with a scrub pad. Always sand in the direction of the wood grain, and try to keep your sanding strokes straight and even. You only need to sand until the wood feels smooth to the touch.

When you're finished, wipe the entire piece with a tack rag, making sure that even the finest grains of sanding residue have been removed from the surface. Don't skip this step; if you do, the residue can make your basecoat look grainy or flawed.

BASECOATING

You can basecoat wood with any color or brand of acrylic or latex paint that you prefer. The most widely available and convenient choice for small projects are 2-ounce squeeze-bottle craft acrylics, which can be purchased at most art supply and craft stores.

Use a natural-bristle or mixed-hair wash brush or glaze/varnish brush to apply the paint. These brushes are more responsive and provide better coverage than the foam-type sponge brushes that are currently popular. Dip the hairs about halfway into the paint, then apply the paint to the surface in smooth strokes. Let this coat of paint dry completely, then assess its finish: If it isn't smooth and opaque, sand it lightly with #400-grit sandpaper, wipe it with a tack rag, then apply a second coat. Allow the second coat to dry completely before proceeding with decorative painting or any other surface treatment.

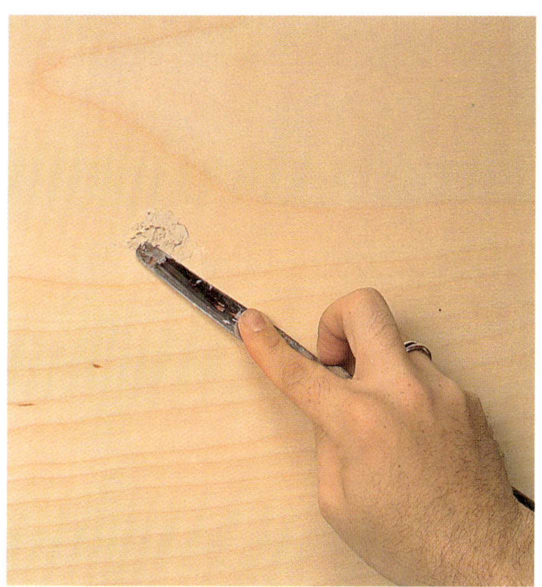

When applying wood putty, smooth out the surface and slightly overfill any concave areas.

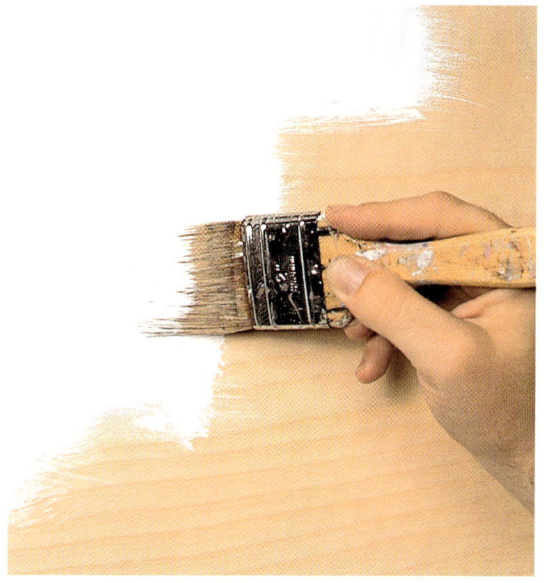

Apply primer to ensure that the grain and any remaining imperfections won't bleed through a light-colored basecoat.

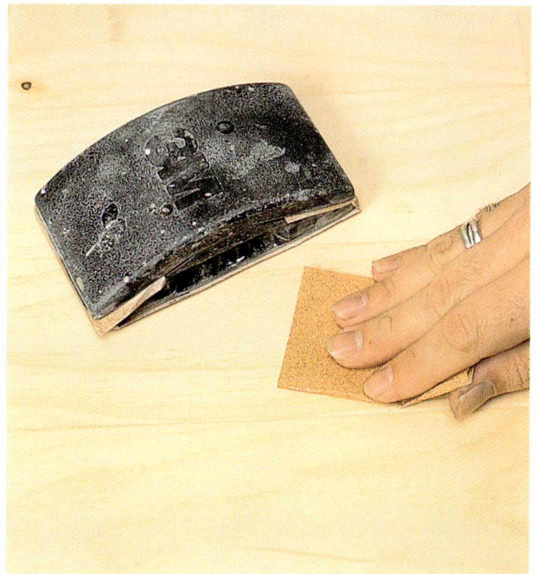

Working with a sanding block—a small rubber or wooden block to which a piece of sandpaper is attached—can make the sanding process a little easier.

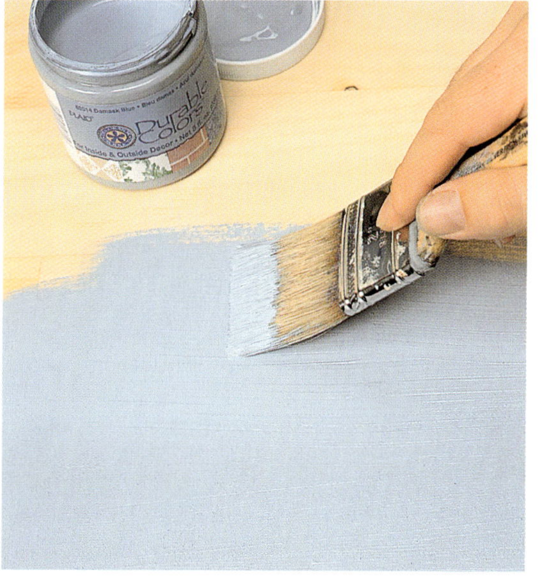

Always apply the basecoat in the direction of the wood grain.

Preparing Metal

Metal is one of the trickiest surfaces to prepare, but when it's prepared correctly it's one of the nicest to paint on. Paint that is applied to an improperly prepared metal surface will flake off, or eventually be overcome by rust, so it's important to get the preparation right from the start.

CLEANING

OLD METAL If an older piece is dirty or rusty, wash it with a pastelike mixture of dishwasher detergent powder and water, or use dishwasher gel straight from the bottle. Be sure to wear rubber gloves, as the detergent can burn your skin. Scrub off as much grime as you can, using a scrub pad, steel wool, or a product like Brillo or SOS to help things along. Rinse the piece thoroughly, allow it to dry, then apply Naval Jelly to remove rust and etch the surface, carefully following the manufacturer's instructions.

To strip already painted metal, use a commercial paint remover. (Naval Jelly alone is often effective.) Never strip or repaint a piece of decorated metalware without first having it evaluated by a reputable antiques appraiser to determine its age and value. Although the condition of an older piece may be fair or poor, which undercuts its decorative appeal, it may in fact be quite valuable.

NEW METAL New pieces are typically finished with a factory-applied oily coating that not only prevents rust but also prevents paint from adhering to the surface. Wash the piece with a 1:1 mixture of vinegar and water to remove the coating, rinse it well, then let dry completely.

PRIMING

Once a piece is clean and dry, it's ready for priming. Use a high-quality enamel primer

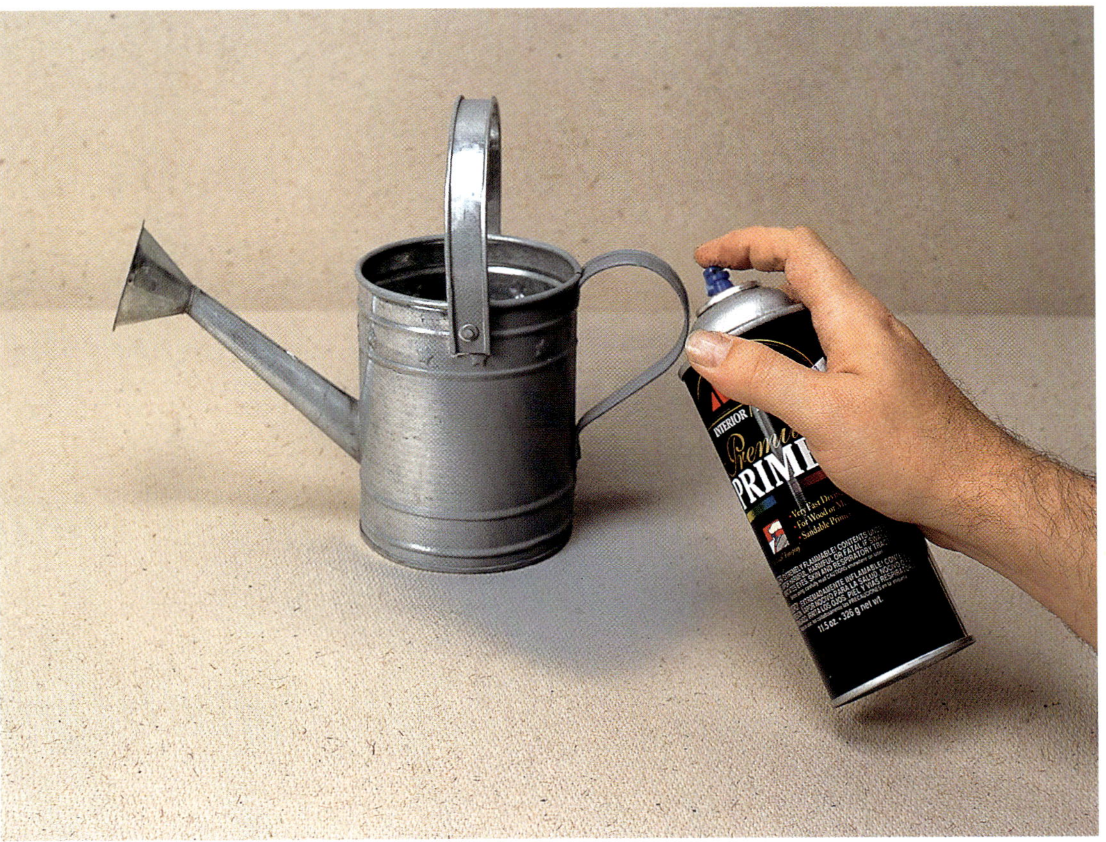

Prime every nook and cranny of your metal project's surface by working the spray in a smooth, side-to-side motion.

formulated specifically for use with metal. I use a spray-on primer that dries to a flat gray finish, which provides an ideal surface for the basecoat. To ensure adequate ventilation while working with the spray, set up outdoors on a warm (but not breezy) day; it's also advisable to wear eye protection, a respirator, and gloves, since the spray generates hazardous mists. Place the piece and the primer in your work area for a few hours (avoiding direct sunlight) to bring them to the same temperature. To apply the primer, hold the can about 8 to 10 inches from the surface and work it in a back-and-forth motion. (If you hold the can any farther away, the primer will actually dry before it lands on the surface.) Minimize runs and drips by applying three or four light coats of primer instead of just one thick one, letting each coat dry before applying the next. Let the final coat dry thoroughly—preferably overnight—before applying the basecoat.

BASECOATING

A basecoat can either be brushed or sprayed on a primed metal surface. Conveniently, you can use acrylic paint straight from the bottle or tube for this purpose. As with primer, it's best to apply a few thin coats rather than a single heavy one.

Once the paint is dry to the touch, and if the piece isn't too large, I like to heat-cure it in an oven, which accelerates the curing process and hardens the surface. Preheat the oven to 200°F, then turn it off before you put the piece in. I usually place my pieces right on the rack, but you can put down a sheet of aluminum foil if you prefer. Remove the piece when the oven is completely cool. While the oven is cooling, attach a note to it advising that it be left off until the piece has been removed, as temperatures above 200°F could blister the paint or melt the solder. Note that heat-curing is optional; you can simply let the piece dry overnight before proceeding.

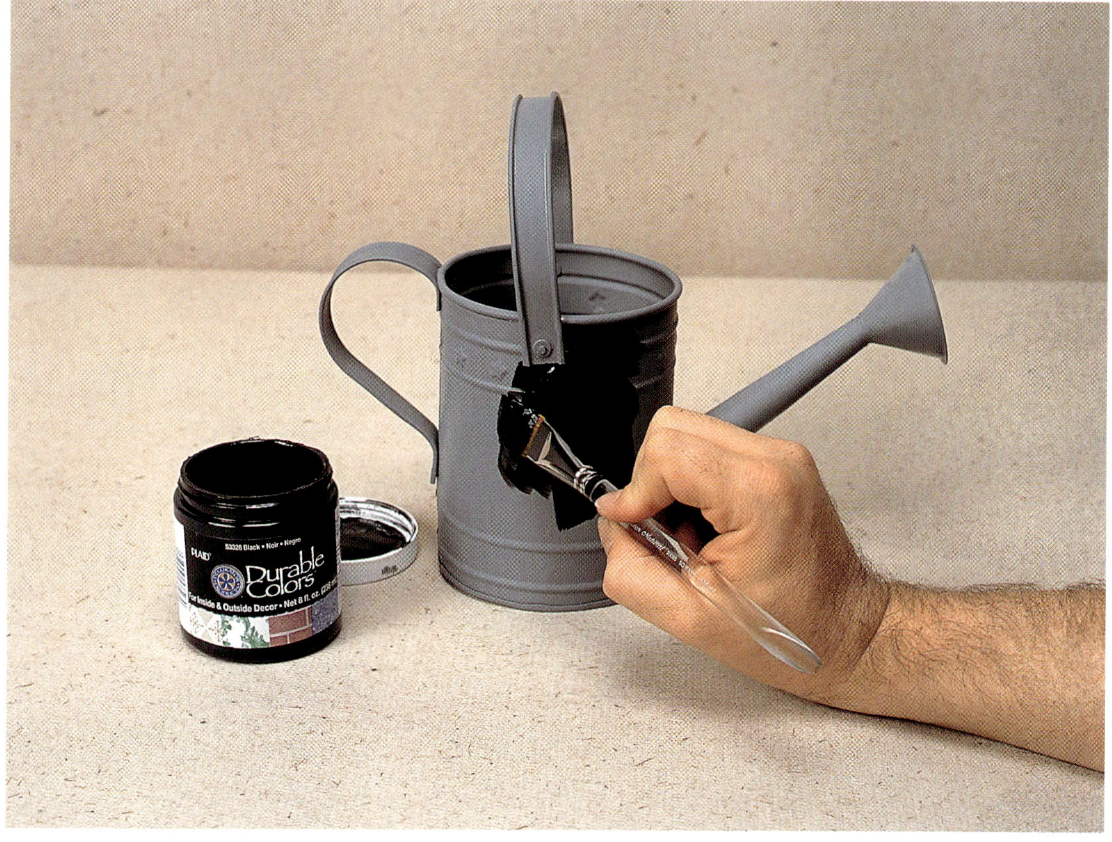

I prefer to basecoat my metal projects with a brush-on paint because it gives the surface a rustic look.

Tracing, Sizing, and Transferring Patterns

The decorative painting patterns at the back of this book are provided for your use and enjoyment. You may use them as is, simplify them by eliminating elements, or embellish them by adding elements from others, or creating your own. Working with an accurately traced, sized, and transferred pattern will make your decorative painting experience more pleasant.

TRACING AND SIZING

Place a sheet of tracing paper over the pattern and carefully outline its contours with a fine-tip black marker. If the traced pattern fits the painting surface, you can simply transfer it using one of the two methods described on pages 39–40. If you need to adjust the size of the pattern to fit the painting surface, you can enlarge or reduce the tracing on a photocopier. To determine the correct percentage of enlargement or reduction, use a *proportional scale,* which consists of two concentric discs whose circumferences are printed with a series of measurements. In one of the disks is a window that, when turned, reveals a sequence of percentages. Simply measure the traced pattern's height or width, then figure out what that dimension should be in order for the pattern to fit on the surface. When you line up these two numbers on the disks, the correct percentage of enlargement or reduction will appear in the window.

I use two transfer techniques: the transfer paper method and the chalk transfer method. Either method can be used with any pattern, but the chalk transfer method is better suited to stroke designs because the chalk dissolves more readily when paint is applied, and can't be seen through the paint even when it doesn't.

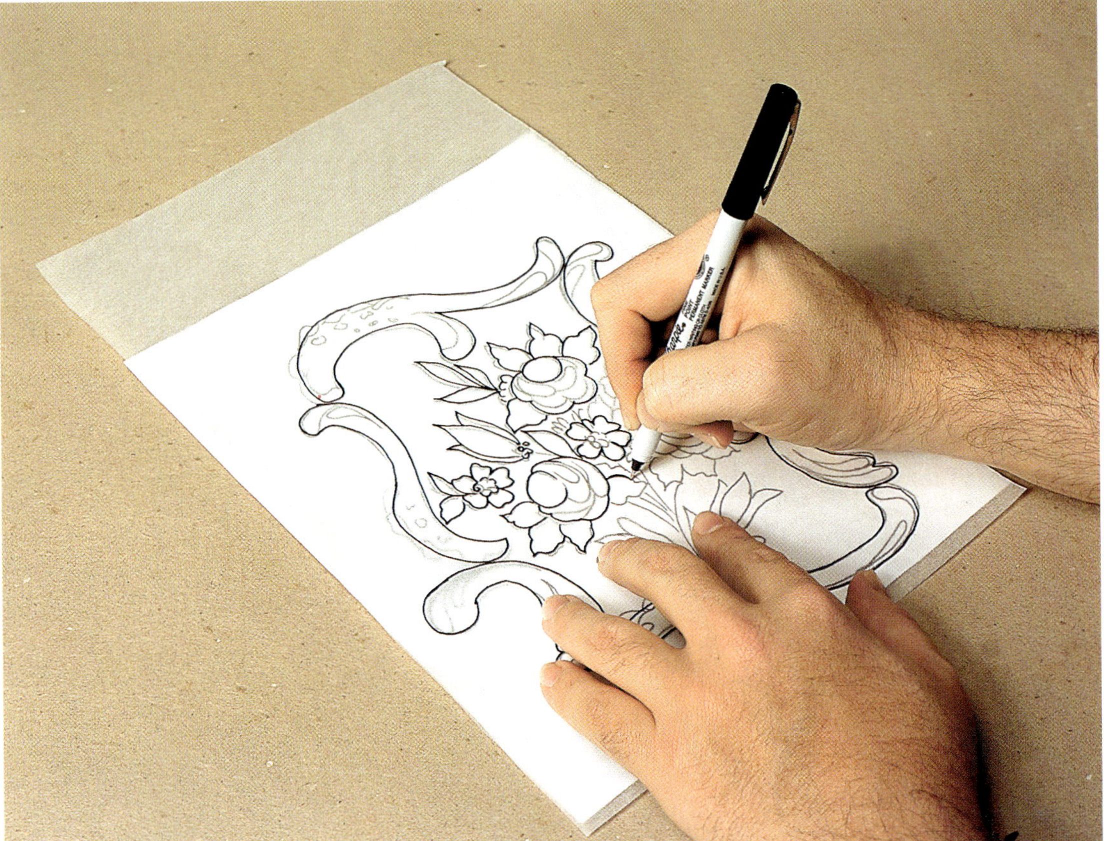

You don't need to trace lines that indicate secondary details like shading, but be sure that you've traced all of the essential lines before removing the tracing paper from the pattern.

TRANSFER METHOD I: TRANSFER PAPER

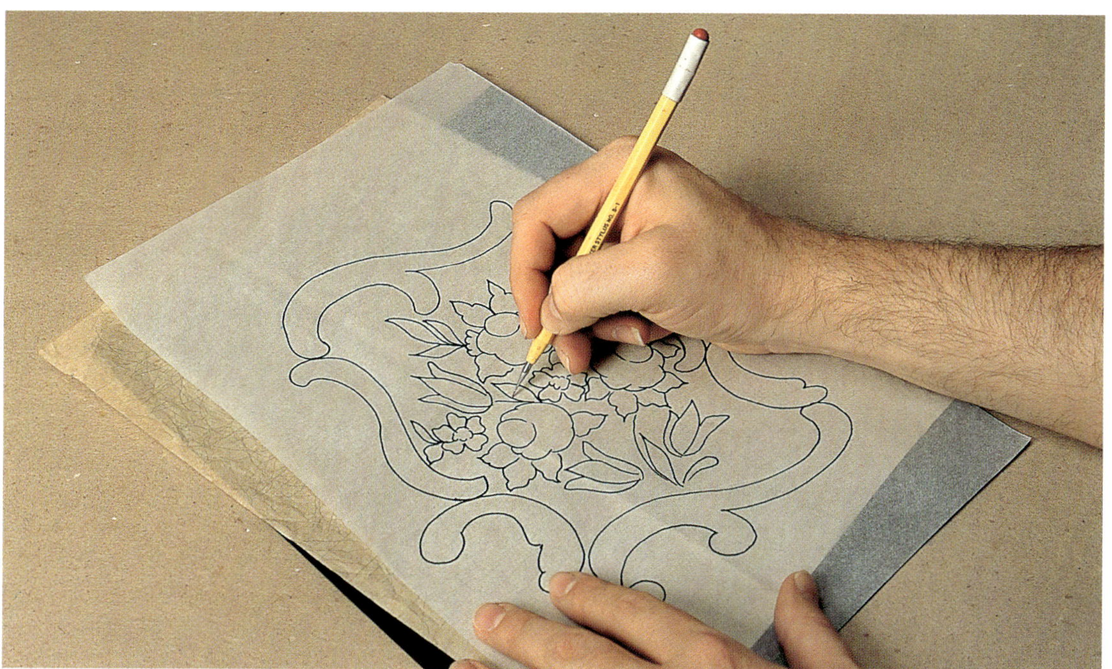

1 Position the correctly sized pattern on the prepared surface. Tape it in place if you think it might slip, but don't affix the tape with much pressure—use just enough to hold the design in place. Slip a piece of transfer paper under the pattern, make a test mark with the stylus, then lift the pattern and the transfer paper to make sure that the right side of the transfer paper is against the surface. (This is an important habit to cultivate, since it's a frustrating waste of time to transfer a pattern to the back of itself.)

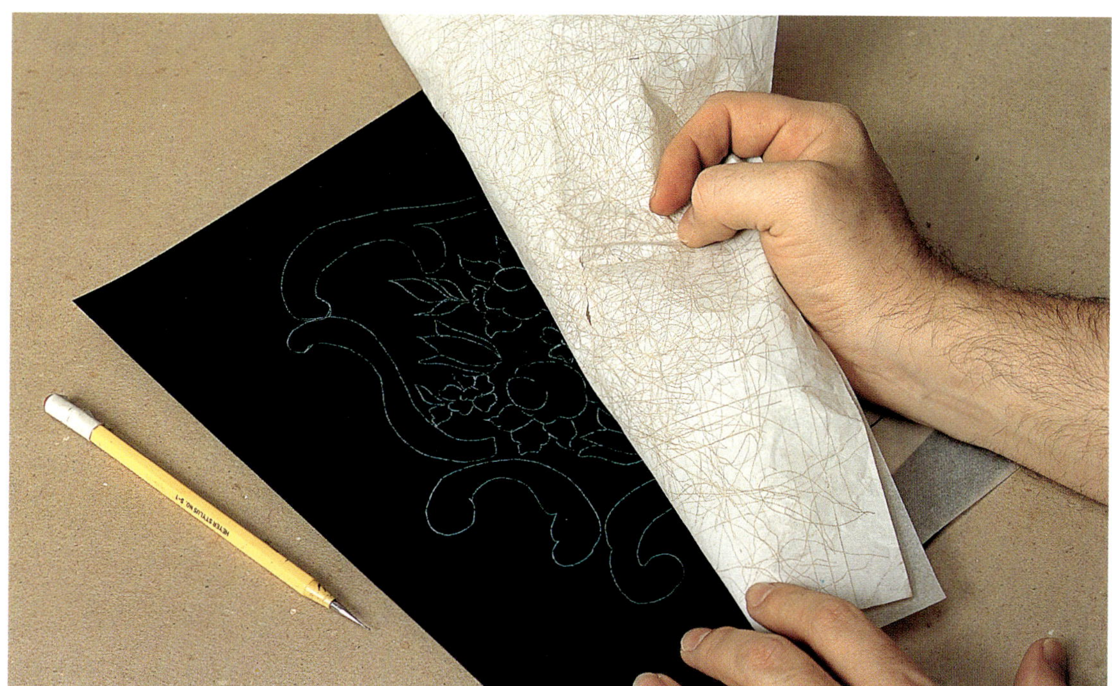

2 Carefully trace all of the pattern lines with the stylus, periodically lifting both the pattern and the transfer paper to see whether you've missed any. One caveat: Don't press hard or you might dent or groove the surface. When you're done, simply remove both sheets and you're ready to paint.

Tracing, Sizing, and Transferring Patterns

TRANSFER METHOD 2: CHALK TRACING

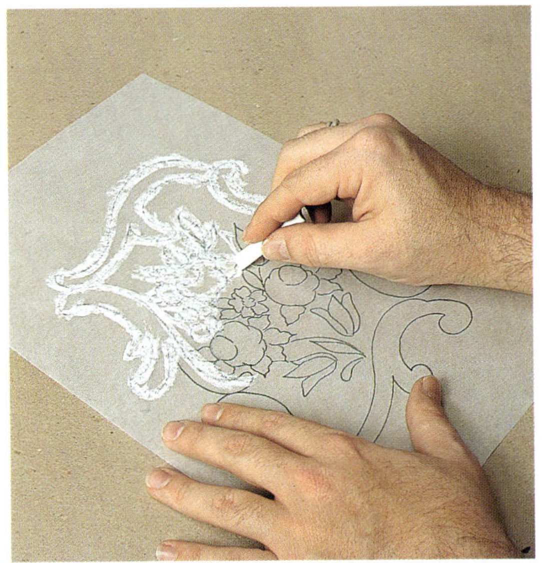

1 Turn the correctly sized pattern face down and carefully trace its lines with a piece of chalk. Do *not* scribble all over the back of the pattern. Gently shake the pattern (but not near the prepared surface) to remove excess chalk.

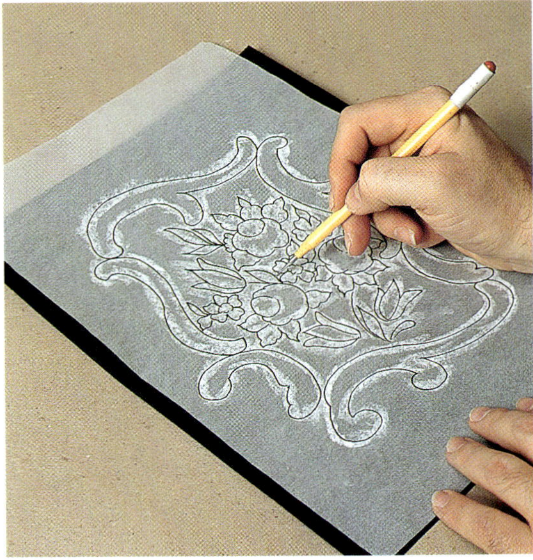

2 Position the pattern chalk-side down on the prepared surface, taping it in place if necessary. Use a stylus to trace over the lines.

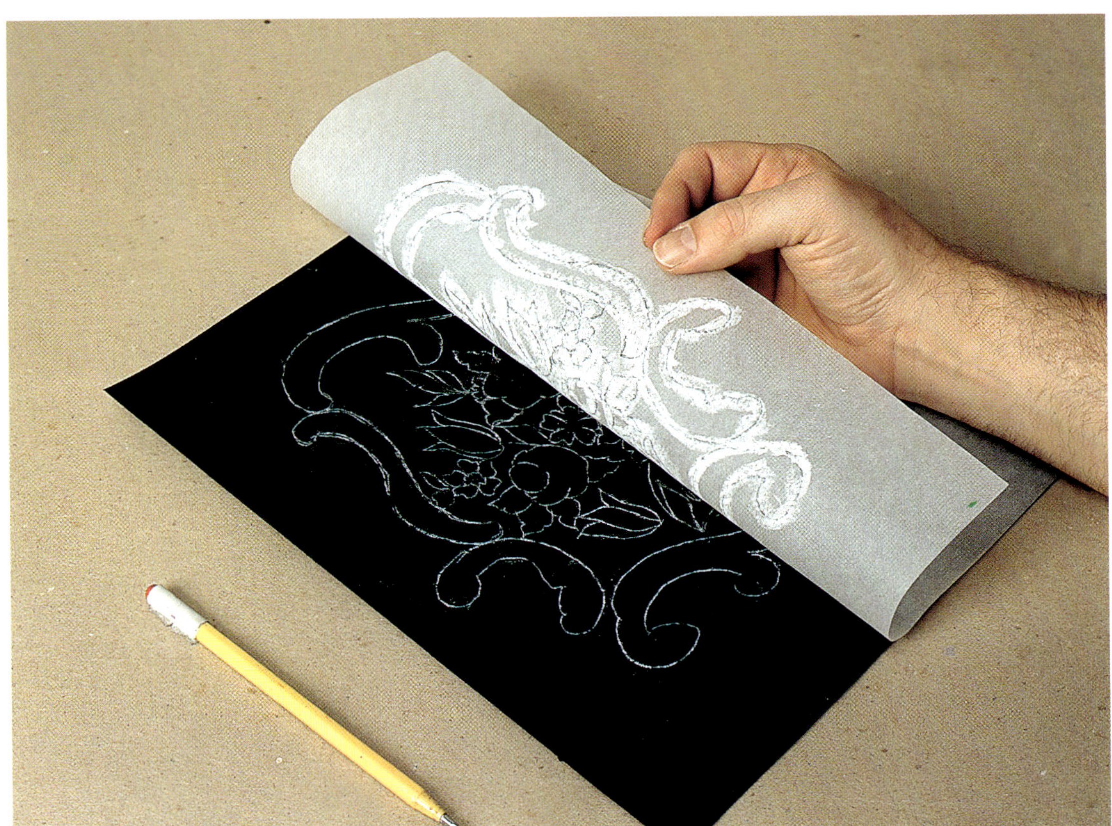

3 Periodically lift the pattern to make sure you've transferred all of its lines, and that the transferred image is clear.

Antiquing

An antiquing glaze—a translucent wash of color applied, then partially removed, to create a patina of age—can add a wonderful, rich look to designs painted on metal and wood. You can apply an antiquing glaze over a basecoat prior to painting a design, or over a completed design.

Before you can begin antiquing, you must create the glaze. Mix equal amounts of paint and Glazing Medium with a palette knife until they are thoroughly combined, and the consistency of the mixture is similar to thick soup. If you want to extend the glaze's working time, add an amount of gel retarder equal to the entire volume of the mixture.

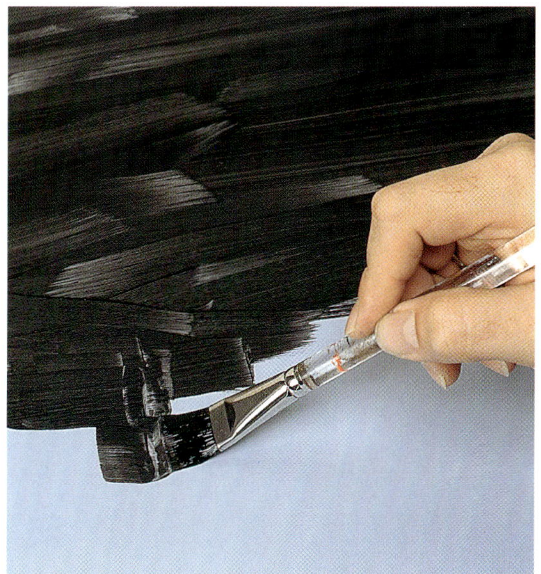

1 Use a wash brush to apply the glaze to the surface in a random manner. Be sure to completely cover the area you want to antique.

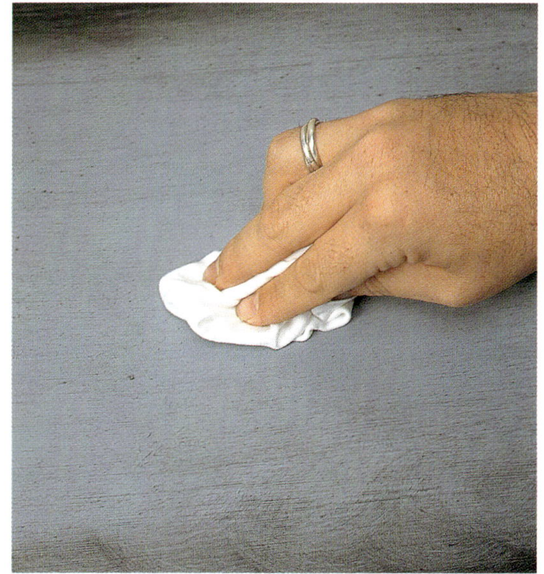

2 While the glaze is still wet, use a soft cotton rag to wipe away the glaze from the center of the surface, working in a circular motion from the center outward to create an attractive highlighted area.

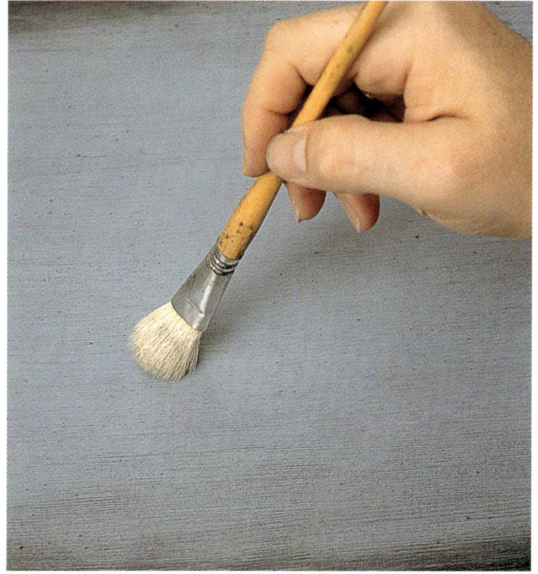

3 To complete the process, use a mop brush to soften and refine the glaze that remains on the surface. Holding the brush so that the bristles just graze the surface, create a subtle gradation from light (in the center) to dark (at the edges of the surface) and eliminate any obvious marks left by the wash brush or rag in steps 1 and 2.

Varnishing

The procedure for varnishing is fairly simple, but you must use the proper tools to achieve satisfactory results. Before you begin, make sure that your painting is sufficiently dry. If you're working with acrylic paints, you should wait at least 24 hours after completing the project before varnishing.

APPLYING BRUSH-ON VARNISH

Use a top-quality natural-bristle brush to apply brush-on varnish. A glaze/varnish brush is an excellent choice for this task, as it holds plenty of varnish and releases it in a controlled and even manner. Never apply varnish with a foam brush, which will leave bubbles on the surface—something you definitely want to avoid.

Using the right kind of brush is essential, but its care is important too. I recommend that you purchase a new glaze/varnish brush and set it aside for varnishing only. In fact, I labeled the handle of one of my glaze/varnish brushes so there would never be any question as to which one should be used for varnishing. Why earmark a brush exclusively for varnishing? The answer is simple: If you use a brush to apply paint, traces of it may remain in the bristles even after it has been cleaned. Good-quality water-based polyurethanes, like the FolkArt and Varathane brands I use, contain chemicals that can loosen and soften this residue, which then may be transferred to the painted surface or leave unsightly streaks of color in the varnish. Wash your varnish brush immediately after applying each coat to prevent a buildup of varnish in the hairs.

Before you begin applying it, stir the varnish thoroughly until none of the cloudy "stuff" (dulling agents) is left in the bottom of the container. (Never shake a can of varnish, as shaking

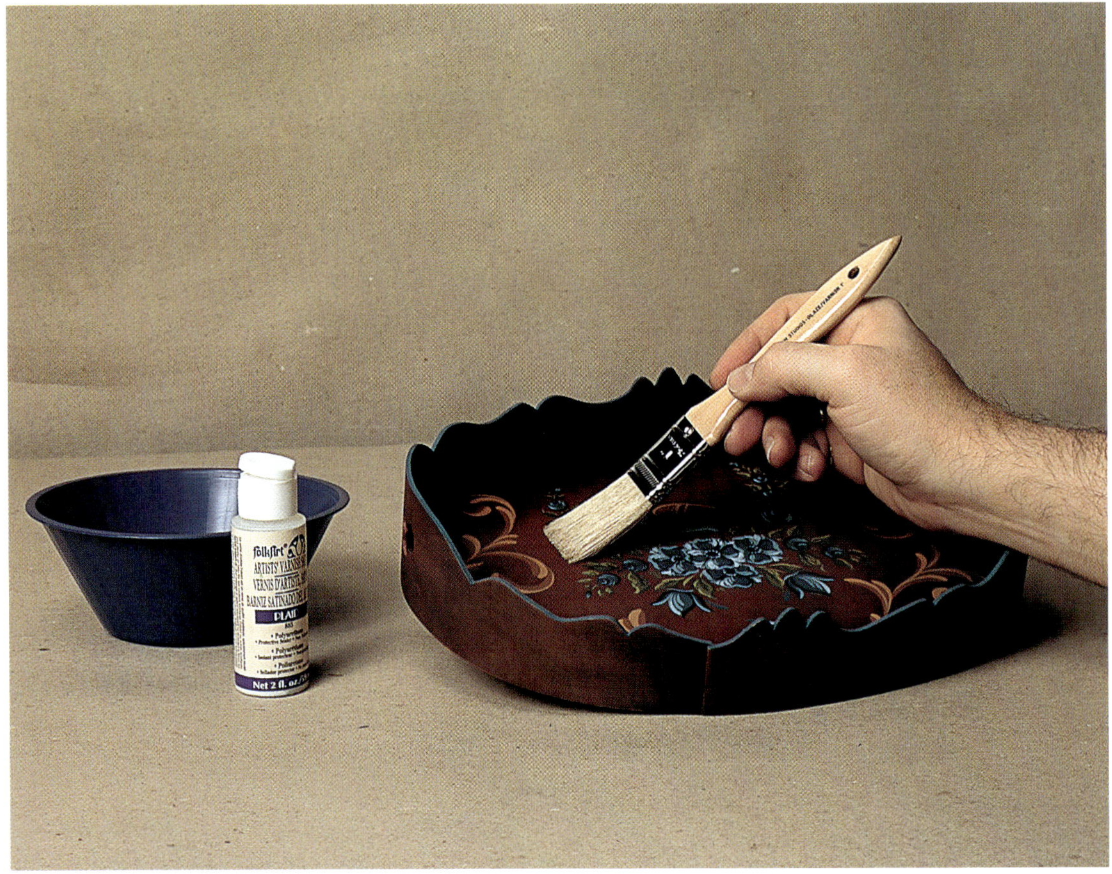

When applying brush-on varnish, flow it on the surface in a uniform layer, working the brush in one direction. Apply a total of three coats, letting each coat dry before applying the next.

produces bubbles.) If you don't distribute the dulling agents throughout the varnish by stirring it, it will become increasingly dull as you use up the can, and will eventually cloud your finish.

After stirring the varnish, dip the brush into it, then even out the load on the hairs by scraping its side against the inner rim of the container. This is done to avoid either "flooding" the surface with varnish or applying so little that you have to scrub it with the brush. Let the first coat dry, then repeat the process to apply two more coats. Three coats of varnish should provide adequate protection for your work.

APPLYING SPRAY VARNISH

When finishing an intricately cut or carved wooden or metal piece, acrylic spray varnish provides a solution to the problem of applying an even coat to every nook and cranny. Spray varnish comes in a range of sheens, from gloss to matte. Choose whichever sheen suits your personal taste, and whatever brand or sheen you use, be sure to read and follow the manufacturer's directions carefully.

The fumes and mists that are by-products of spray varnish can be dangerous if your work area isn't properly ventilated—the rooms in most homes aren't designed for this task—so set up outdoors on a balmy but not breezy day. Leave the piece and the spray in your work area for a few hours to bring them to the same temperature. Apply a light coat of varnish, holding the can at least 8 inches, but no more than 10 inches, from the surface, moving it with a sweeping back-and-forth motion. As with brush-on varnish, it's best to apply three or four light coats rather than one or two heavy ones.

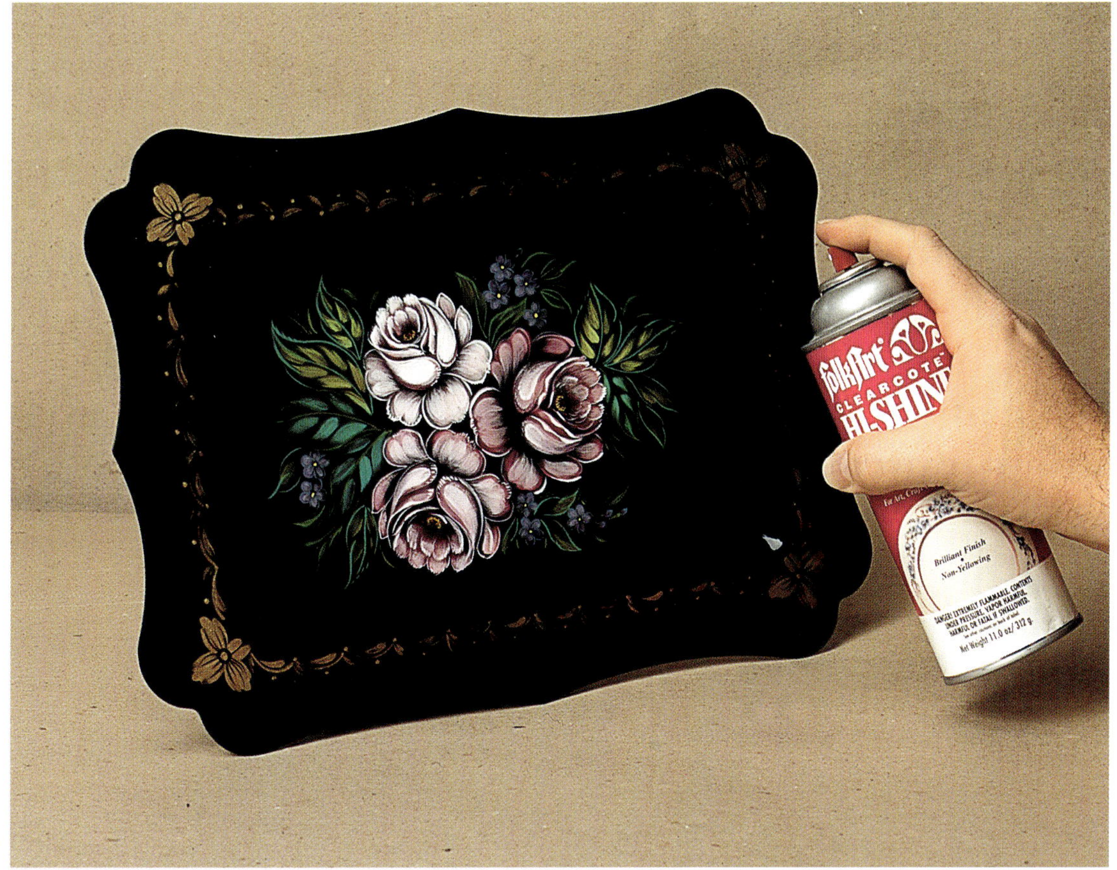

If you hold the can of spray varnish closer than 8 inches from the surface, the solvent in the varnish may reactivate the paint; if you hold it farther than 10 inches, some of the varnish may dry before it can even make contact with the surface.

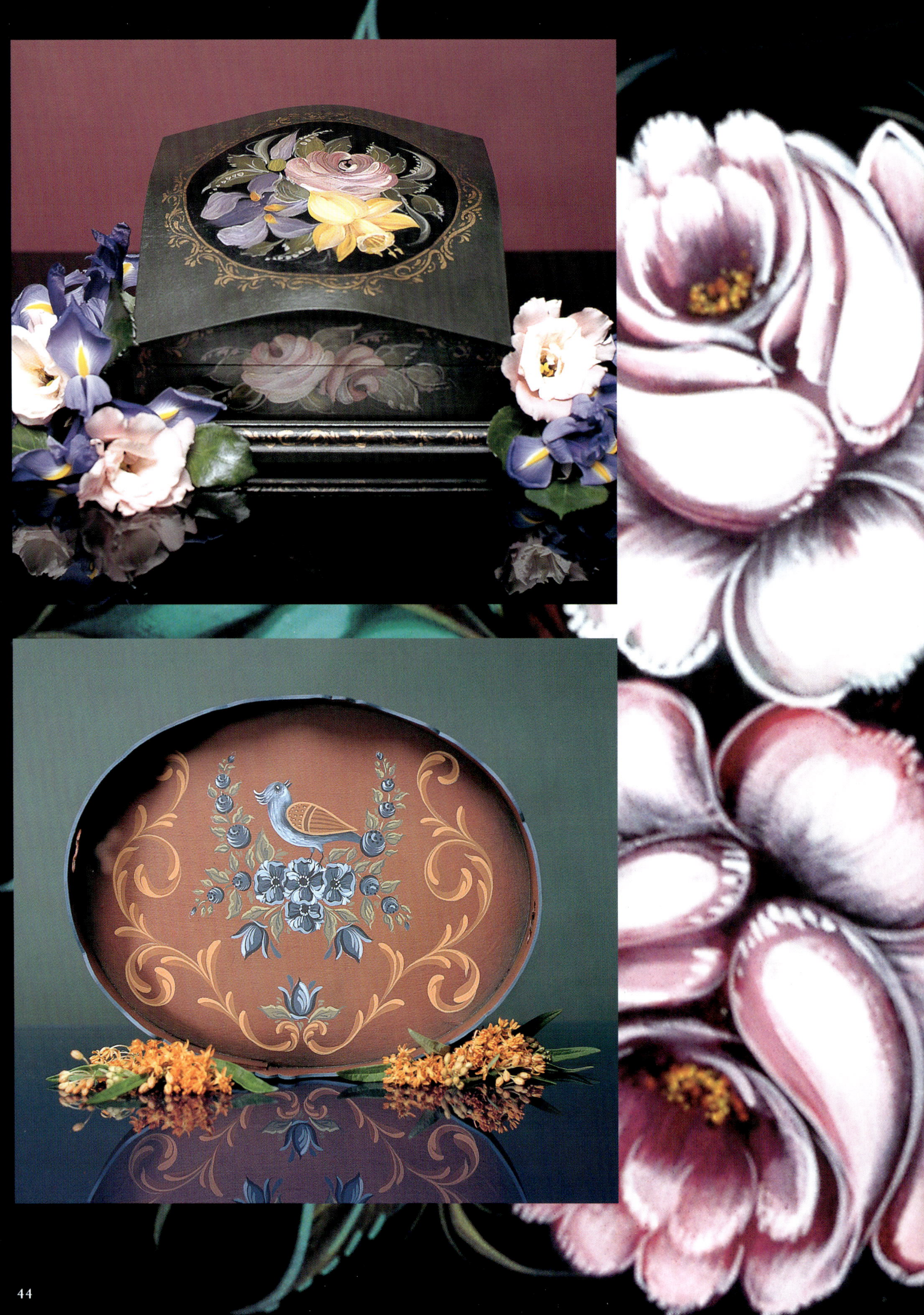

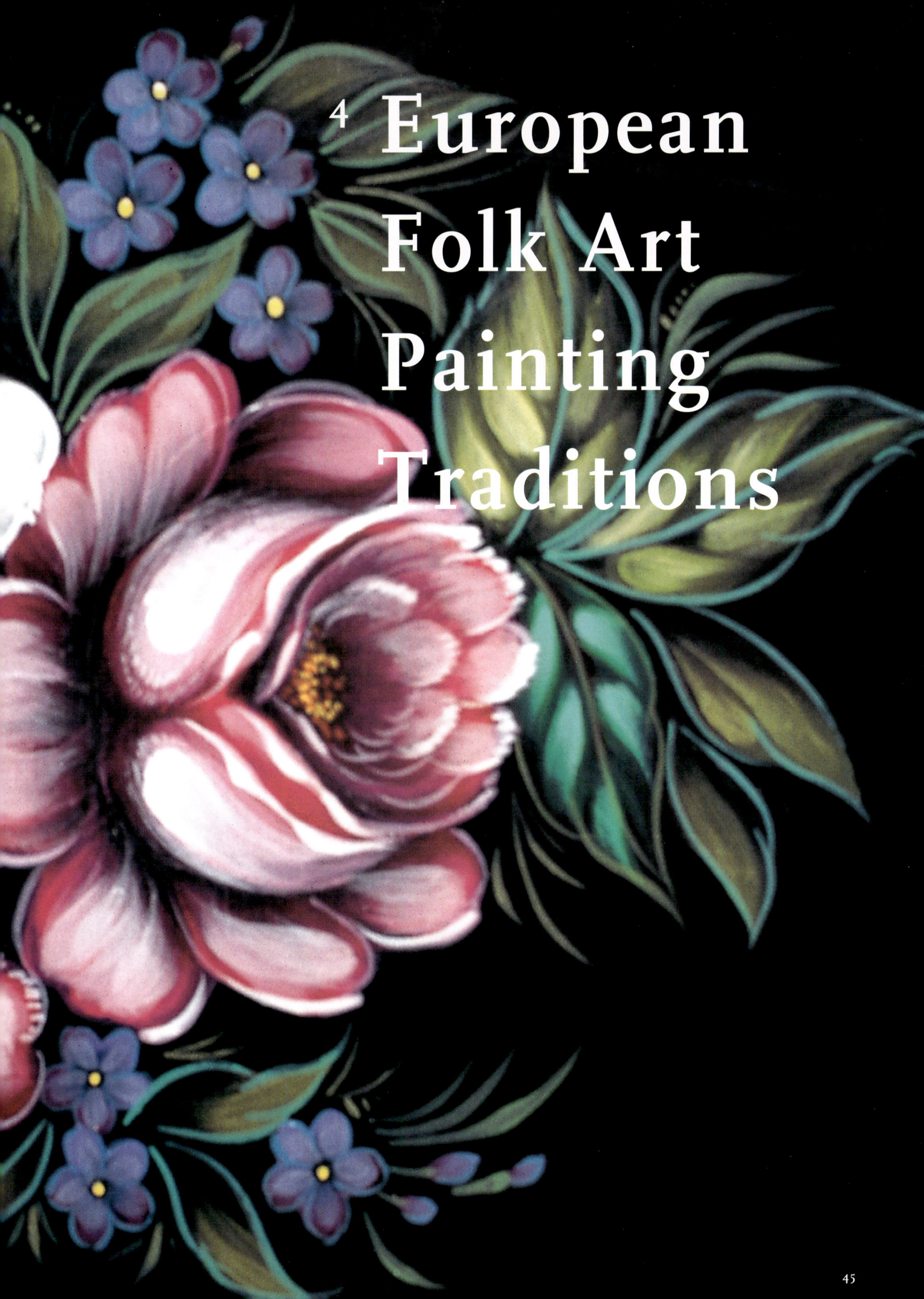

4 European Folk Art Painting Traditions

Narrow Boat Painting

Degree of Difficulty

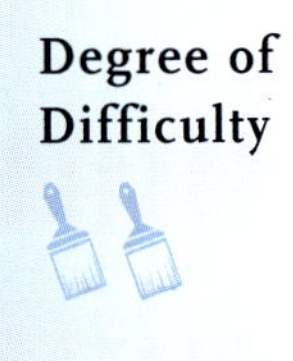

The surface for this piece is a traditional metal buckby *or water can. This vessel was always highly decorated and given a place of honor on the narrow boat. The original buckby cans were anywhere from 14 to 28 inches tall, but the one I've painted here is only 12 inches tall.*

If you can't locate an authentic buckby can, you can adapt the design to a pitcher or coffeepot. You can also place the rose motifs on boxes or other accent pieces. Never let your imagination be limited to the way a piece is presented in this book. Folk art is a living art form and can be interpreted in many ways. The narrow boat painting presented here is my own interpretation of the traditional art form.

WHAT YOU'LL NEED

Pattern

Page 102

Project

Buckby by Lola Gill *(see page 111 for ordering information)*

Supplies

SURFACE PREP

- Scrub pad
- Naval jelly
- Gray primer
- Tack cloth
- Basecoat paint: pure black *(see list of artists' acrylics)*

TRACING AND TRANSFERRING

- Tracing paper
- Fine-tip black marker
- Chalk
- Stylus

ARTISTS' ACRYLICS

- Titanium white
- Medium yellow
- Turner's yellow
- Yellow ocher
- Raw sienna
- Naphthol crimson
- Asphaltum
- Burnt umber
- Burnt carmine
- Hauser green light
- Hauser green dark
- Pure black

CRAFT ACRYLICS

- Light blue

BRUSHES

- Wash brush: 3/4-inch
- Round: no. 4
- Flat: no. 8
- Script liner: no. 2

BASIC PAINTING SUPPLIES

- Water container
- Palette knife
- Sta-Wet palette
- Paper towels

FINISHING

- Satin-sheen spray polyurethane varnish

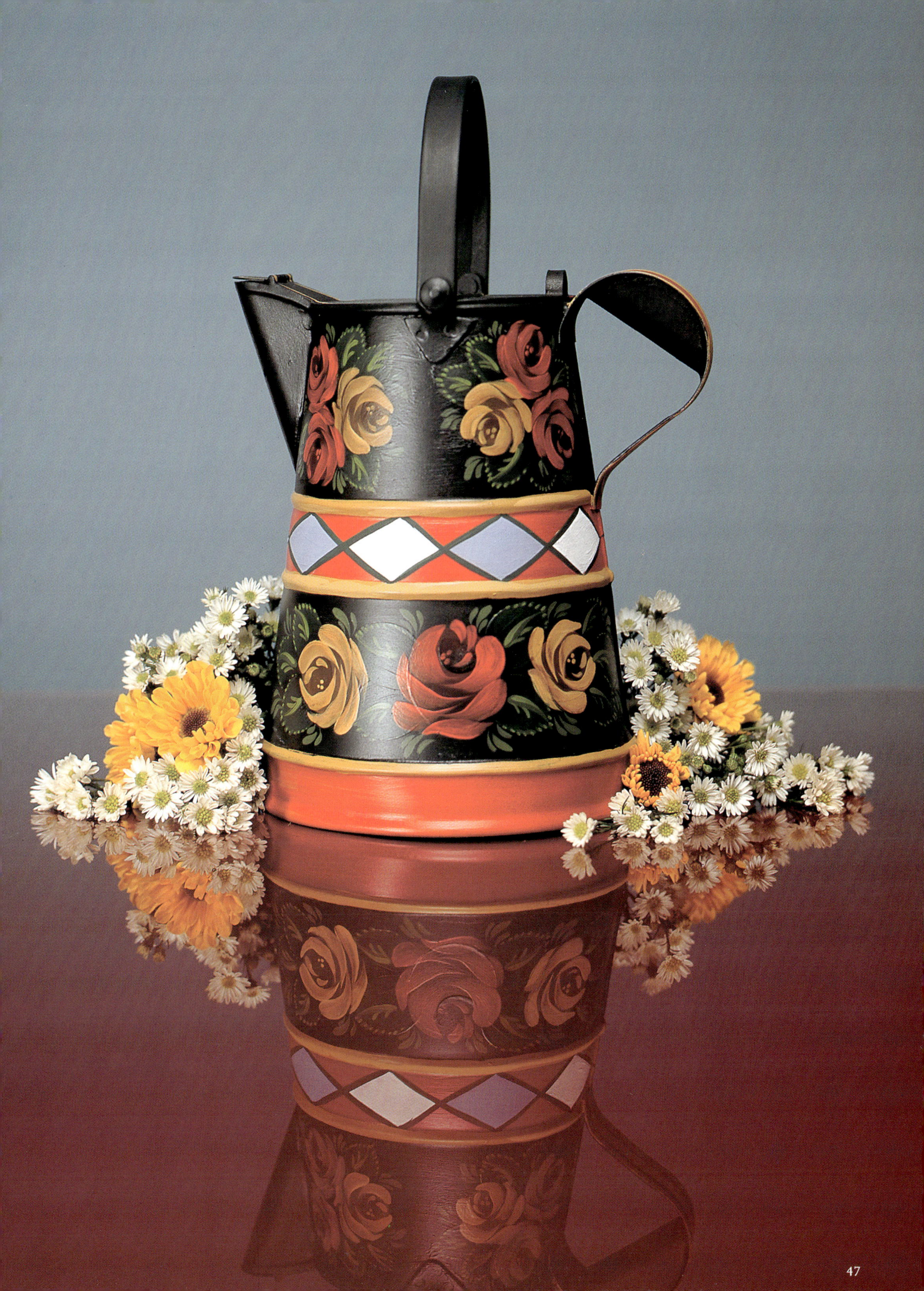

Narrow Boat Painting

GETTING READY

Clean and prime the buckby according to the instructions on pages 36–37, then basecoat it with pure black using either spray paint or the wash brush. After letting it dry completely, undercoat the two wide bands with yellow ocher. Apply two or three coats in order to achieve an opaque coverage of paint, letting each coat dry completely before painting the next. Then paint the bands' centers with naphthol crimson, again applying two or three coats.

Use the script liner to paint a stripe around the edges of the lid with yellow ocher + Turner's yellow. Then paint a green stripe on the handle with Hauser green dark.

Finally, transfer the patterns to the water can using the chalk tracing method described on page 40.

LEAVES

1 Using the flat brush, undercoat the leaves with Hauser green dark. Let dry.

2 Sideload the same brush with pure black and apply the dark shading at the base of the leaf where the leaf goes behind a rose or another leaf. Let dry.

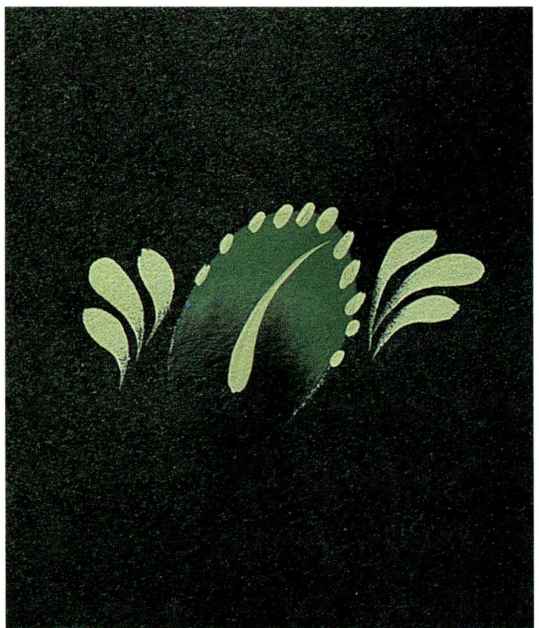

3 Paint the center vein using the script liner and thinned Hauser green light. Let dry. Add small dots or dabs along the top edge of the leaf with the same color. At this time, add the small green comma strokes that complete the design. Let dry.

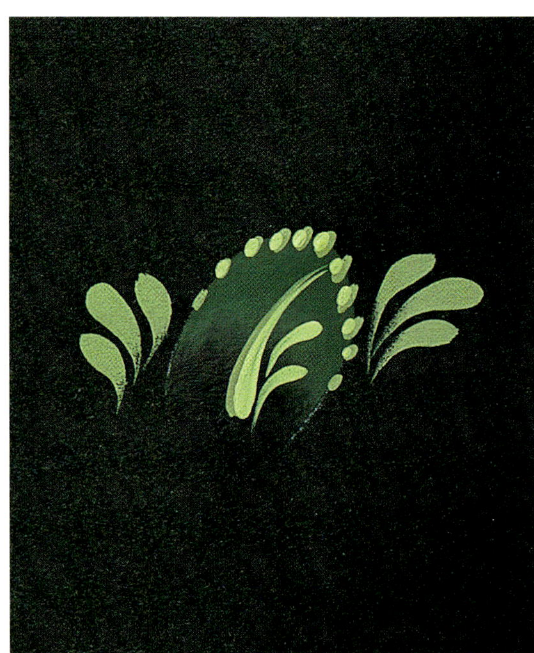

4 Add a smaller center vein and two side strokes of Hauser green light + medium yellow to the leaves. Add highlight dabs to the top edge of the leaves. Let dry.

RED ROSES

1 Using the flat brush, undercoat each red rose with a circle of naphthol crimson. Let dry.

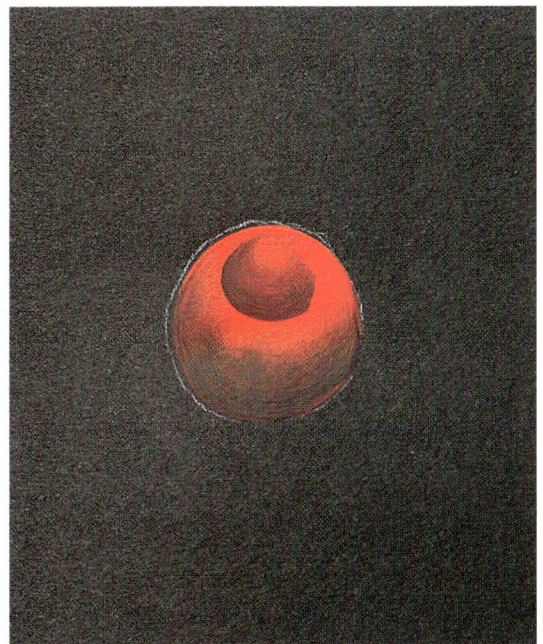

2 Sideload the flat with burnt carmine, then shade the rose by placing one U stroke at the bottom of the circle and a second, smaller U stroke near the top.Let dry.

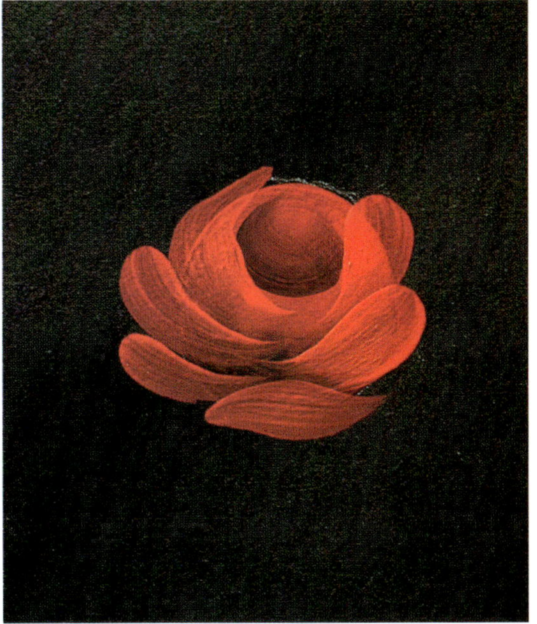

3 Using the round brush, form the petals of the rose with naphthol crimson by painting a sloppy U stroke and a comma stroke. Do not restroke the petals. You should see some of the undercoat through them. Let dry.

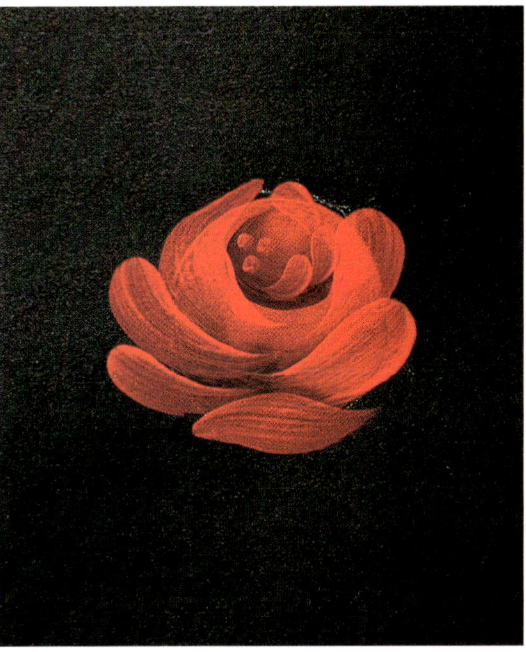

4 To finish the rose, switch to the script liner filled with naphthol crimson and apply a few tiny comma strokes to the throat of the rose. If desired, add a few red dots in the same area.

YELLOW ROSES

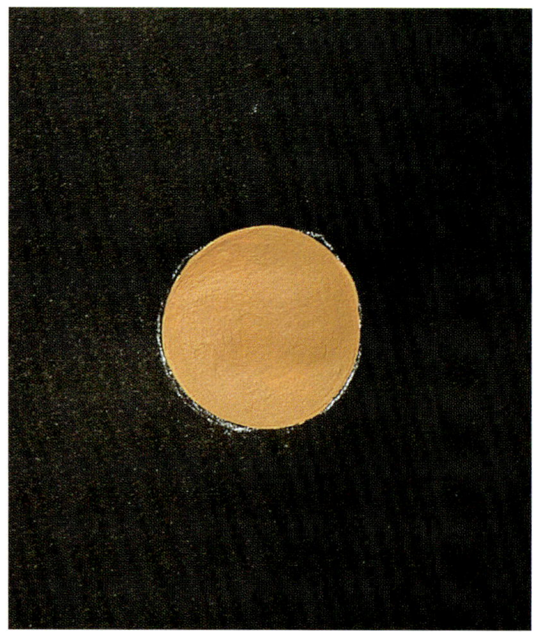

1 Use the flat brush to undercoat the yellow rose with a circle of raw sienna. Let dry.

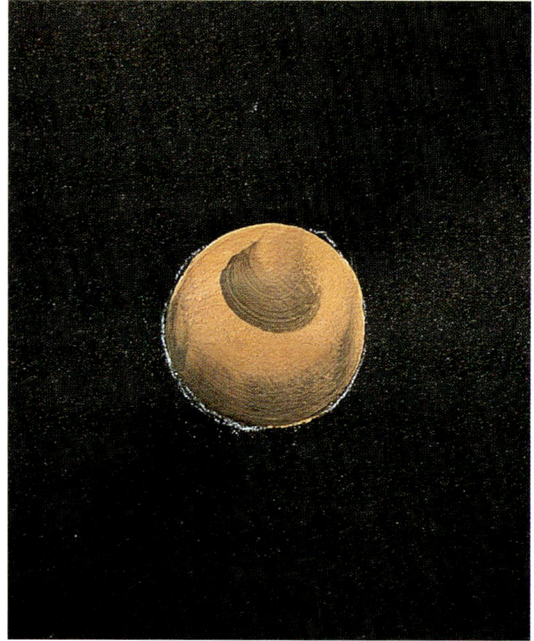

2 Shade the circle with the flat brush side-loaded with asphaltum + a little burnt umber. As you did when painting the red roses, apply one U stroke along the bottom of the circle and another near the top of the circle. Let dry.

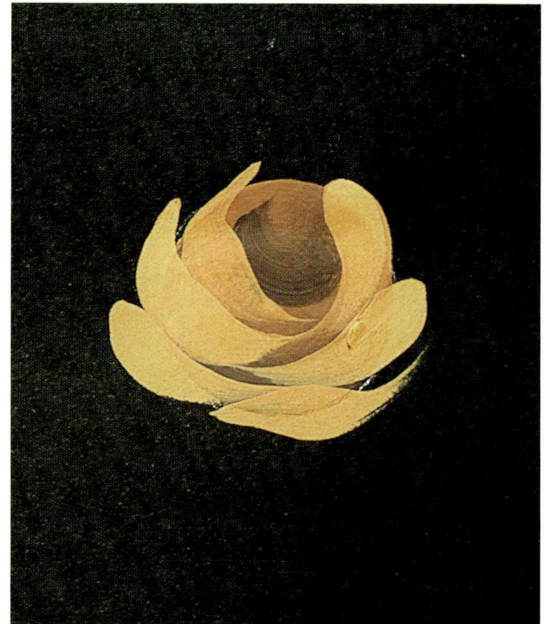

3 Form the petals of the rose using the round brush filled with yellow ocher and a bit of Turner's yellow. Since you do not want the two colors to blend on the brush, it's a good idea to first load the brush with ocher and then stroke it through the Turner's yellow. Form the petals with sloppy U strokes and comma strokes. Let dry.

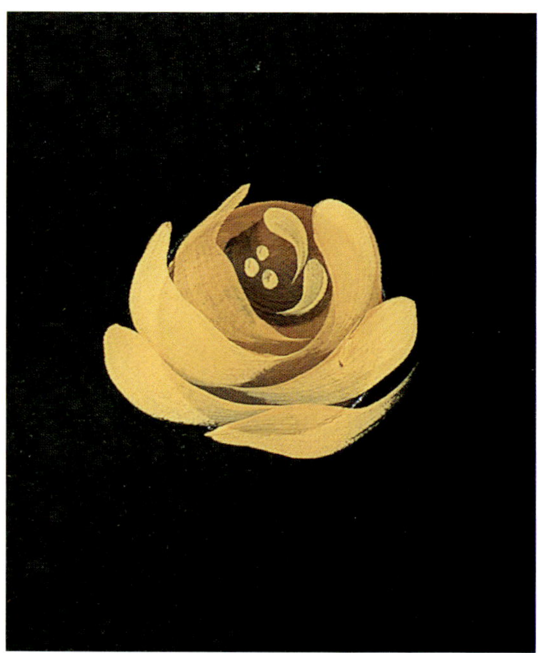

4 Switch to the script liner and finish the rose with a few tiny yellow comma strokes and dots in the throat.

TRIM

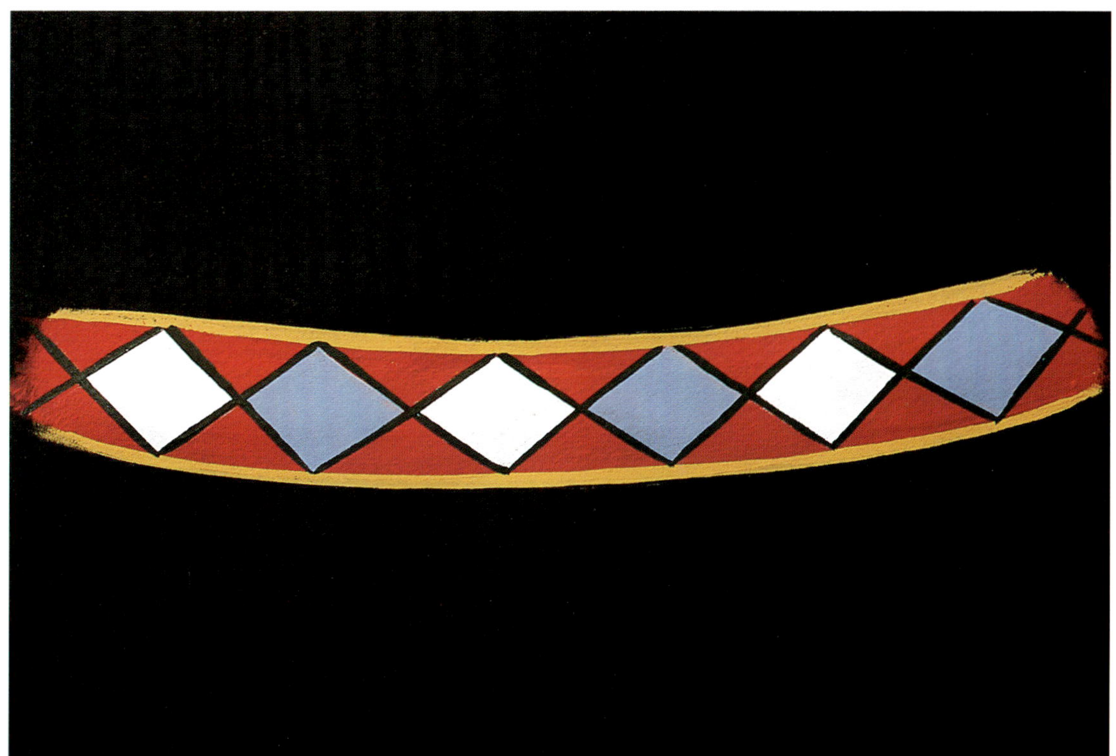

To complete the center stripe, either transfer or draw the diamond shapes. Paint the white diamonds with titanium white and the blue diamonds with light blue. You may need to apply two coats in order to achieve opaque coverage. Let dry, then use the script liner to paint the dark green stripes around the diamonds with Hauser green dark.

FINISHING

Finish the buckby with two coats of spray varnish, letting the first coat dry before applying the second.

Bauernmalerei

Degree of Difficulty

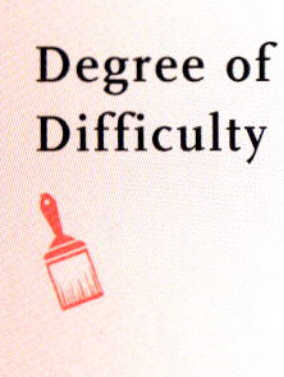

Peasant paintings in the Bauernmalerei style were influenced by the fine art of their day. The herb cabinet that I have painted shows the influence of the elaborate rococo style of the 18th century, especially in the scroll border with its shell motif. However, the painting itself is quite simple. When painting the piece, don't be alarmed by the bright, even garish appearance of the colors. The antiquing process will give the piece a rich, warm feeling by toning down the colors and revealing the textural quality of the strokework.

A relaxed mindset is essential to paint in the Bauernmalerei style. While each stroke is important, the overall effect is still more important.

WHAT YOU'LL NEED

Pattern

Page 103

Project

Herb cabinet from Custom Woods by Dallas *(see page 111 for ordering information)*

Supplies

SURFACE PREP

#400-grit sandpaper
Tack cloth
Basecoat paints: engine red *(bright red)* and light blue *(pale baby blue)*

TRACING AND TRANSFERRING

Tracing paper
Fine-tip black marker
Chalk
Stylus

ARTISTS' ACRYLICS

Titanium white
Warm white
Yellow ocher
Red light
Naphthol crimson
Burnt carmine
Ice blue
Green umber
Burnt umber
Payne's gray
Pure black

ACRYLIC MEDIUMS

Dimensional Brush Stroke Gloss Medium
Gel retarder
Glazing Medium

BRUSHES

Glaze/varnish brushes: two 1-inch *(one for basecoating, one for varnishing)*
Wash brush: 3/4-inch
Script liner: no. 2
Rounds: nos. 4 and 6
Filbert: no. 6
Mop brush: 3/4-inch

BASIC PAINTING SUPPLIES

Water container
Palette knife
Sta-Wet palette
Paper towels

FINISHING

Brush-on satin-sheen polyurethane varnish

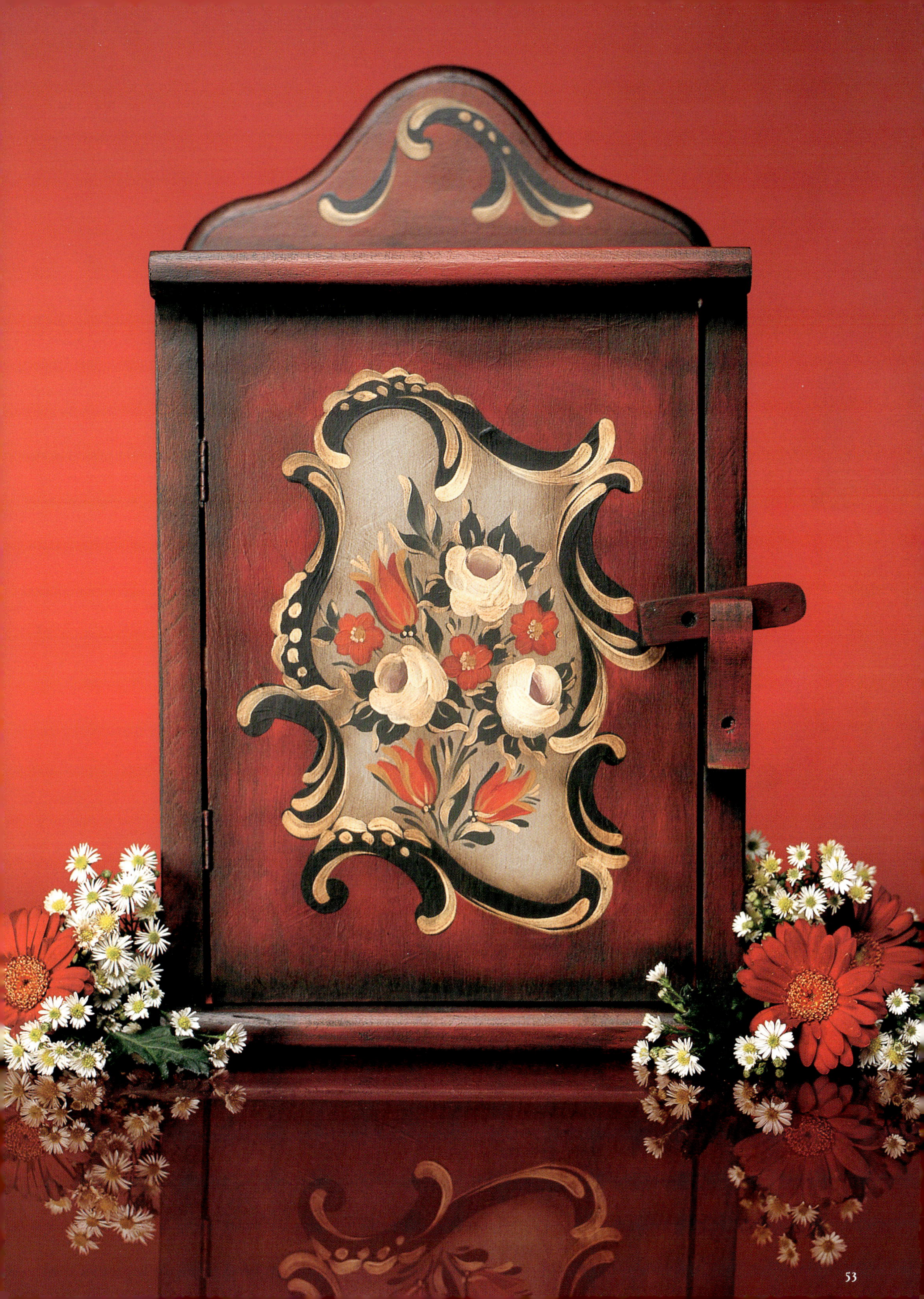

GETTING READY

Sand and basecoat the cabinet according to the instructions on page 34. Using a glaze/varnish brush, apply two coats of engine red. For the second coat, use a heavily loaded brush so that your brushstrokes are visible.

Transfer the scroll design using the chalk tracing method. Use a wash brush to paint the area surrounded by the scrolls light blue. It's okay to paint a little bit inside the scrolls themselves. Make sure to achieve opaque coverage. If necessary, let dry and apply a second coat.

Paint the scrolls with the no. 4 round brush filled with green umber + Payne's gray. Let dry, then add the light strokes using the script liner and a mixture of warm white + a tad of yellow ocher. To paint these large strokes with the script liner, the brush must be very full of paint. Add some Dimensional Brush Stroke Gloss Medium to the paint to make the strokes more textural.

Transfer the rest of the design using the chalk tracing method.

LEAVES

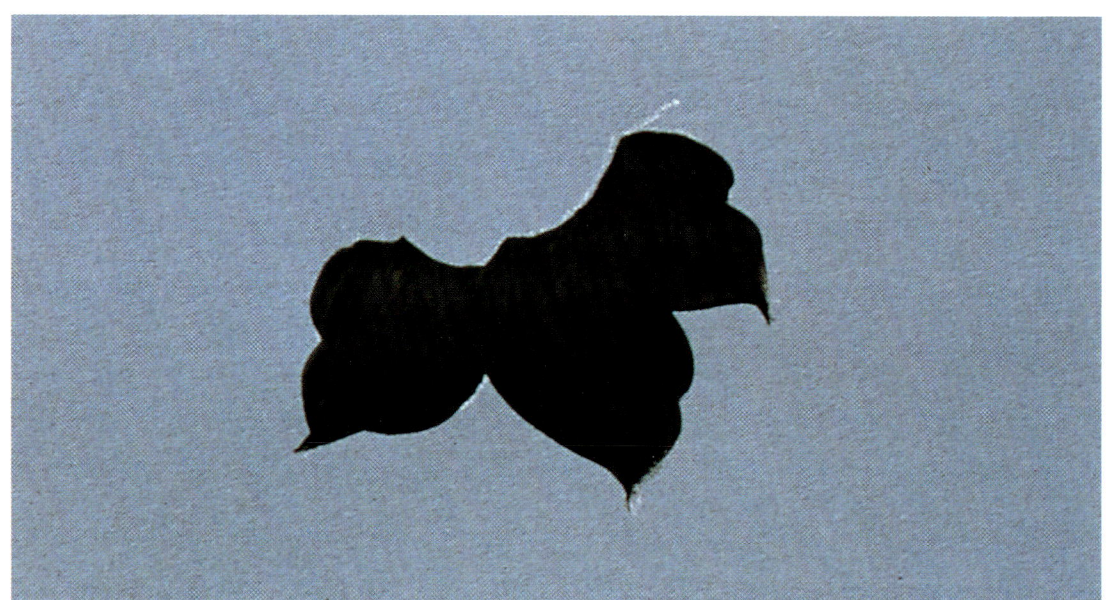

1 Undercoat the leaves using the no. 4 round brush and a 3:1 mixture of green umber + Payne's gray. At this time, you should also use the script liner loaded with this paint mixture to paint the green comma strokes that embellish the design. Try to paint the strokes with confidence and ease. Don't worry if each stroke isn't perfect. Let dry.

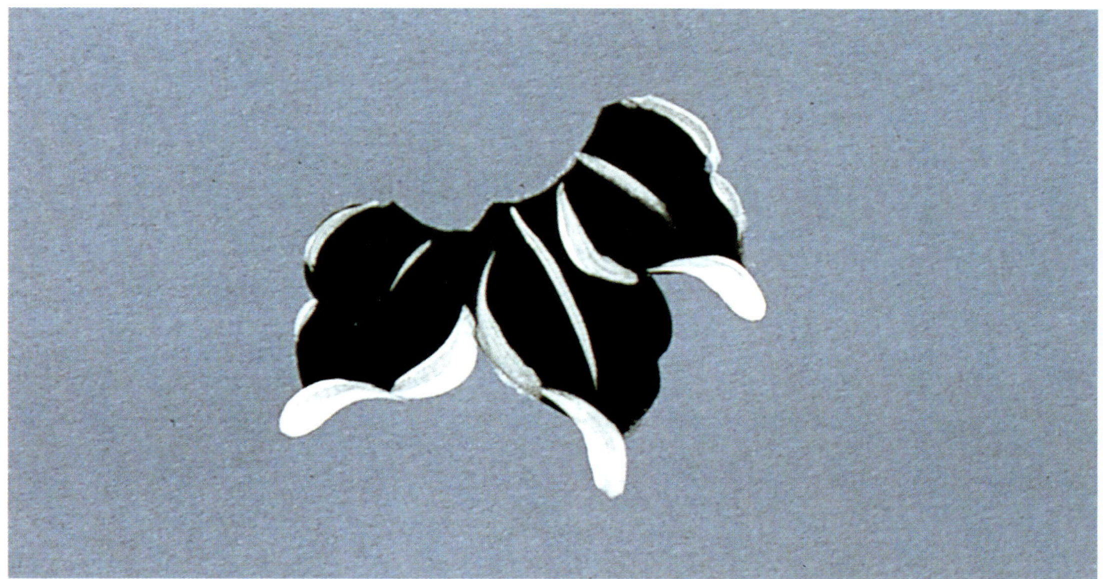

2 Fill the script liner with Dimensional Brush Stroke Gloss Medium, then load it again with a mixture of warm white + just a tad of yellow ocher. Paint comma-stroke highlights on the edges of the leaves. Let dry, then paint the veins on the leaves with the same color.

RED BLOSSOMS

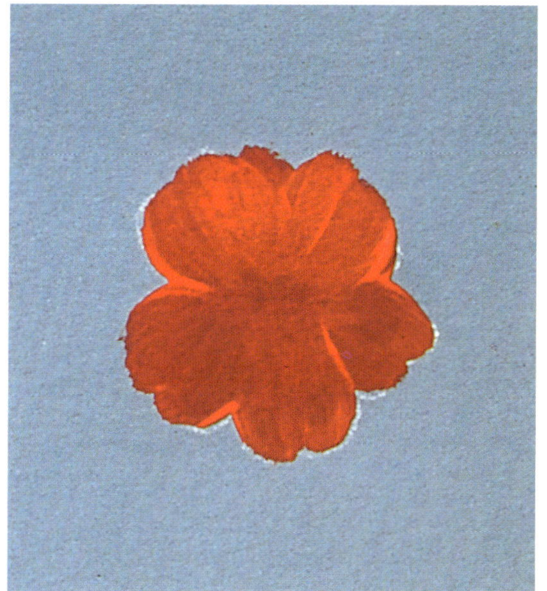

1 Use two strokes to undercoat each petal using the filbert brush loaded with naphthol crimson. Begin at the outside edge of the petal and stroke toward the center. The edges of the petals should have a scalloped look. Be sure to fill in the center of the flower when you have completed the petals. Let dry.

2 Load the filbert with red light and restroke the petals. Do not cover the undercoat at the center of the flower, and let a little of it show at the outer edges of the petals. Let dry.

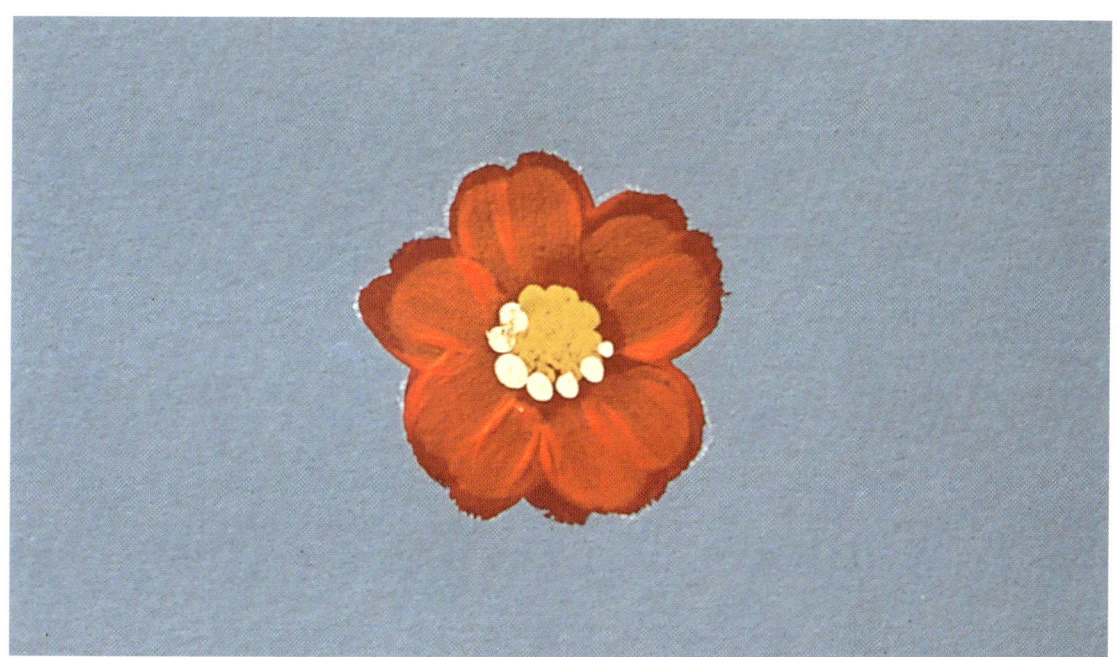

3 Use the script liner to paint the center of the flower. Mix some yellow ocher with Dimensional Brush Stroke Gloss Medium and make a circle of dots, then fill in the circle with the same mixture. Let dry. To highlight the center, mix warm white + a touch of yellow ocher. Pick up both this mixture and some Dimensional Brush Stroke Gloss Medium and apply several dots along the left side of the center and let dry.

RED TULIPS

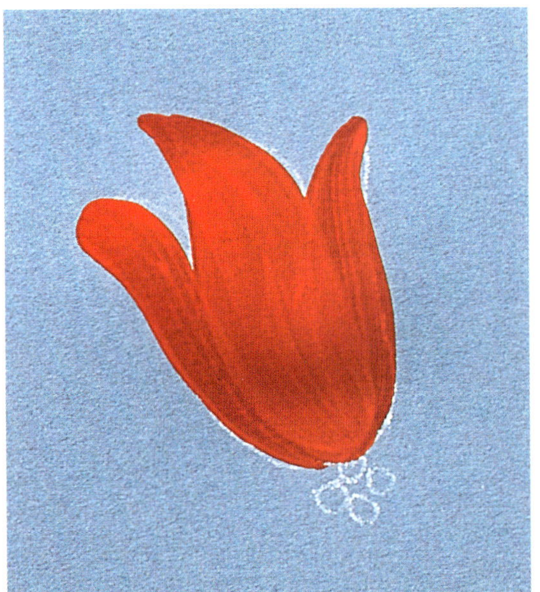

1 Undercoat the tulip shape with three large strokes of naphthol crimson. Begin with the two side petals, painting from tip to base with the no. 6 round brush. Use the same brush to paint the large center stroke, this time moving from the base of the tulip toward the tip. Let dry.

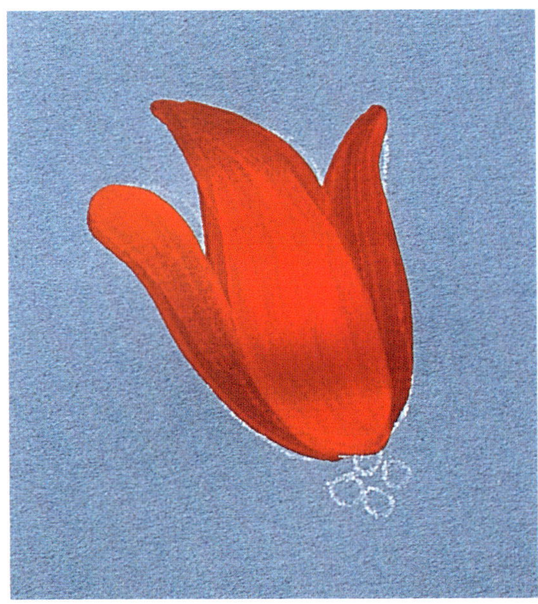

2 Highlight the tulip with red light, once again using the no. 6 round brush. The strokes should be applied in the same way as the undercoat strokes, but should not completely cover them. You do not have to restroke the entire tulip; I find it more interesting if a petal here and there is not highlighted. Let dry.

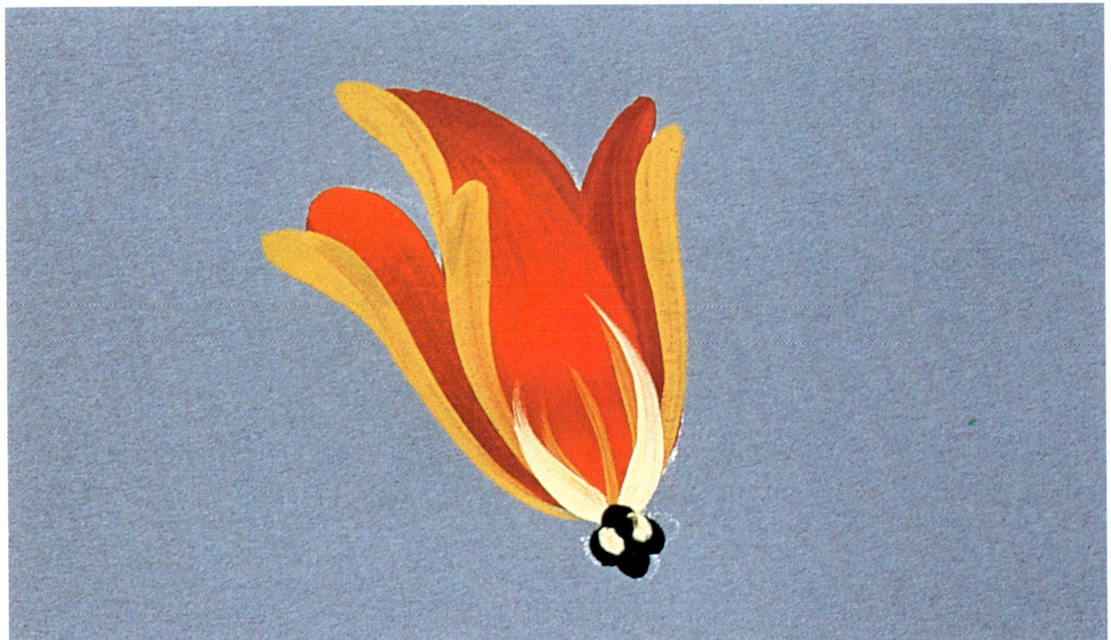

3 Paint the final highlight strokes with the script liner. Use yellow ocher for the gold strokes, let dry, then use the mixture of warm white + a tad of yellow ocher you used for the leaves for the white strokes. Mix some Dimensional Brush Stroke Gloss Medium into each of the colors so the strokes retain their dimension and texture.

To paint the tulip's base, use the script liner to make four large dots of dark green (green umber + Payne's gray). Let dry, then add a couple of light dots using the mixture of warm white + a tad of yellow ocher. Let dry.

WHITE ROSES

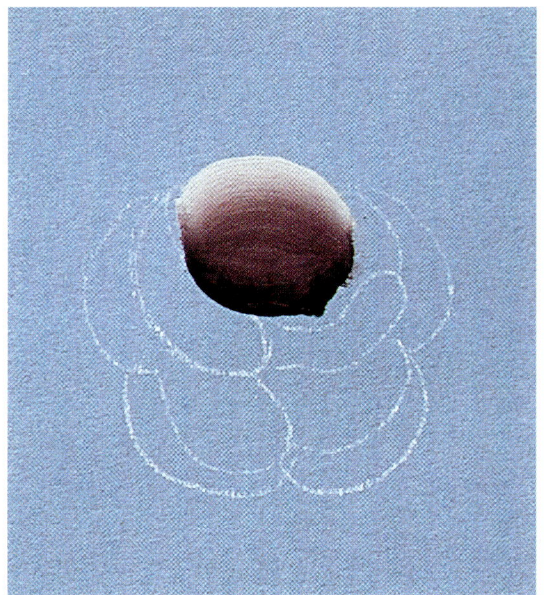

1 These roses should be painted using the second wet-in-wet technique described on page 29. Work quickly and paint one rose at a time.

Load the no. 4 round brush with burnt carmine and place a stroke to form the dark area at the center of the rose. Wipe the brush, load it with ice blue, and stroke across the top of the area you have undercoated. Then wipe the brush again, pinch it into a flat shape, and stroke between the two colors to blend them together.

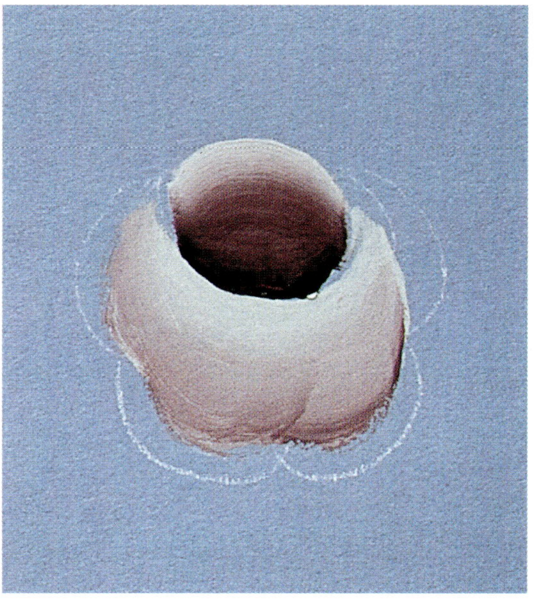

2 Using the no. 4 round, paint the front of the center of the rose with ice blue, then wipe the brush and stroke one of its edges through burnt carmine. Apply a stroke across the bottom of the rose to shade it. Wipe the brush again and quickly blend the two colors together.

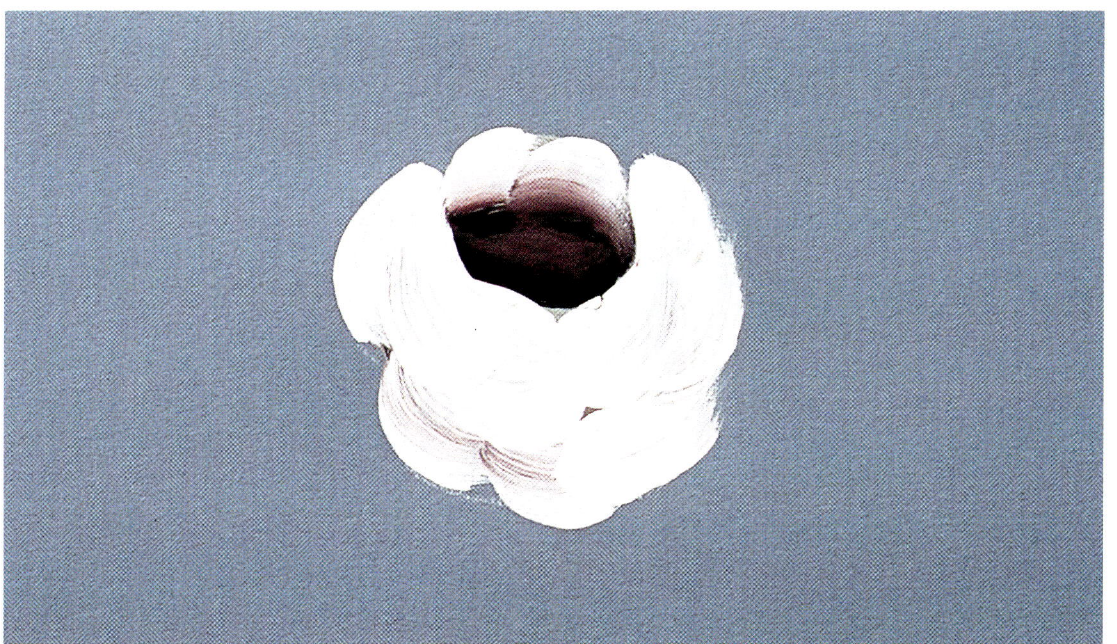

3 For the outer petals, load the filbert with titanium white + Dimensional Brush Stroke Gloss Medium. Begin at the top of the rose and stroke on some scalloped strokes. Apply more strokes at the front and bottom of the flower. Don't reload the brush after each stroke; this will help you vary the strokes' appearance, which is desirable. Let dry.

FINISHING

Using a mixture of burnt umber + a little pure black, prepare an antiquing glaze according to the instructions on page 41. Apply the glaze to the cabinet one section at a time. I like to remove more antiquing glaze from the center and leave the edges darker. You can also remove more glaze from the center of an individual flower and leave the edges of the flower darker.

Allow the antiquing glaze to dry overnight, then finish the cabinet with two or three coats of varnish, letting each coat dry before applying the next.

Assendelfter

Degree of Difficulty

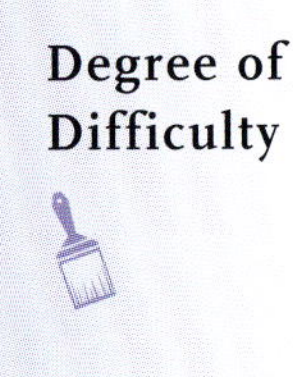

Over the years, the popularity of the Assendelfter style of painting gradually decreased. For a long time, it was considered to be less refined than traditional Dutch still life painting, and therefore of less interest to serious artists. It was not until the 1980s that a resurgence of interest occurred, due in large part to the efforts of Jacques Zuidema. Zuidema was a charismatic artist who loved life and the art of his native Holland. He taught and lectured extensively on Assendelfter painting and the history of Dutch folk art in general, and was given the title of "Dutch National Flower Painter" by Prince Bernard of the Netherlands.

My interpretation of the Assendelfter style of painting is based on my experiences meeting Mr. Zuidema and watching him demonstrate his approach to this fascinating art form. When you paint in this style, relax, feel free, and enjoy. As you'll see, there are surprises with each brushstroke in this technique due to the tipped brush loading technique used to create the different elements of the designs.

WHAT YOU'LL NEED

Pattern

Page 104

Project

Butterfly box from Valhalla designs *(see page 111 for ordering information)*

Supplies

SURFACE PREP

#400-grit sandpaper
Tack rag
Basecoat paints: green umber and Hauser green medium *(see list of artists' acrylics)*

TRACING AND TRANSFERRING

Tracing paper
Fine-tip black marker
Chalk
Stylus

ARTISTS' ACRYLICS

Titanium white
Yellow light
Medium yellow
Yellow ocher
Pure orange
Alizarin crimson
Burnt carmine
Burnt umber
Raw sienna
True burgundy
Dioxazine purple
Asphaltum
Hauser green medium
Green umber
Pure black

CRAFT ACRYLICS

Metallic gold

ACRYLIC MEDIUMS

Pearlizing Medium

BRUSHES

Glaze/varnish brush: 1-inch
Wash brush: 3/4-inch
Rounds: nos. 4 and 6
Script liner: no. 2
Mop brush

BASIC PAINTING SUPPLIES

Water container
Palette knife
Sta-Wet Palette
Paper towels

FINISHING

Brush-on satin-sheen water-based polyurethane varnish

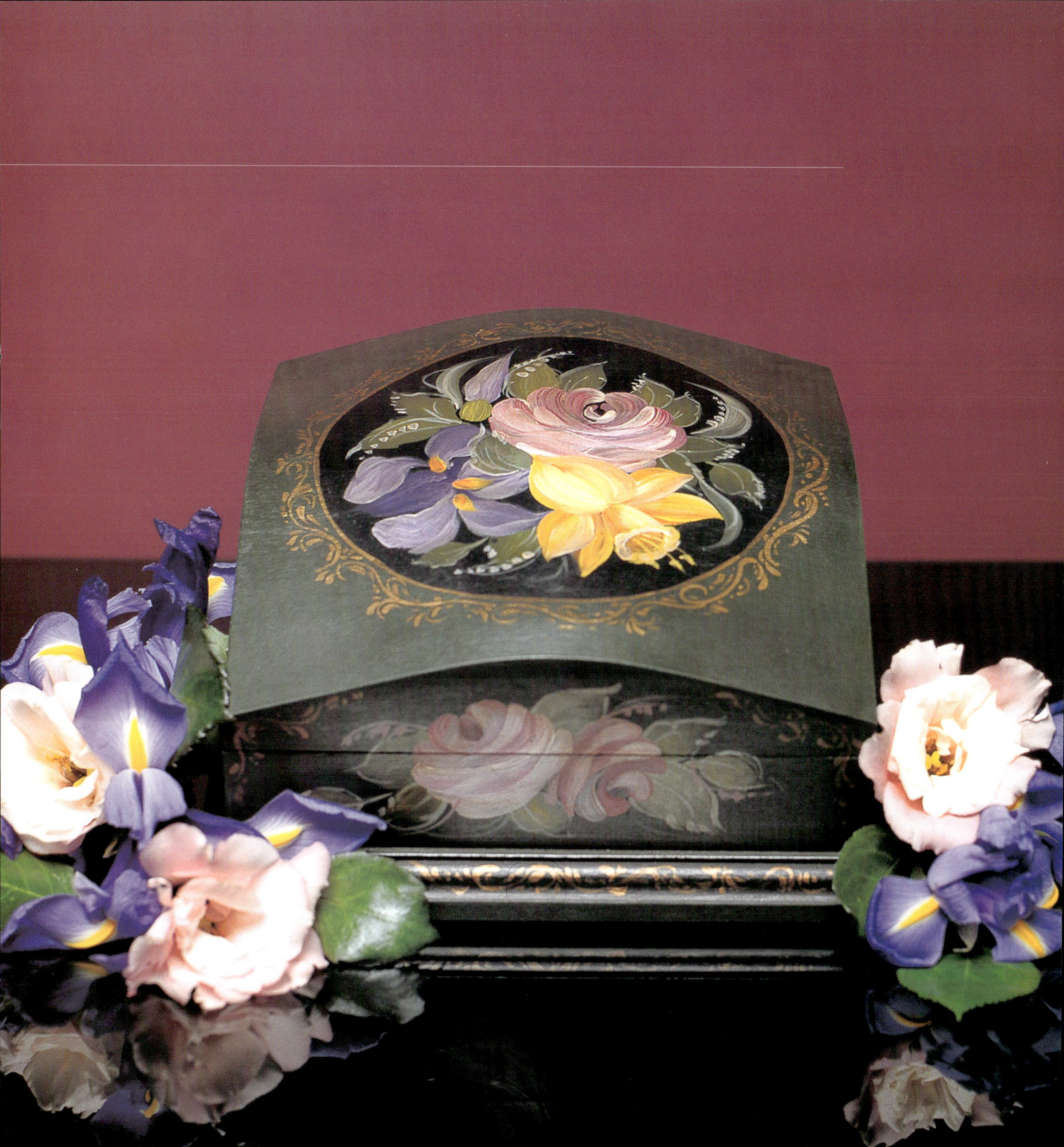

Assendelfter

GETTING READY

Basecoat the box using the glaze/ varnish brush and a mixture of greenish umber + a touch of Hauser green medium. Let dry. Lightly sand the box and apply a second coat.

Transfer the circle to the top of the box and paint it with pure black using the wash brush. You may need to apply two coats to insure opaque coverage. Let dry. Paint the routed edge of the bottom of the box with pure black.

Transfer the design using the chalk transfer method.

LEAVES

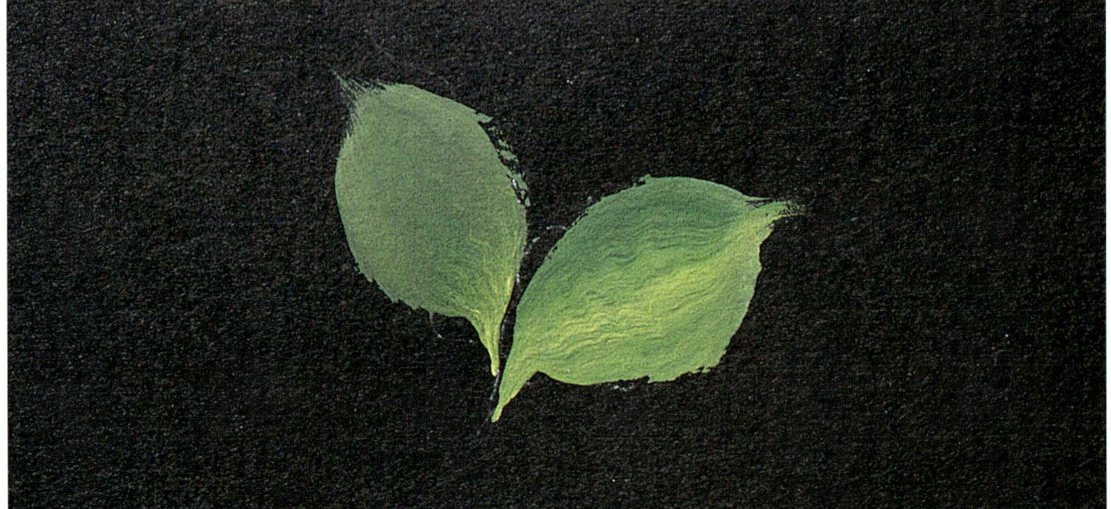

1 Use a tipped brush (see instructions on page 26) to paint the leaves. Load the no. 4 round brush with Hauser green medium, then stroke the tip of the brush into some greenish umber. Pat the brush on the palette to mix the two colors slightly, but make sure you can still see both colors distinctly. Now tip the brush into a little medium yellow paint. Twirl the brush on the palette to bring the tip back into a point.

To form the leaf, touch the tip of the brush to the surface and pull slightly, then press the brush down fully, giving it a slight wiggle to spread the bristles. Begin to pull the brush and wiggle it to form the leaf size you want. When you have formed a little more than half of the leaf, begin to release the pressure on the brush as you form the tip of the leaf. Don't worry if the edge or tip is a bit ragged—that's part of the Assendelfter charm! Let dry.

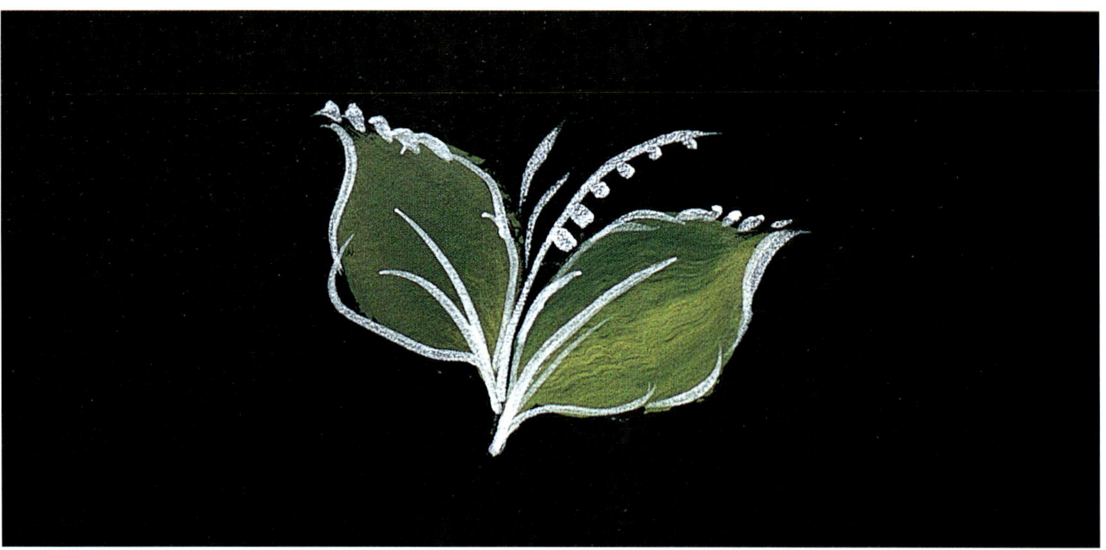

2 Paint the details with the script liner and thinned paint. Outline the leaves and add veins with titanium white or a mixture of titanium white and Pearlizing Medium. You can add some extra dots or dabs for variety. Be sure that your outlines are broken and not a solid line of color. A shaky outline will look better than a perfect one!

Another way to add variety is to paint the leaves with different color combinations. For example, you may want to load the brush with green and tip with some Pearlizing Medium for a lighter shade. You can also use a touch of purple if desired. Experiment. The leaves are easy and quick to paint.

ROSE

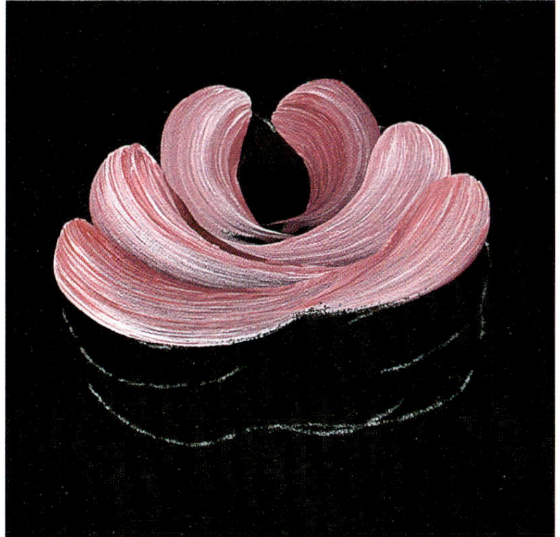

1 Using the no. 4 round brush, place a dot of burnt carmine + true burgundy in the center of the rose. Then, load the brush with alizarin crimson and true burgundy. Simply stroke the brush through both colors without mixing them together. You'll find that sometimes the brush will have more burgundy, while at other times it will carry more crimson. The variety will add interest to your roses. With the brush loaded with the reds, tip the brush into titanium white.

Begin by forming two comma strokes around the dot of red. Continue forming comma strokes on either side of the rose with the tipped brush.

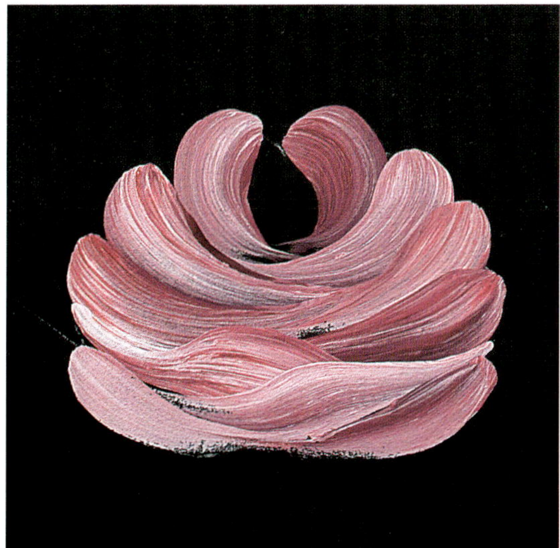

2 As you continue down the rose, add a couple of S strokes with the tipped brush. They will add some variety to the strokes forming the rose.

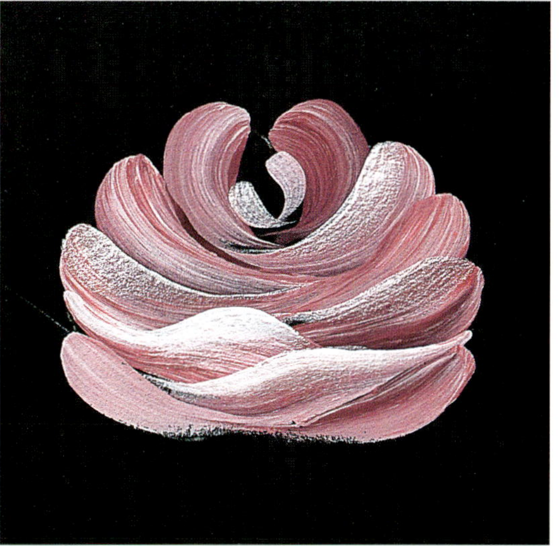

3 Finish the rose with a few more comma strokes. Let dry.

To add some highlights and shimmer to it, load the round brush with a little thinned Pearlizing Medium and apply a few strokes over some of the strokes you've already painted. I like to side-load the brush with the Pearlizing Medium when adding these strokes so only half of the underneath stroke gets highlighted.

You may pick up some of the pinks and tip the brush with white and add some small strokes in the center of the rose if the dark dot seems too dark.

IRIS

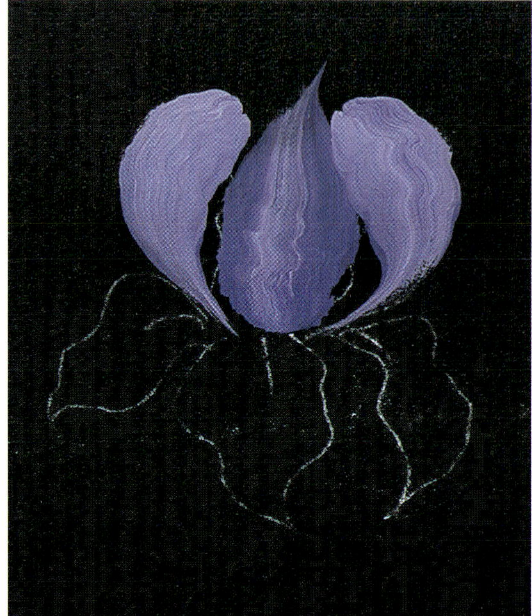

1 Load the no. 6 round brush with some dioxazine purple + just a little titanium white. Tip the brush into more white and place a straight comma stroke to form the center standard (upright) petal. You will want to wiggle the brush to help form the stroke and allow the tipped color to create a beautifully shaded stroke.

Form the other two standard petals using the same coloration (with a bit more white in the brush) as the first stroke. Remember to apply pressure on the brush and wiggle it slightly for some variation in the coloration.

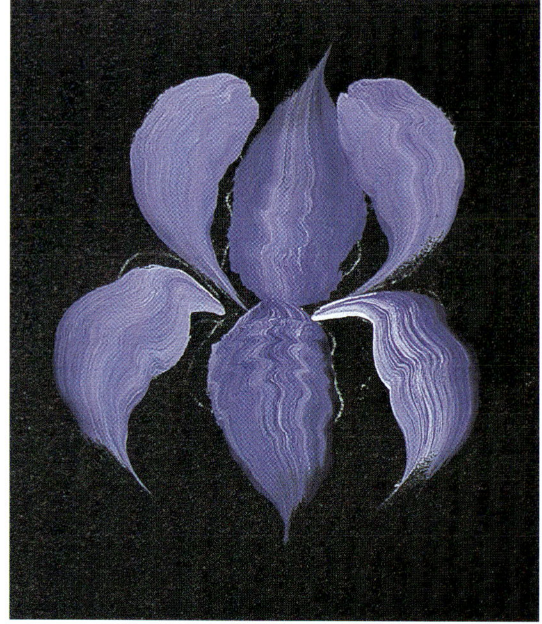

2 The fall petals also require only one stroke each. To form the center fall, reload the brush with the same mix of paints you've been using and paint a straight comma stroke. For the two side fall petals, use loose U strokes. Throughout the painting of the iris, the brush is tip loaded. Let dry.

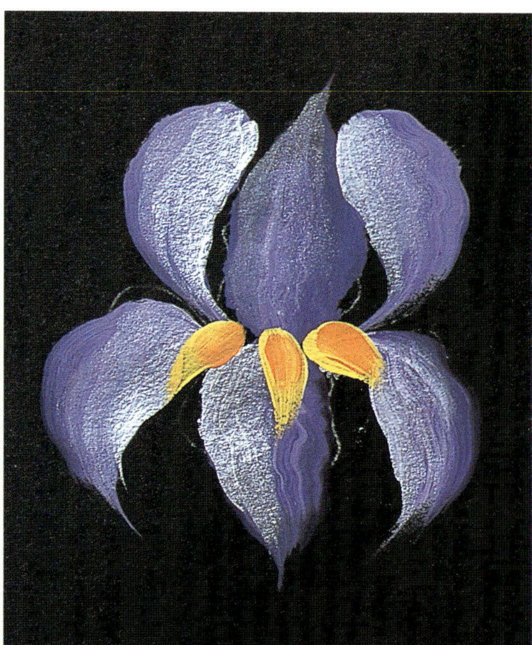

3 Highlight the iris with a round brush side-loaded with Pearlizing Medium. This will help lift the two side standards and two side falls.

Paint the iris "beards" with loose comma-like strokes. Apply medium yellow first, let dry, then cover with pure orange, allowing some of the yellow to show through.

DAFFODIL

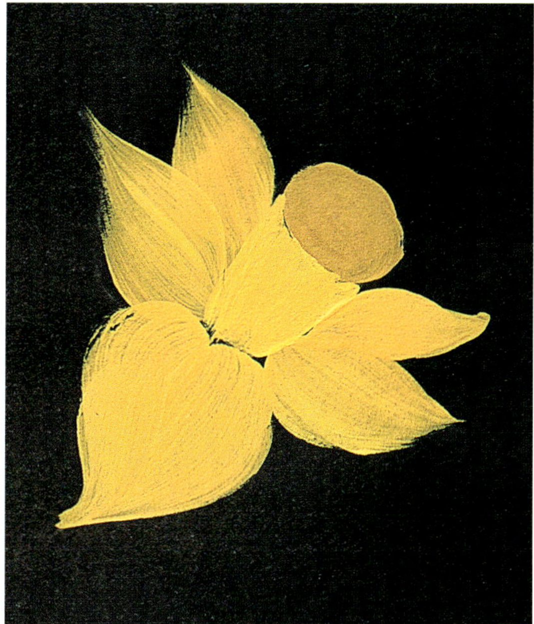

1 With graceful strokes, undercoat the daffodil's petals using the no. 4 round brush and medium yellow. Use yellow ocher for the flower's throat. Let dry.

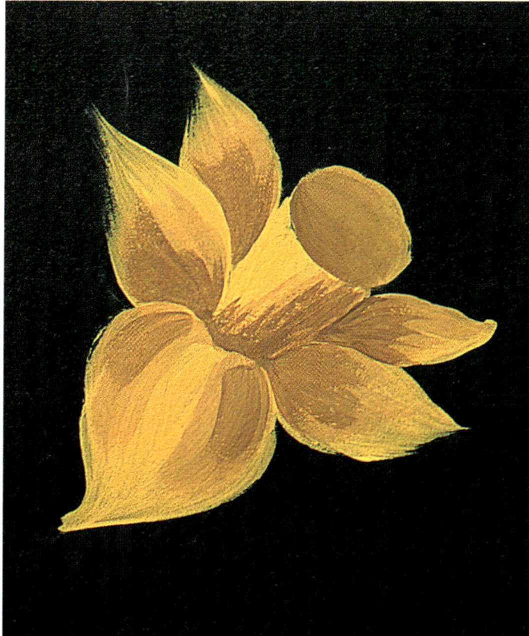

2 Using the no. 4 round brush and some yellow ocher, stroke on some shadows where one petal overlaps another. Then, while the ocher is wet, stroke on some raw sienna to deepen the shading. Let dry.

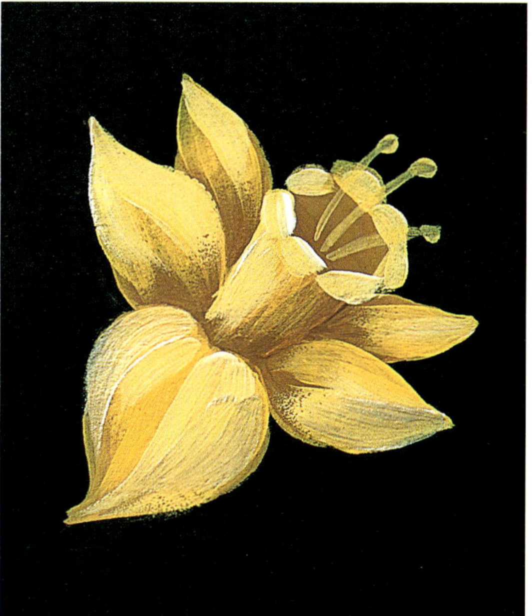

3 To highlight the four side petals of the daffodil, load the no. 4 round brush with medium yellow and stroke from the outside edges toward the center. Then, wipe the brush, pick up some yellow light, and restroke some of the petals to lighten them even more. Finally, without wiping it, tip the yellow brush into titanium white and add some final highlights. You may let the flower dry and add some highlights of Pearlizing Medium to enhance the brightness of the flower.

Repeat this process to highlight the larger petal in the front, but this time, stroke from the top of the petal toward the tip. Be certain your strokes curve to follow the contour of the petal.

Highlight the trumpet of the daffodil in the same manner. Add some short, scalloped strokes around its opening to represent the flower's ruffled edge.

Finally, paint the stamens using the script liner and yellow light.

FINISHING

Using the script liner, add some lines and dabs of paint to represent small wildflowers. Use some titanium white or a light pink made from titanium white + true burgundy. These dabs and stems will fill in the design.

Paint the gold border with metallic gold using the script liner. After painting the basic circle, surround it with serpentine (S-shaped) line segments. Then add small comma strokes around the curves. You may group them together in graduated sizes and embellish with some dots. The goal is to create a filigree effect. Study the finished painting to make sure there is variety in the border. Let dry. Repeat the border on the bottom, routed edge and on the top front corners of the box.

When the design is finished and dry, antique the box to give it a mellow quality. Using Glazing Medium and equal amounts of asphaltum and burnt umber, prepare the glaze according to the instructions on page 41. Apply it to the box one section at a time. Let dry, then apply two or three coats of varnish, allowing each coat to dry before applying the next.

Hindeloopen

Degree of Difficulty

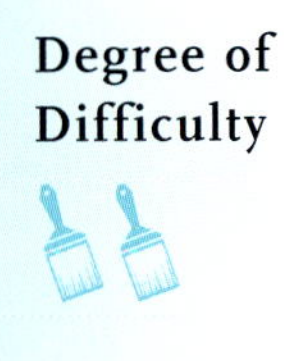

I have chosen to decorate this piece in the Roosje style, which is the older and more primitive of the two Hindeloopen styles. The Roosje style is based on motifs that were typical in the Dutch woodcarving tradition, which predates the decorative painting tradition. The designs in this type of folk art are more or less symmetrical. Common motifs include open flowers, poppy pods, tulips, birds, and fruit.

Most of the colors used in Hindeloopen painting are rather muted. If you choose to use brighter colors, keep in mind that the "authentic" look of your piece will be lost.

Traditionally, Hindeloopen pieces were painted with oils. Because no blending is required, the layers of oil paint were allowed to dry before reapplication; this makes the Hindeloopen style particularly well suited to being painted with acrylics.

WHAT YOU'LL NEED

Pattern

Page 105

Project

Oval Hindeloopen tray from Valhalla Designs *(see page 111 for ordering information)*

Supplies

SURFACE PREPARATION

#400-grit sandpaper
Tack cloth
Basecoat paint: autumn leaves *(rust color)*

TRACING AND TRANSFERRING

Tracing paper
Fine-tip black marker
Chalk
Stylus

ARTISTS' ACRYLICS

Titanium white
Medium yellow
Pure orange
Light red oxide
Burnt umber
Burnt carmine
Prussian blue
Pure black

ACRYLIC MEDIUMS

Gel retarder

BRUSHES

Script liner: no. 2
Flats: nos. 4 and 8
Glaze/varnish brush: 1-inch

BASIC PAINTING SUPPLIES

Water container
Palette knife
Sta-wet palette
Paper towels

FINISHING

Brush-on semi-gloss or satin-sheen polyurethane varnish

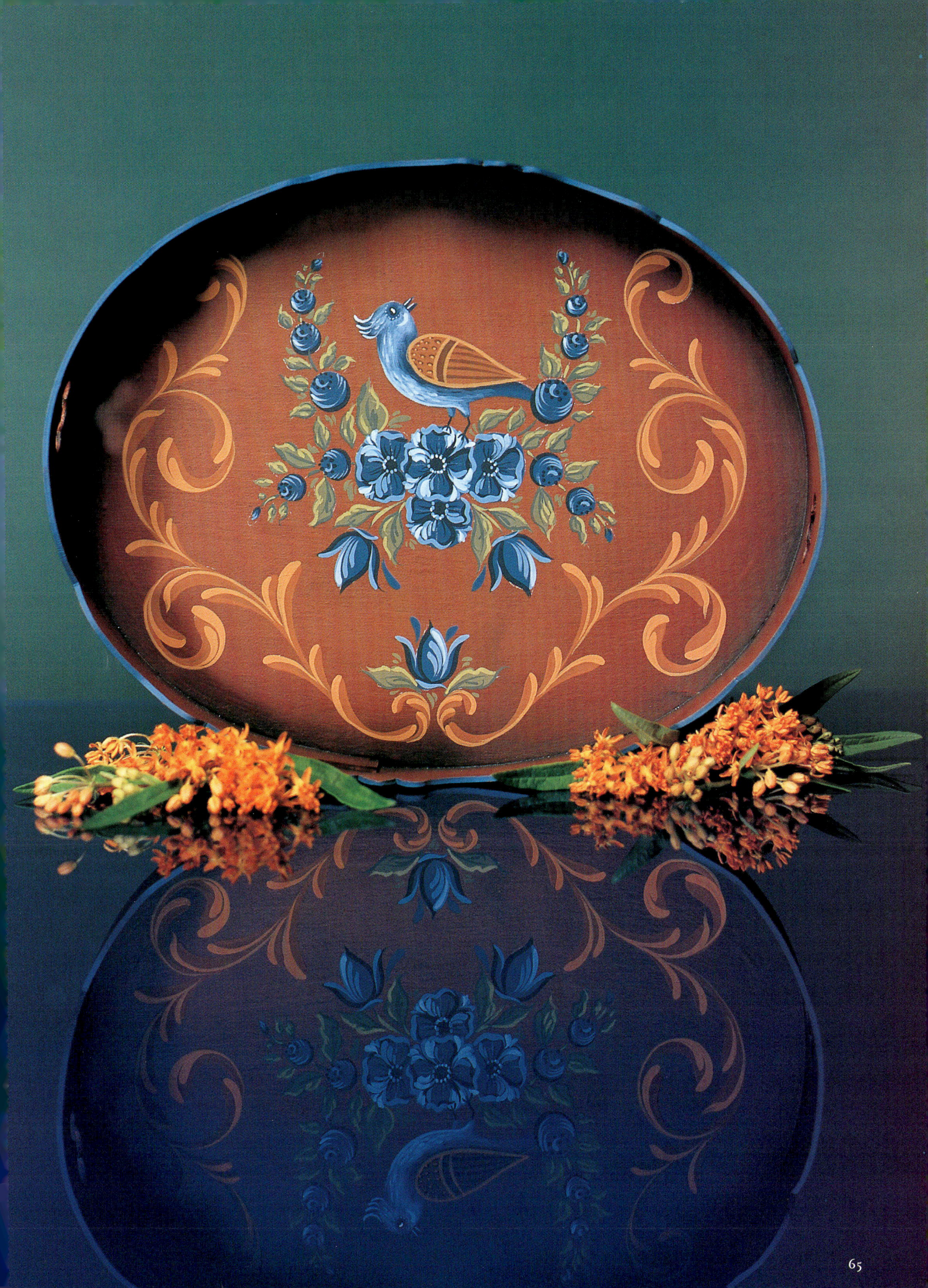

Hindeloopen

GETTING READY

Paint the tray with two coats of autumn leaves using the glaze/varnish brush. When the tray is dry, antique the background color to tone and darken it, using a mixture of burnt umber + a little burnt carmine paint (see page 41 for instructions).

Trace the pattern following the instructions on page 38, then use the chalk transfer method on page 40 to transfer the main design elements to the tray. Do not transfer any detail.

PREPARING THE PALETTE

For this painting, use a palette of toned colors. I find it easier to mix the palette before beginning the project. Mix the palette in the following order:

- Dark blue: burnt umber + Prussian blue 1:1, then add a touch of titanium white.
- Medium blue: dark blue + titanium white + a touch of pure orange
- Light blue: medium blue + titanium white
- Dark rust: light red oxide + burnt umber + burnt carmine
- Medium rust: pure orange + dark rust
- Light rust: medium rust + pure orange + titanium white
- Light green: yellow medium + dark blue
- Medium green: light green + pure black
- Dark green: medium green + pure black + Prussian blue

These colors are referred to by the mixture names throughout the instructions.

SCROLLS

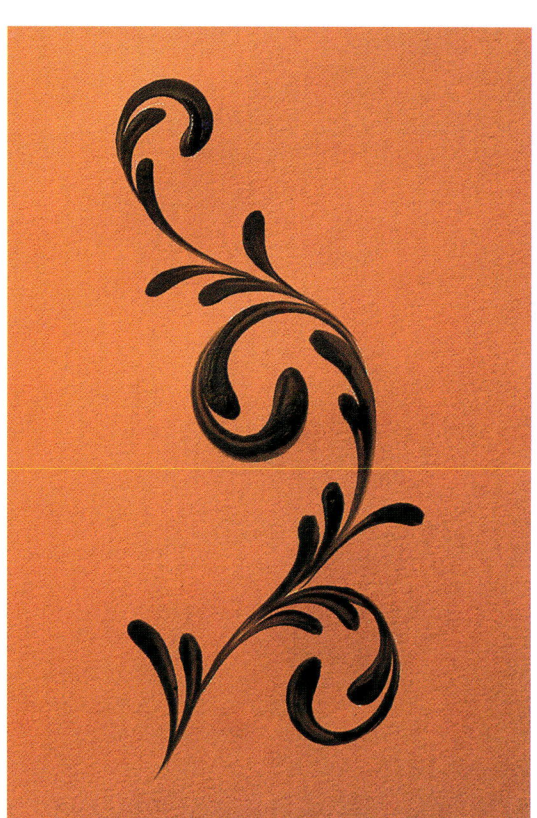

1 Paint a series of large comma strokes with the script liner *fully* loaded with medium rust. Work slowly and carefully as you develop the scroll, beginning at the top and working your way down. Be sure that there are no gaps between strokes. Let dry.

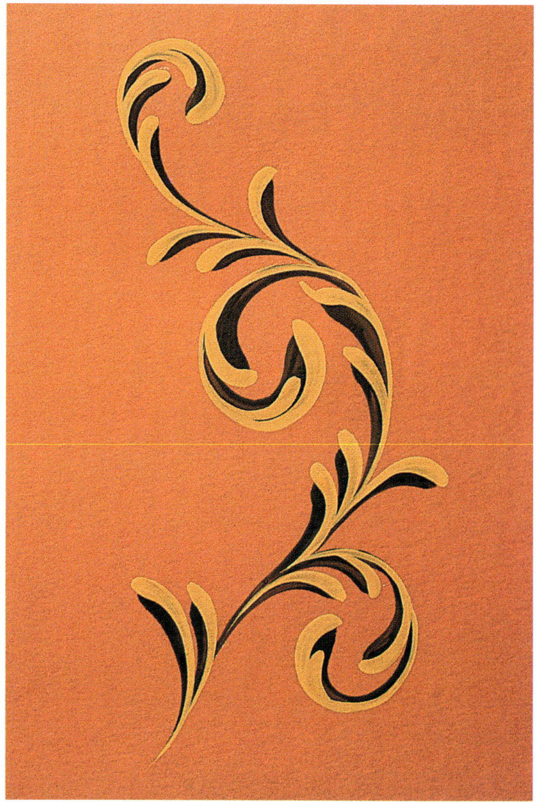

2 Paint the highlights in the same fashion, using the script liner loaded with light rust. Begin at the end of the medium rust strokes and let the new strokes taper to a graceful tail. Where two light strokes are placed on a dark stroke, paint the longer stroke first, then nestle the smaller stroke under it. Let dry.

LEAVES

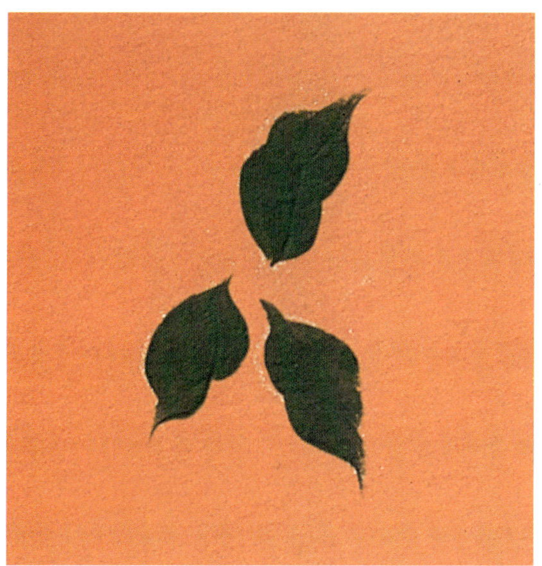

1 Using the no. 4 flat, undercoat the leaf forms with medium green. Let dry.

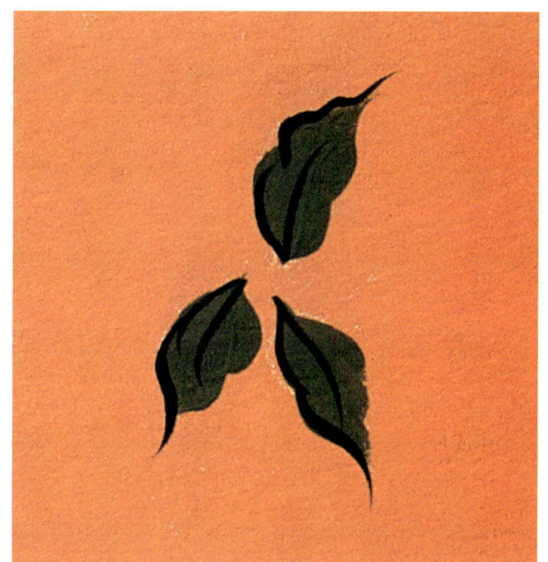

2 Shade the leaves using the script liner. Load the brush with dark green, then apply an outline on one side of each leaf. Add a center vein and any dark accent strokes you desire. Let dry.

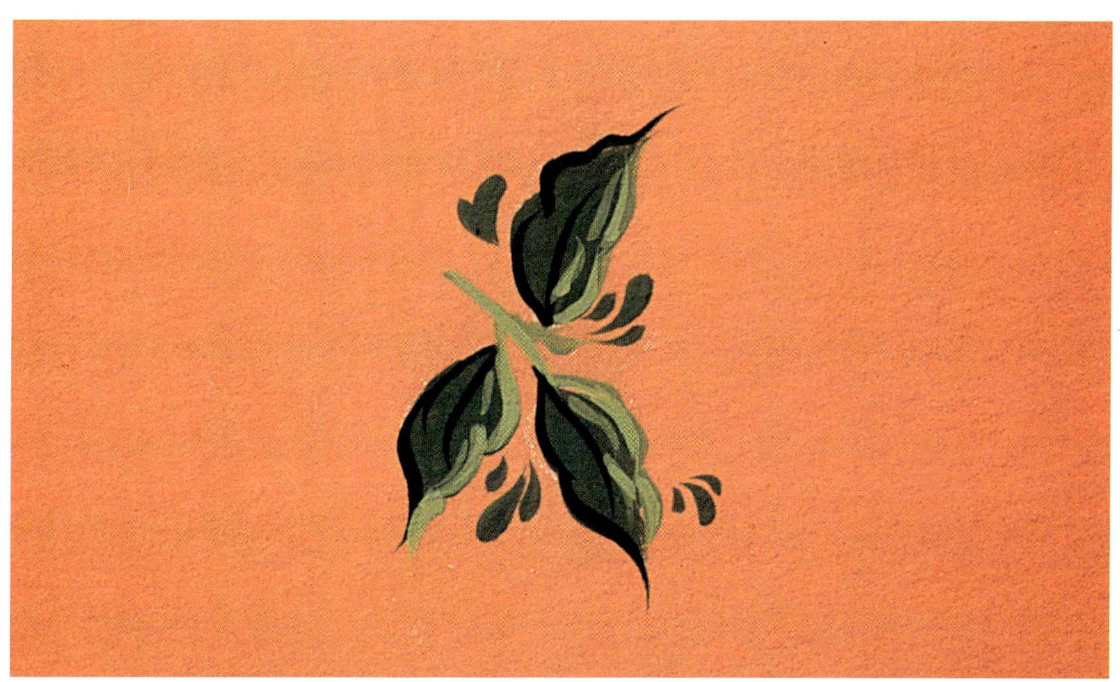

3 To highlight the leaves, load the script liner with light green and outline the light side of each leaf. The highlight should not be a solid line, but rather a broken line—almost like small or thin comma strokes. Let dry.

Add additional "fill in" strokes of medium green here and there between the leaves to flush out the design.

OPEN FLOWERS

1 Use the no. 8 flat to basecoat the open flowers with a circle of medium blue. Let dry.

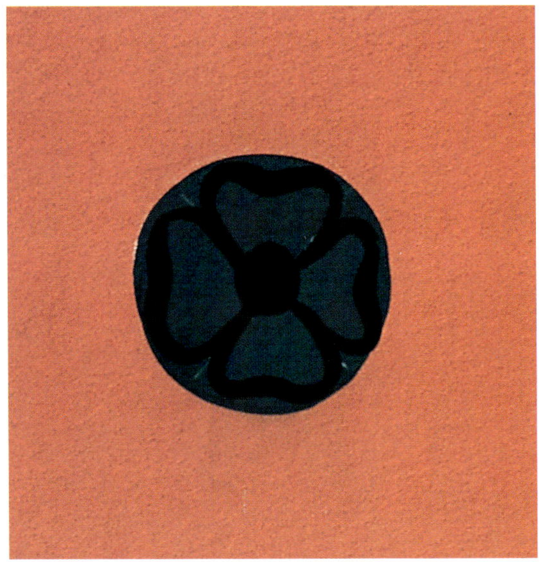

2 Since blending techniques are not used in the Hindeloopen style, the appearance of shading on the flowers is created simply by adding strokes to the petals. Load the script liner with dark blue and paint four petal shapes. Then paint a small circle in the center of the flower. Let dry.

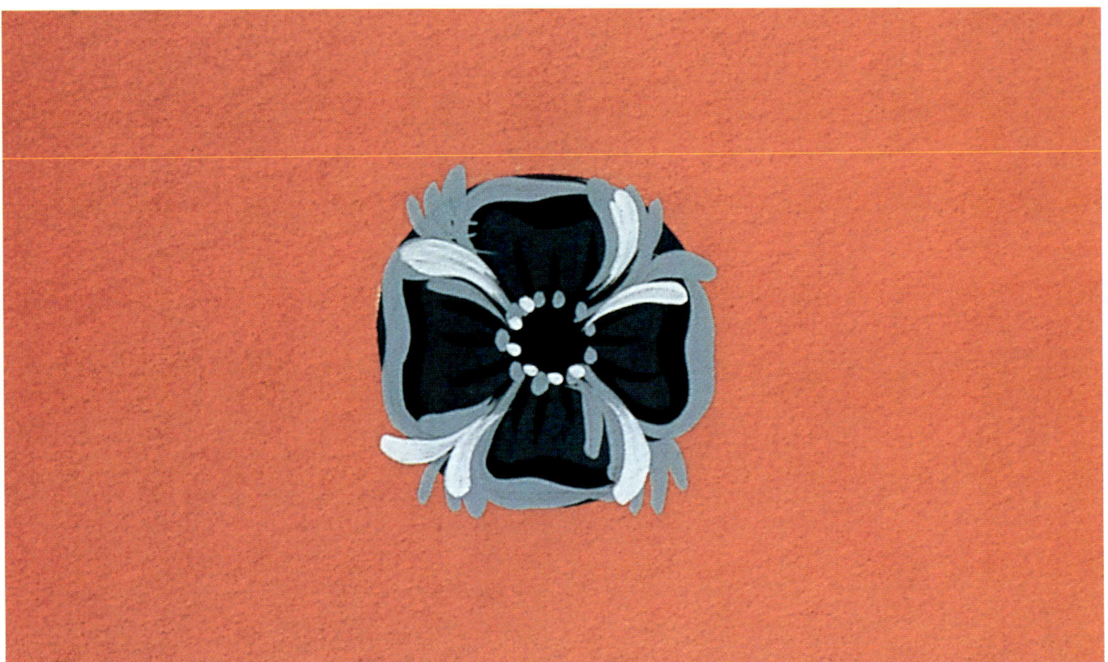

3 To highlight the open flower, outline the dark blue petal shapes with light blue. Next, form small comma strokes of light blue at the corners of the petals. You may want to pick up titanium white and apply a few very light strokes on the edges of the petals for variety.

To paint the center of the flower, use the script liner to make a circle of dots with light blue. Then use titanium white to apply another half circle of dots. Let dry.

POPPY PODS

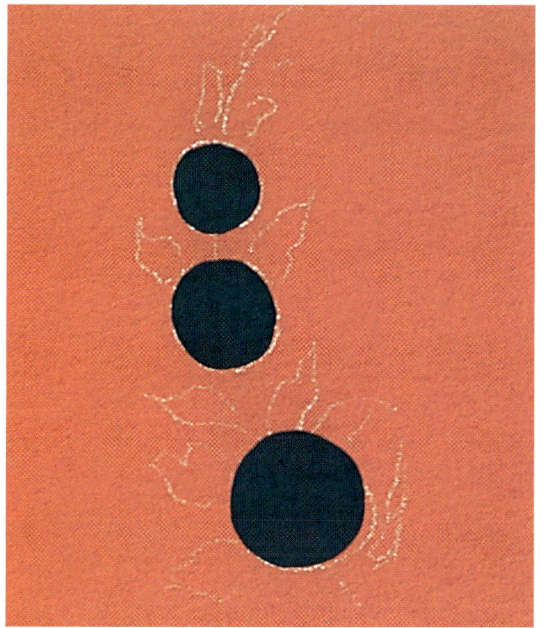

1 Undercoat the poppy pods with medium blue using the no. 4 flat brush. Let dry.

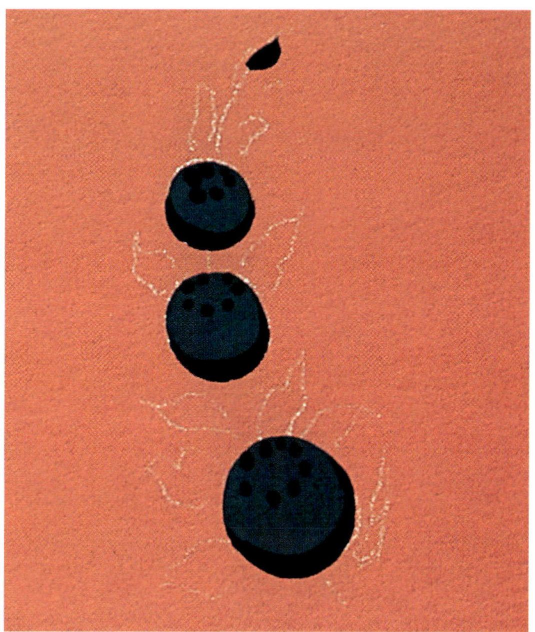

2 To shade the pods, paint a line of dark blue at the base of each one. Then place a ring of dark blue dots near the top of each circle.

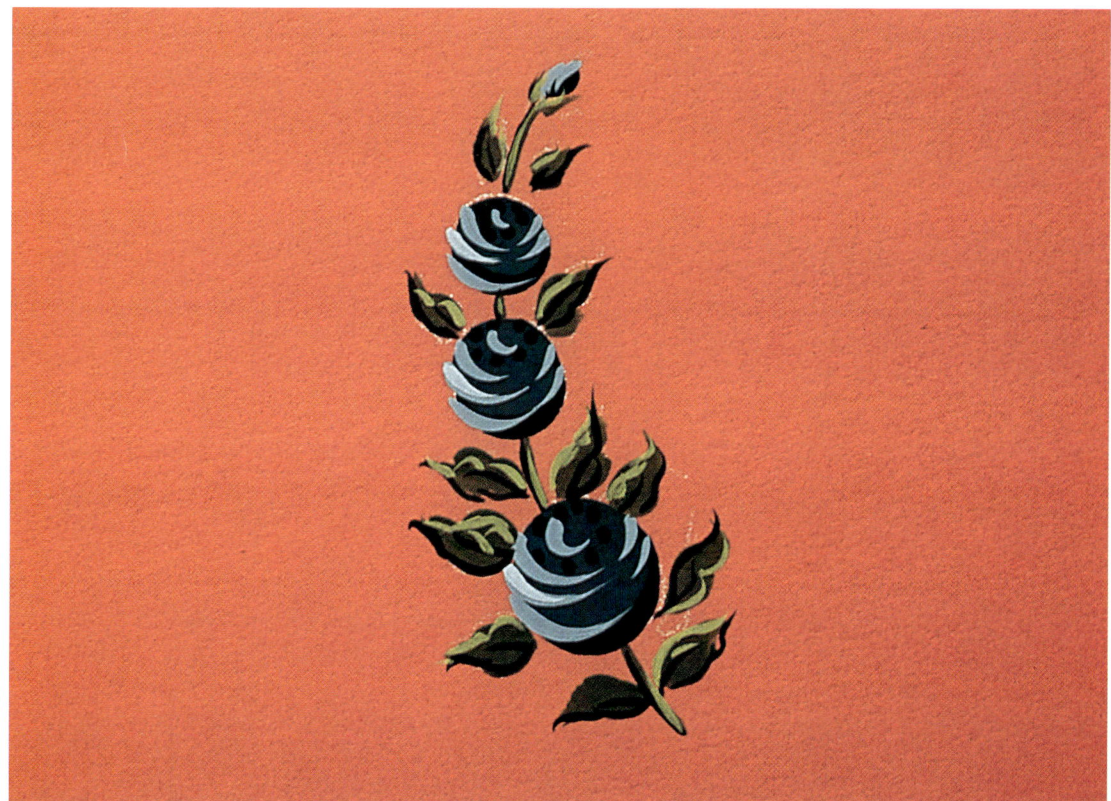

3 Highlight the pods by placing light blue comma strokes on each one. Begin the strokes at the outside edge of the pod and stroke inward. Be sure the strokes curve downward toward the base of each pod. Place a light blue comma stroke within the ring of dots at the top of the pod.

You can also highlight some of the light blue strokes by adding accent strokes of light blue + titanium white. Let dry.

TULIPS

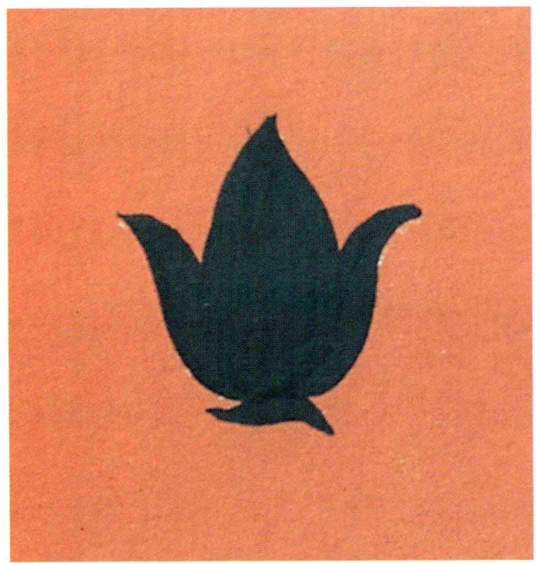

1 Undercoat the tulip forms with medium blue using the no. 4 flat brush. Let dry.

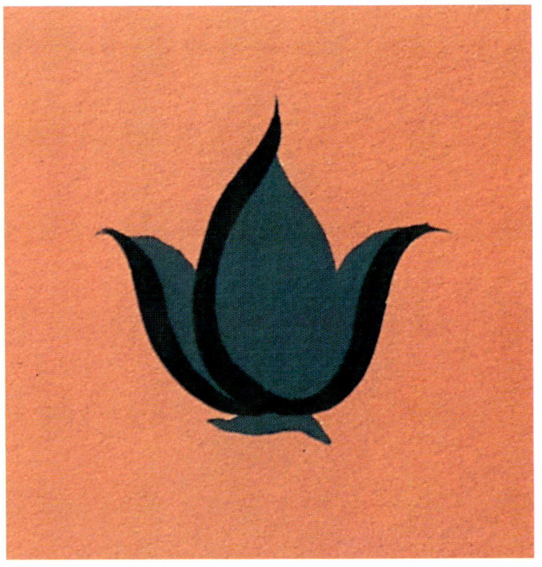

2 Shade the tulips with dark blue. Load the script liner and outline the outer edge of the two side petals and one side of the center petal. Let dry.

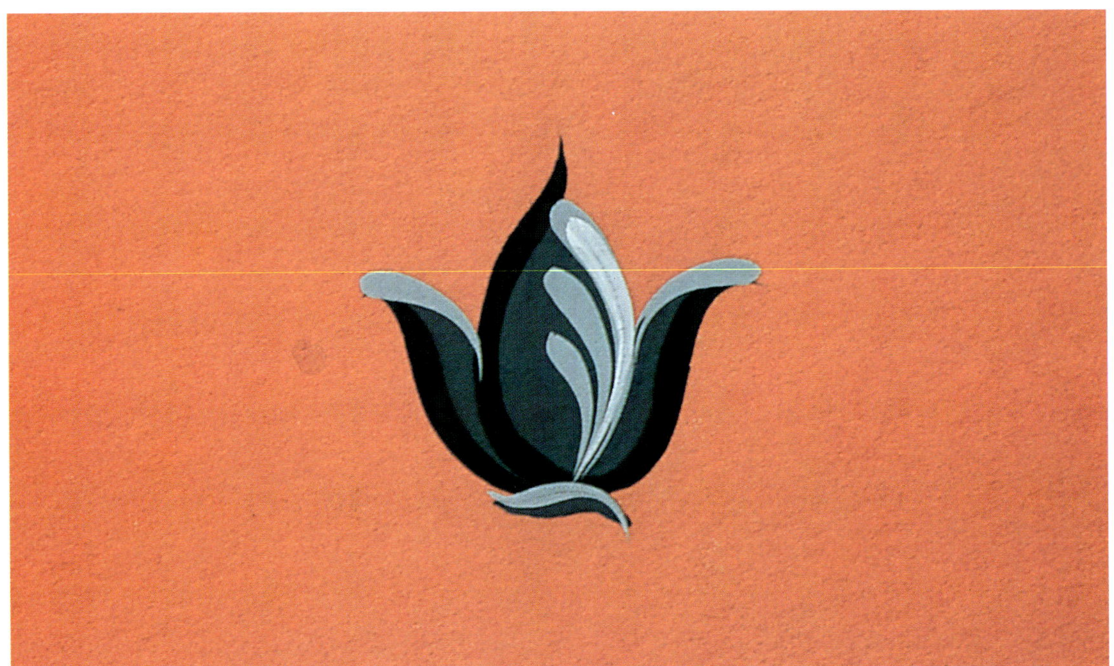

3 Using the script liner loaded with light blue, highlight each of the side petals with a comma stroke along the top edge. Place another highlight on the small petal at the bottom of the tulip. On the center petal, paint three light blue comma strokes and an additional stroke of light blue + titanium white. Let dry.

BIRD

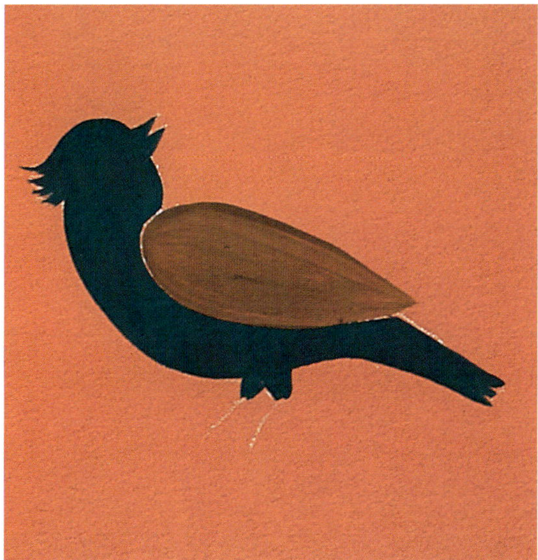

1 Undercoat the head, breast and tail of the bird with medium blue using the no. 8 flat. Let dry, then undercoat the wing with medium rust. Let dry.

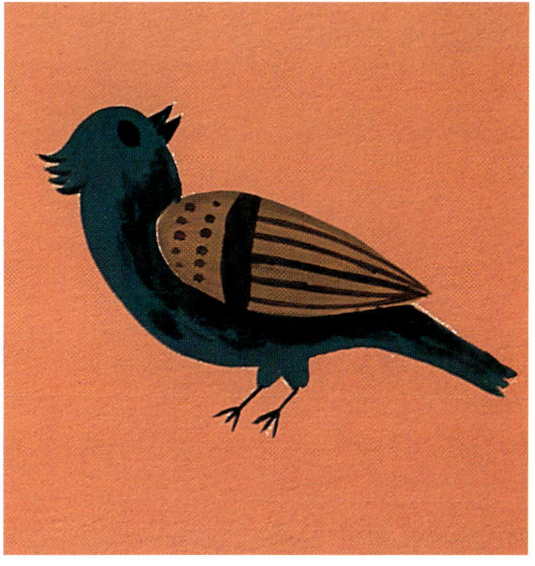

2 Sideload the no. 8 flat with dark blue and shade the bird's body on the neck and under the wing. Then use the script liner with the same color to paint the eye, beak and feet. Let dry. Paint the stripe, lines, and dots on the bird's wing with dark rust. Let dry.

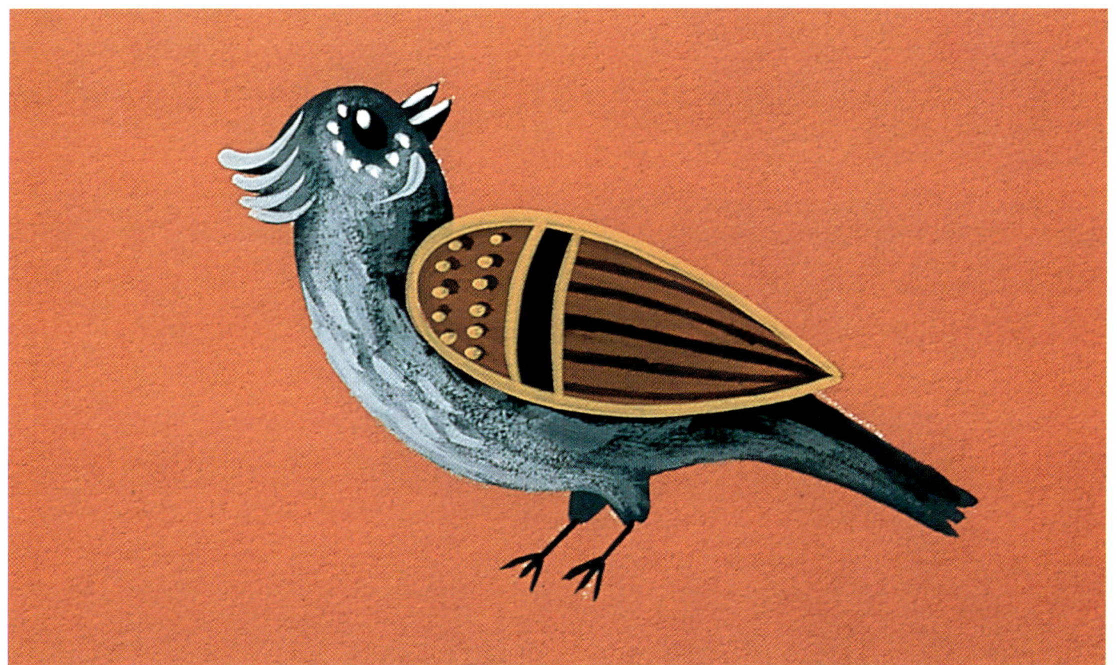

3 Using the no. 4 flat, apply a small amount of light blue paint to highlight the bird's body. Scuff the color onto the surface to simulate folk art feathers. You may need to add a touch of titanium white to the blue to create another value of blue highlights. Let dry.

Add the outline and highlight dots to the wing using the script liner and light rust. Let dry.

Make a dot with titanium white for the eye, then surround the eye area with a semicircle of light blue dots. You should also use light blue for the highlights on the beak and the bird's crest. Let dry.

FINISHING

Using the no. 4 flat, paint the top edge of the tray with medium blue + a tad of light blue. When the piece is dry, apply two coats of varnish, allowing the first coat to dry completely before applying the second.

Gzhel

Degree of Difficulty

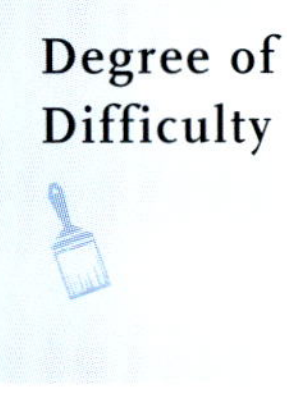

Gzhel pieces vary widely in size and function, ranging from plates and bowls to large, elaborate tea and coffee services. The most common motifs are floral: roses, daisies, and leaves. All of the pieces are adorned with elaborate strokework embellishments that leave none of the surface without decoration.

Traditional Gzhel is done with underglazes on ceramic or porcelain bisque. The pieces are fired and glazed several times. My interpretation is done using acrylic paints on bisqueware, and cannot be fired. You can paint on any white or slightly off-white surface of your choice.

WHAT YOU'LL NEED

Pattern

Page 106

Project

Teapot with hole from J.C.'s Pour 'n More *(see page 111 for ordering information)*

Supplies

SURFACE PREP

Scrub pad
Tack cloth
Basecoat paint: titanium white *(see list of artists' acrylics)*

TRACING AND TRANSFERRING

Pencil

ARTISTS' ACRYLICS

Titanium white
Prussian blue
Payne's gray

ACRYLIC MEDIUMS

Gel retarder

BRUSHES

Script liner: no. 2
Flat: no. 8
Wash brush: 3/4-inch

BASIC PAINTING SUPPLIES

Water container
Palette knife
Sta-Wet palette
Paper towels

FINISHING

Spray high-gloss polyurethane varnish

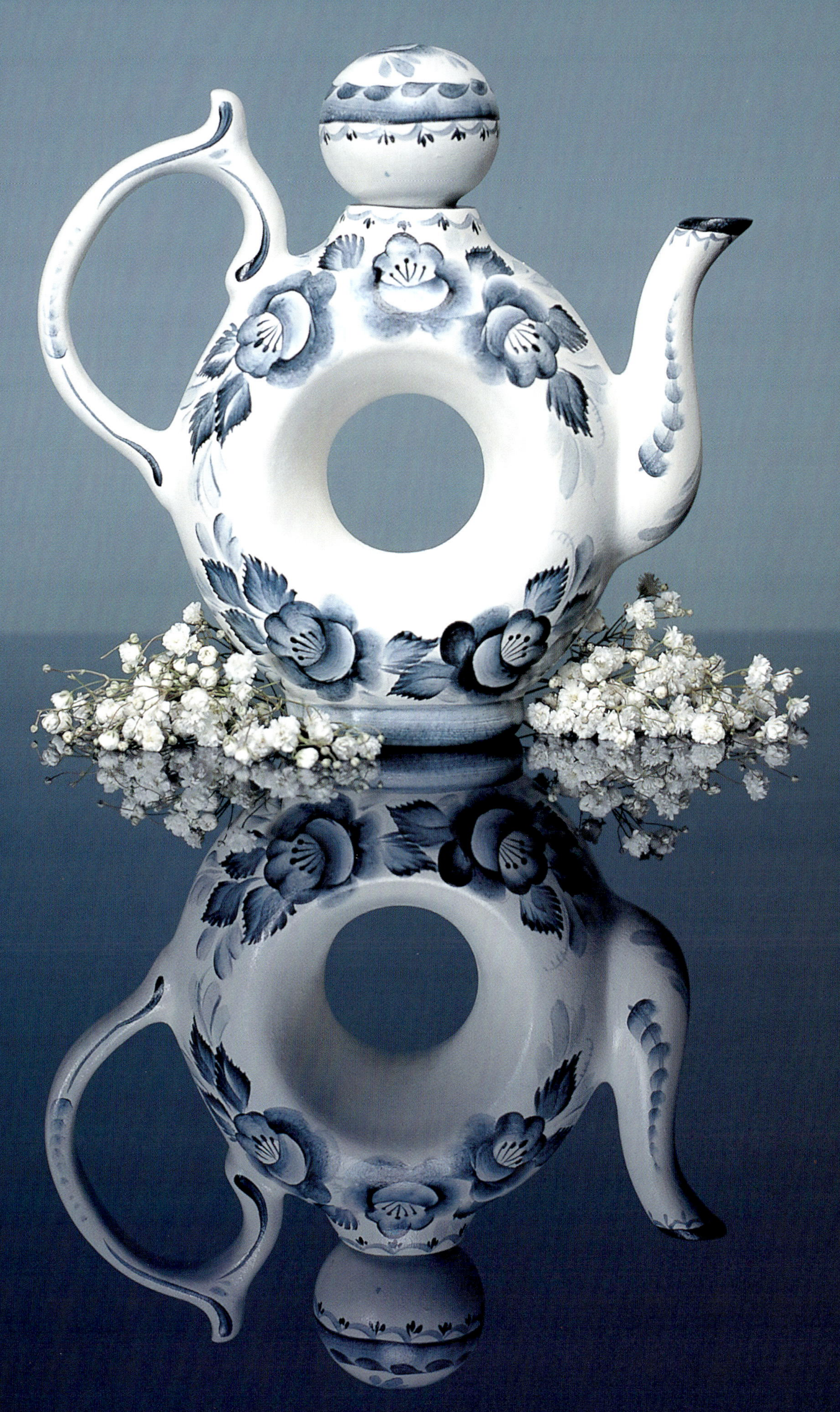

Gzhel

GETTING READY

Sand the teapot with the scrub pad to smooth the surface, then apply two coats of titanium white to the entire surface using the wash brush. Be sure to let each coat dry before applying the next.

Since transferring a design to a rounded surface such as this teapot can be difficult, I suggest that you do *not* try to follow my general instructions on tracing and transferring using transfer paper. Instead, try to sketch the design very loosely onto the surface with a pencil. The design is composed primarily of stroke work, so you need only the most basic of design guidelines on the surface. Make sure to sketch very lightly; otherwise, your pencil lines will be visible on your finished piece.

LEAVES

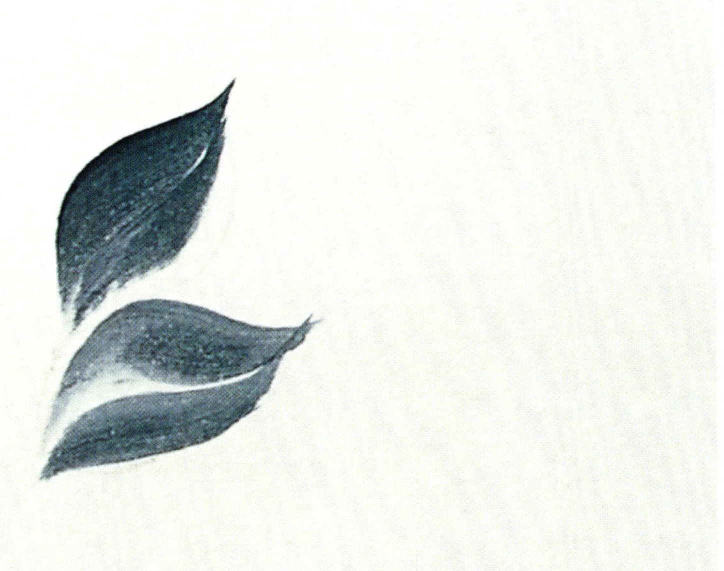

1 Mix Prussian blue and Payne's gray in a 2:1 proportion. This blue color is used for the entire painting. When painting with transparent color and creating a design of strokes, it is imperative to use a correctly loaded brush. Sideload the flat brush with blue paint following the instructions on page 30, but use gel retarder instead of water. Blend on the palette to soften the color. The color on the brush should range from a strong, yet transparent blue on one side to clear gel on the other side.

Apply two S strokes, one below the other, to form the leaf.

2 Reload the brush the same way to paint the jagged edges of the leaves. Holding the brush upright, making a slight slicing motion with it. The dark color should always be on the outside edge of the leaf.

Add a blue vein to the leaf with the script liner.

ROSES

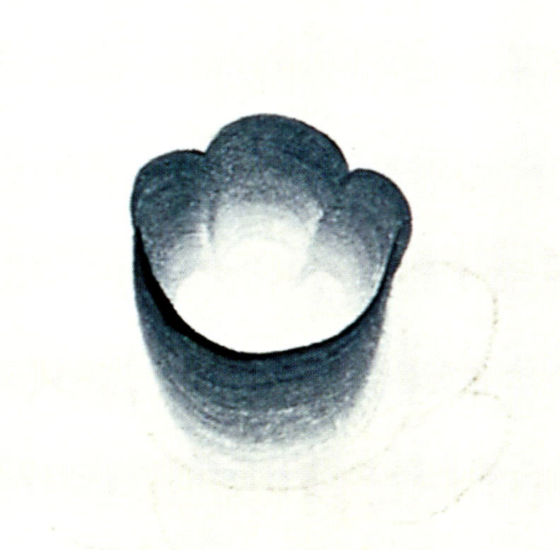

1 Sideload the flat brush as you did in step 1 of the instructions for painting the leaves, then begin to paint a rose by placing three scalloped strokes across the top of the flower. The dark blue should be on the outside edge of the rose. Next, paint the front of the rose with a U stroke. Again, make sure the dark blue is on the top (outer) edge.

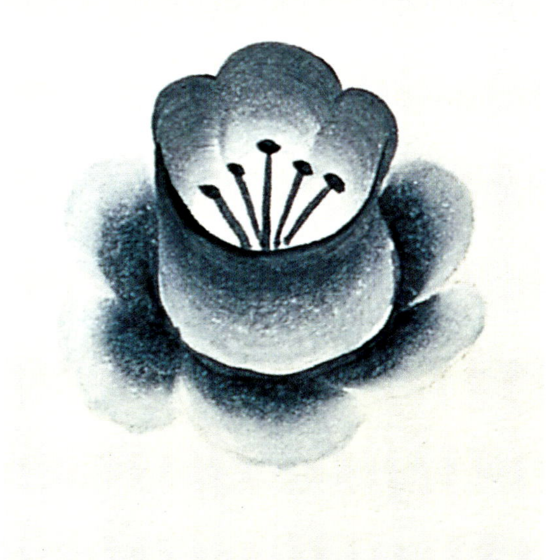

2 Doubleload the same flat brush with paint and gel retarder to paint the outside petals of the rose. Be sure that the dark blue is toward the bowl of the rose and that the bowl of the rose maintains a nice curve. The gel retarder should have a slight tint of blue so that the petals show up against the white of the background.

Paint the stamens with the script liner. Top each stamen with a dot.

STROKE EMBELLISHMENTS

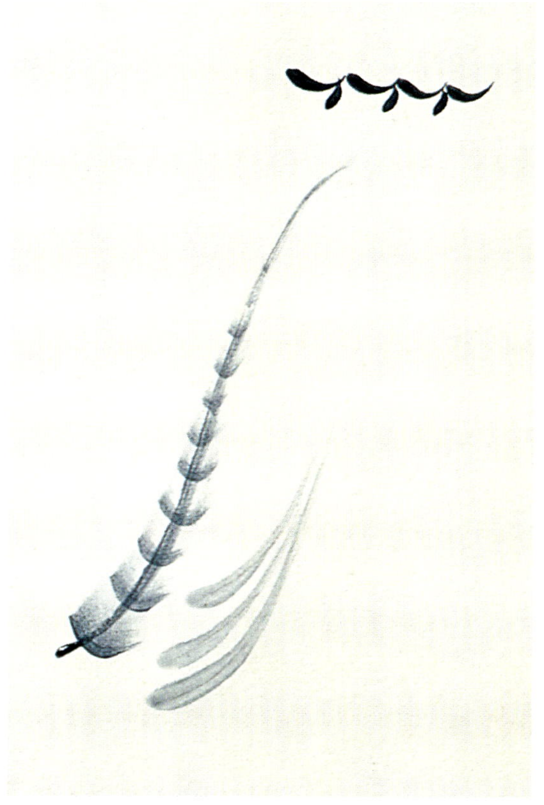

1 To paint the stroke embellishments, add more gel retarder to the blue paint mixture to create some other shades of blue. Use both the script liner and the flat brush (both sideloaded and loaded normally) to paint the strokes. Be creative in both the formation of your strokes and their placement. Studying the example of Gzhel porcelain on page 1 may be helpful as you try to come up with ideas for embellishments.

FINISHING

Apply several coats of a high-gloss spray varnish to emulate the glazed surface of porcelain. Let each coat dry completely before applying the next.

Mstera

Degree of Difficulty

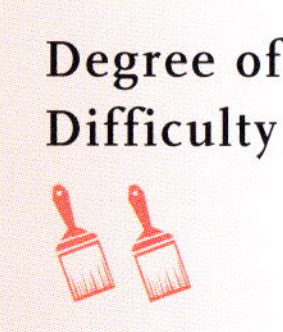

I will admit without shame that my painting skills fall far short of the Russian artists who have inspired me. Their work is without question among the very best in the world. What I hope to show you is that you can take inspiration from an art form and create an interpretation of it.

The work of the Mstera artists often utilizes very delicate gold filigree work. I have adapted a typical floral ornament design that includes gold flourishes and linework. At some point, I suggest you take the time to find some original Russian lacquer miniatures and study them. I have no doubt that you will admire them and take some measure of inspiration from them.

WHAT YOU'LL NEED

Pattern
Page 106

Project
Ball box from PCM Studios *(see page 111 for ordering information)*

Supplies

SURFACE PREP
#400-grit sandpaper
Tack cloth
Basecoat paint: pure black *(see list of artists' acrylics)*

TRACING AND TRANSFERRING
Tracing paper
Fine-tip black marker
White transfer paper
Stylus

ARTISTS' ACRYLICS
Red light
Naphthol crimson
True burgundy
Hauser green dark
Prussian blue
Aqua
Pure black

CRAFT ACRYLICS
Metallic gold

BRUSHES
Wash brush: 3/4-inch
Flat: no. 4
Script liner: no. 2

BASIC PAINTING SUPPLIES
Water container
Palette knife
Sta-wet palette
Paper towels

FINISHING
High-gloss spray varnish

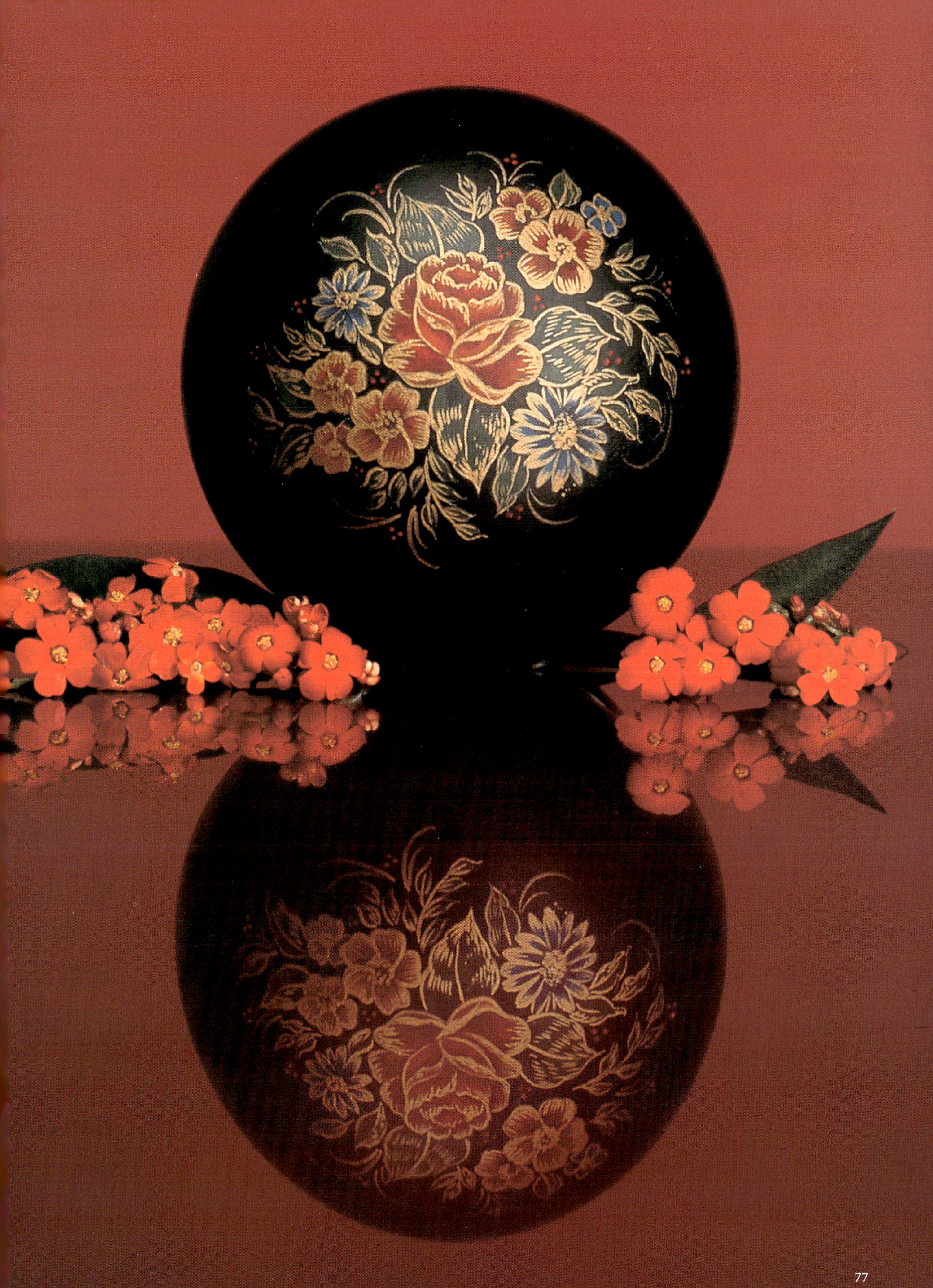

Mstera

GETTING READY

Use the wash brush to basecoat the ball-shaped jewelry box with pure black. Then transfer the design to the surface with white transfer paper following the instructions on page 39. You may find it helpful to snip the design around the edges to help it conform to the spherical shape of the box.

LEAVES

1 Use the flat brush to undercoat the leaves with Hauser green dark. Let dry.

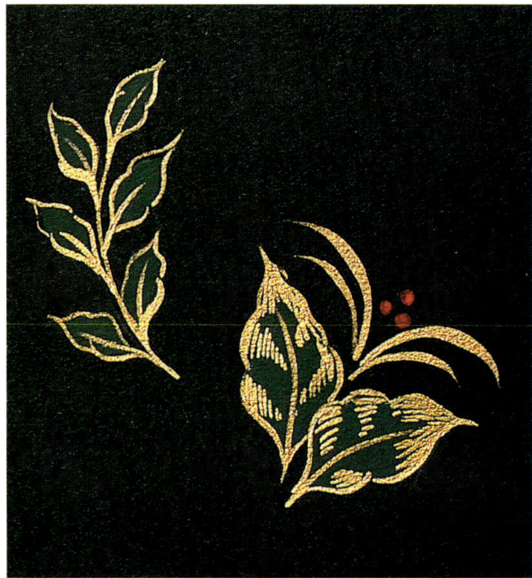

2 Load the script liner with metallic gold and outline the leaves. Make a series of short parallel lines to indicate the ripples of the leaves, then add the veins.

With the same brush, paint some small, curving gold lines radiating from the design. Then apply clusters of three naphthol crimson handle dots to create floral forms. These details will flesh out the design.

BLUE DAISIES

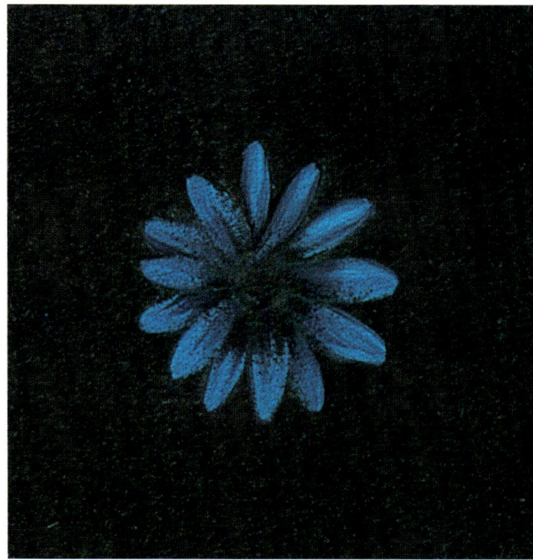

1 Using the script liner, stroke on a petal of the daisy with Prussian blue. Wipe the brush and load it sparsely with aqua. Restroke the petal with aqua to highlight the tip of the petal. Repeat this for each petal. Let dry.

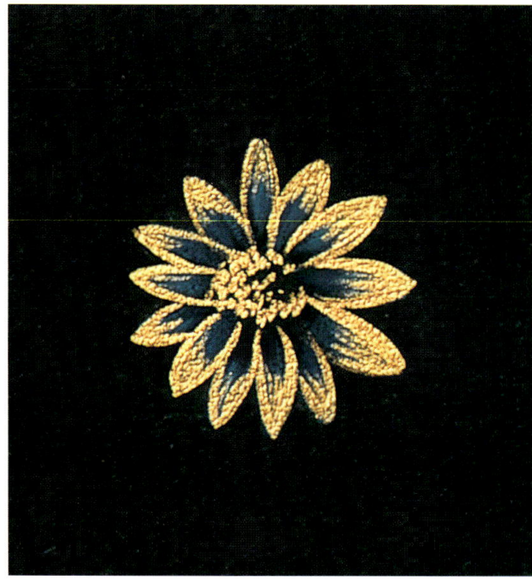

2 Load the script liner with metallic gold, then outline each petal of the daisy. Make a few pulls of gold from the tip toward the center of the flower to highlight the tips of the petals. Let dry. The center is composed of small dots of metallic gold applied with the tip of the script liner.

RED BLOSSOMS

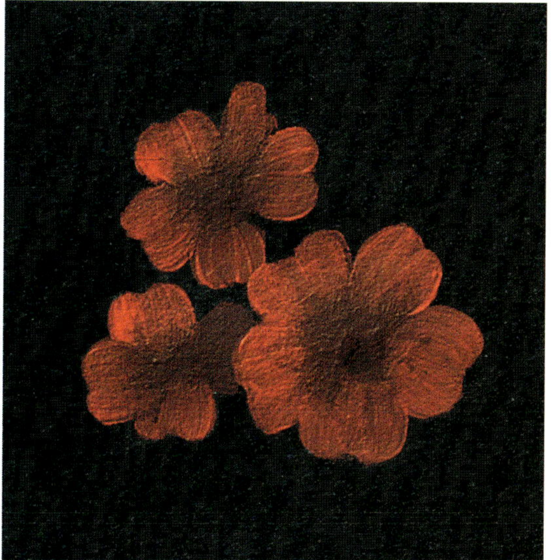

1 Undercoat the petals using the flat brush and true burgundy paint. While the petals are wet, stroke on highlights of naphthol crimson. Paint only one petal at a time. Let dry, then fill in the center of the flowers with true burgundy. Let dry.

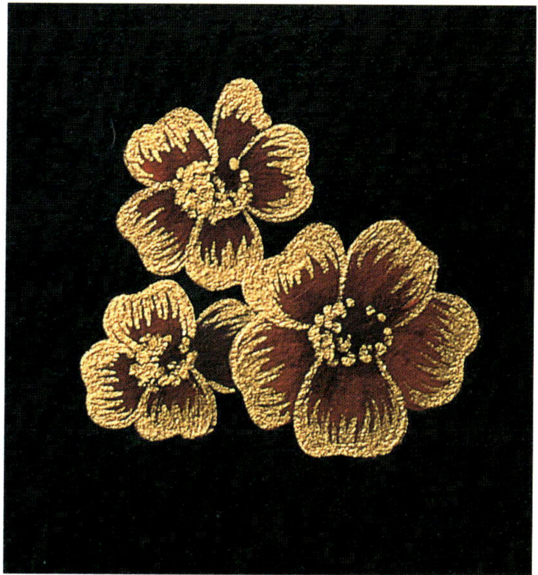

2 Highlight the flowers by first outlining the petals with metallic gold using the script liner. Then make a series of small lines to indicate a lighter area near the ends of the petals. The centers are a series of dots made with the same brush and paint. Paint a higher concentration of dots on one side of the center to indicate highlights and shading.

ROSE

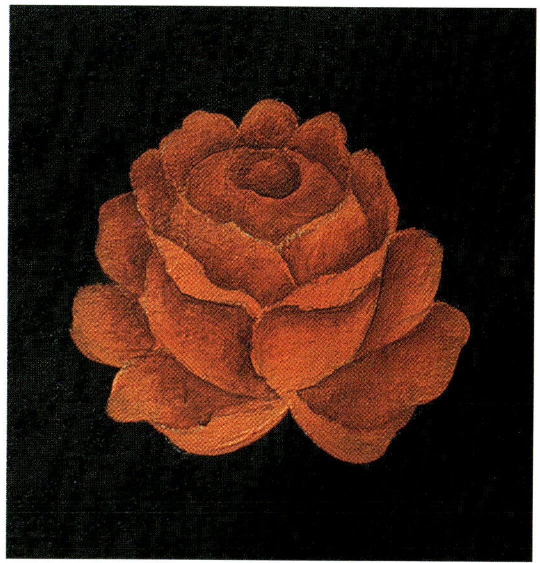

1 Undercoat the entire rose with red light using the flat brush. You will need to apply three or four coats to achieve an opaque coverage. Let dry, then transfer the petal lines to the rose.

Sideload the flat brush with true burgundy and shade the areas where one petal falls behind another petal. Let dry.

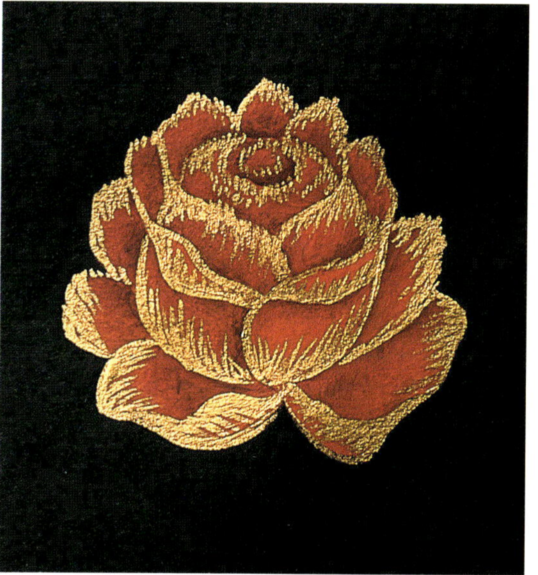

2 Beginning at the top of the rose and working down, apply metallic gold highlights using the script liner. I find it helpful to outline the petals, then go back and apply the hatch lines to indicate stronger highlights.

FINISHING

In order to simulate the highly polished surface of Russian lacquerware, finish the box with high-gloss spray varnish following the instructions on page 43.

Zhostovo

Degree of Difficulty

Zhostovo artists don't use patterns when they paint, but create designs in their minds and begin execution directly on the piece. The process begins with an undercoating of the main design elements with white. The skillful application of this basecoat begins the development of the flower or fruit's form. When this layer has dried, the artist paints the object's local color. The object is then shaded with other deep, transparent colors and allowed to dry again. Next, highlights are applied in several layers using a wet-in-wet technique. Finally the details are added. The piece is then usually sent to another artist who specializes in the rich gold border work.

Zhostovo artists typically paint their pieces with a variety of different leaf shapes and colors. For this project, paint all of the leaves using the same technique, but use two different colors. Feel free to alter the colors shown to make your leaves more olive green or more blue-green to suit your taste. You'll notice that the roses on my finished tray are several different shades of pink. Again, adjust the coloration to suit your own taste. Try painting several different-colored roses using the same technique.

Zhostovo trays are truly an inspiration in terms of color, design, and execution. My example is a rather simplified version. Once you are comfortable with the basic painting technique you can apply it to other designs or create your own.

WHAT YOU'LL NEED

Pattern

Page107

Project

Tin Chippendale tray from Barb Watson's Brushworks *(see page 111 for ordering information)*

Supplies

SURFACE PREP
- Scrub pad
- Tack cloth
- Basecoat paints: satin-sheen black spray paint

TRACING AND TRANSFERRING
- Tracing paper
- Fine-tip black marker
- Chalk
- Stylus

BRUSHES
- Filberts: nos. 4, 6, and 8
- Script liner: no. 2
- Flats: nos. 4, 8, and 10

ARTISTS' ACRYLICS
- Titanium white
- Alizarin crimson
- True burgundy
- Burnt carmine
- Medium yellow
- Hauser green dark
- Hauser green medium
- Hauser green light
- Aqua
- Payne's gray
- Dioxazine purple
- Pure black
- Brilliant ultramarine

CRAFT ACRYLICS
- Metallic gold

ACRYLIC MEDIUMS
- Gel retarder

BASIC PAINTING SUPPLIES
- Water container
- Palette knife
- Sta-wet palette
- Paper towels

FINISHING
- Spray high-gloss polyurethane varnish

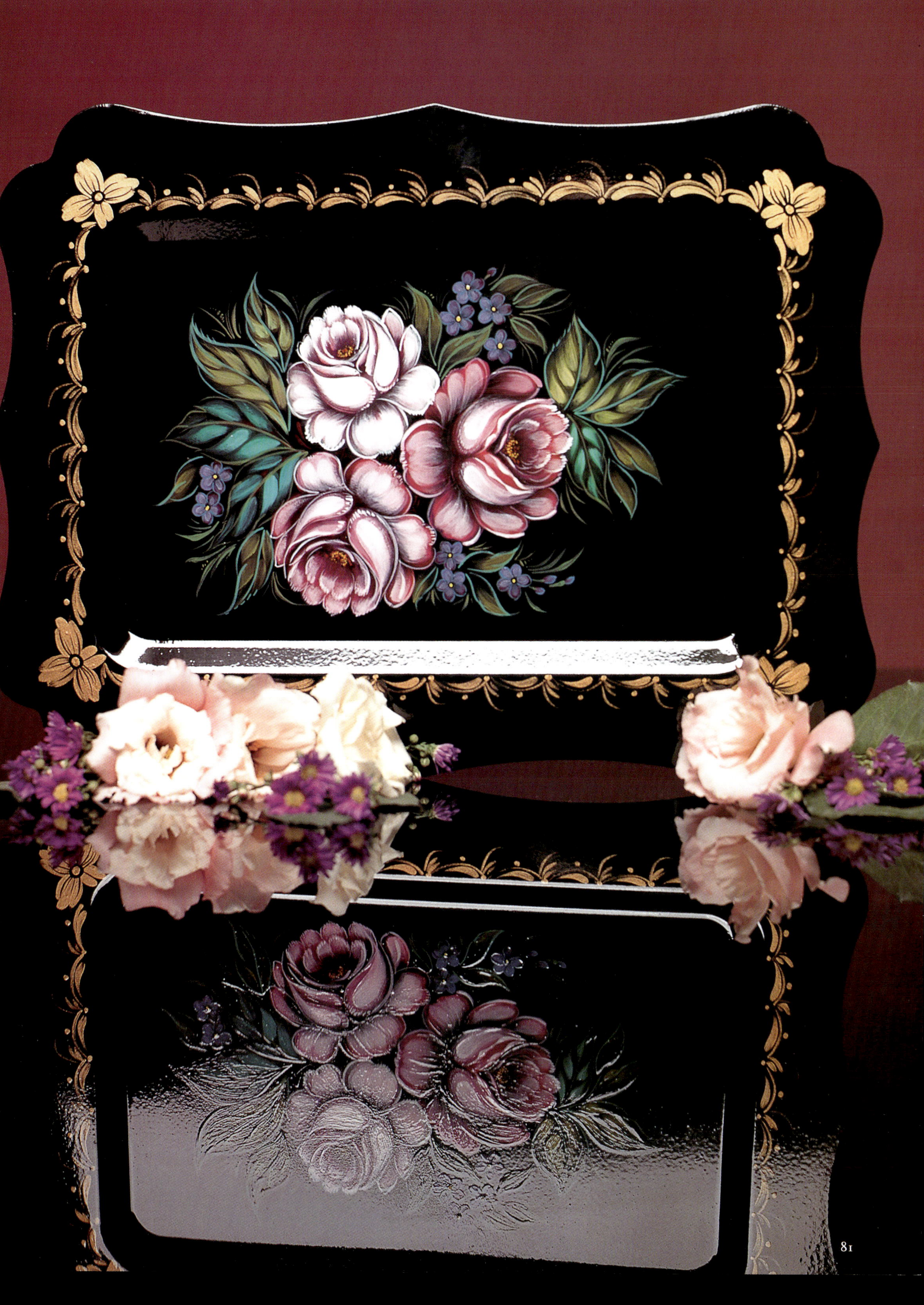

Zhostovo

GETTING READY

Prepare the tray according to the instructions on page 36. Since the tray I used comes pre-primed from the manufacturer, I simply rubbed it lightly with a scrub pad and wiped it with a tack cloth.

Next, basecoat the tray using black satin-sheen spray paint. For this technique a very smooth background is essential. Be sure the paint coverage is even and opaque.

Trace the pattern following the instructions on page 38, then transfer only the main design elements—not the border pattern—to the tray using the chalk tracing method described on page 40.

LEAVES

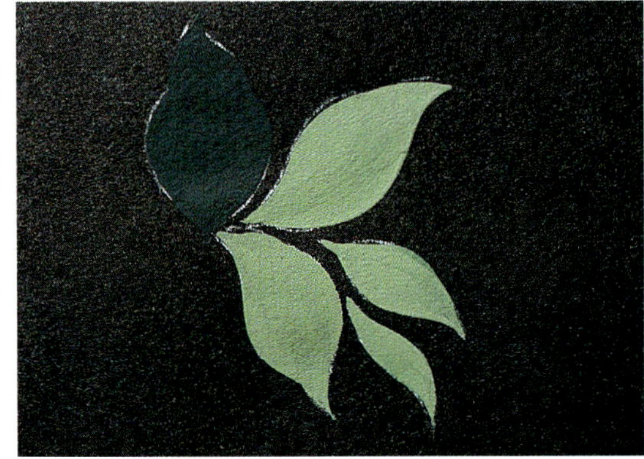

1 Undercoat the leaf forms using the no. 8 flat brush. Use Hauser green medium for the green leaves and Hauser green dark for the blue-green leaves. Let the first coat dry and apply a second coat if needed. Let dry.

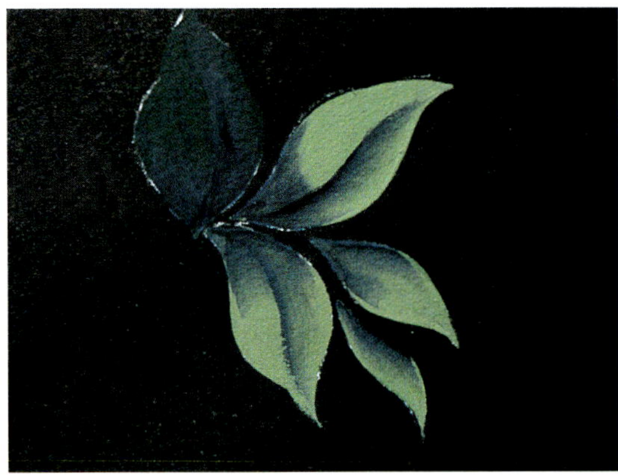

2 Using gel retarder, sideload the flat brush with Payne's gray. Shade the base of the leaf and let dry. Then, with the brush loaded the same way, create the center vein area by applying a graceful S stroke to the center of the leaf. Let dry.

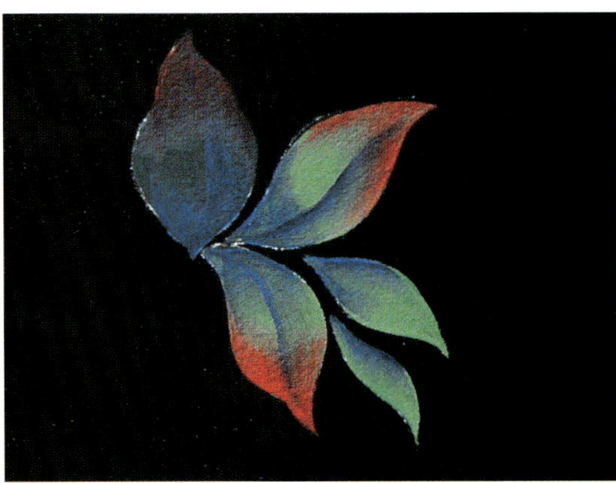

3 Sideload the same flat brush with alizarin crimson and apply some paint to the tips of some of the leaves. Do not apply the crimson to every leaf. Let dry.

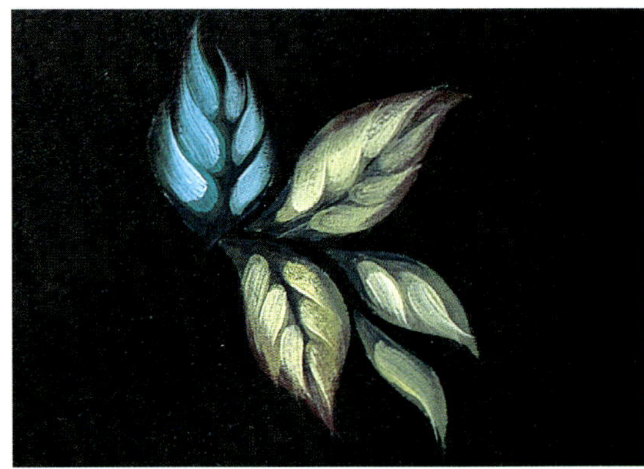

4 Using the same brush, apply a coat of gel retarder to the leaves. Switch to the no. 6 filbert and brush a thin coat of Hauser green medium on the green leaves and Hauser green dark on the blue-green leaves. While the green is wet, load the filbert with Hauser green medium + a touch of Hauser green light for the green leaves and Hauser green dark + aqua for the blue-green leaves and paint some loose comma or S strokes as highlights. Continuing into the wet gel, make another series of smaller strokes over the ones you've just made using Hauser green light on the green leaves and aqua on the blue-green ones. Finish the highlights by placing yet another layer of highlight strokes, with Hauser green light + yellow medium on the green leaves and aqua + a little titanium white on the blue-green leaves. Let dry.

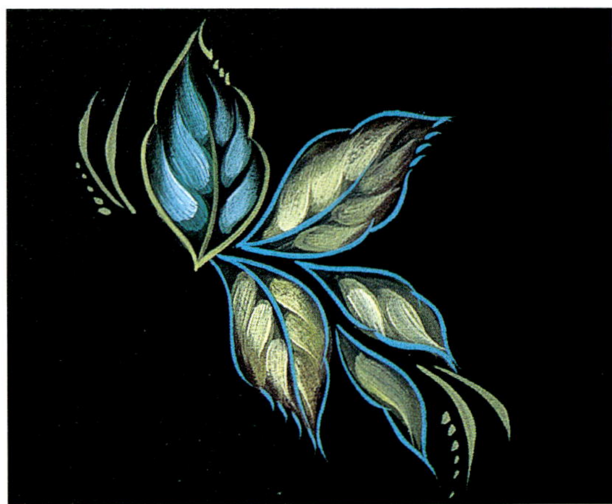

5 To finish the green leaves, outline them using the script liner and aqua + yellow medium paint. To make this color a bit more opaque, add a touch of titanium white to the mix. For the blue-green leaves, do the same thing using Hauser green medium. Again, add a touch of titanium white to increase the opacity of the color. On all of the leaves, be sure to break up the outline so it isn't a solid line. Study the photographs of this step and of the finished tray for reference.

ROSES

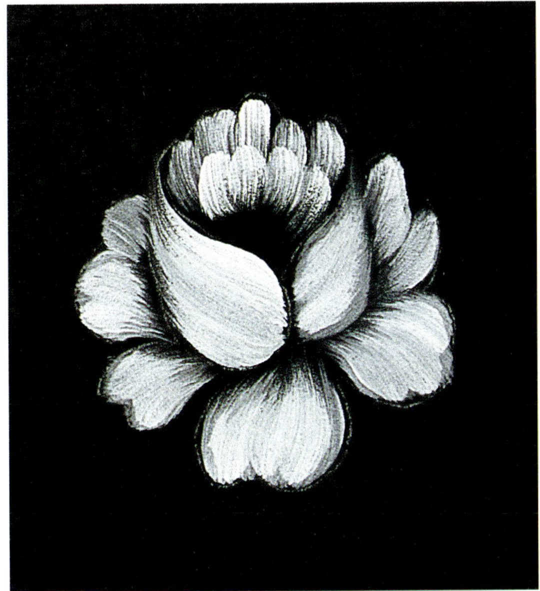

1 Using the no. 8 filbert, undercoat the rose with a thin coat of gel retarder, then apply a layer of titanium white while the gel is still wet. Beginning at the top of the rose, make a series of short "pull" strokes to form the back row of petals. Drop down and create a second, overlapping row of petals. For the outer petals, stroke from the outside in toward the bowl of the rose. Create the bowl itself by applying large comma strokes to the front of the rose. While the paint is wet, pick up more white and re-stroke some of the front petals to make them more opaque. (Study the photo to see which petals should be brighter.) Let dry completely.

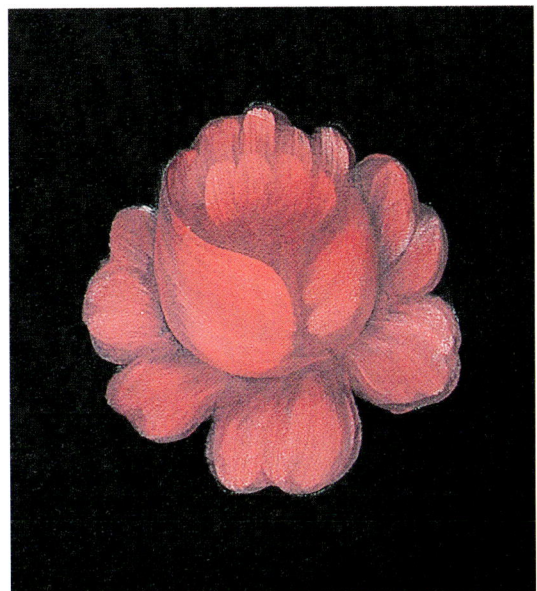

2 Using the no. 10 flat brush, apply a coat of titanium white + alizarin crimson. Thin the paint with a little water so that is slightly translucent. You should be able to see your white undercoat clearly. Let dry.

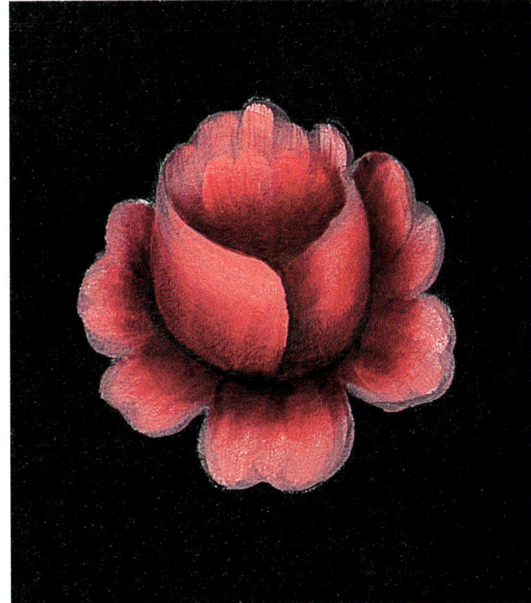

3 Sideload the same brush with true burgundy and shade the rose. Apply the shading in the throat of the rose, where the front petals overlap, and at the base of the rose where the outside petals join the bowl of the rose. Let dry. Enhance the shading by sideloading the brush with burnt carmine and reapplying the shading. Be sure the burnt carmine does not completely cover the crimson shading. Let dry.

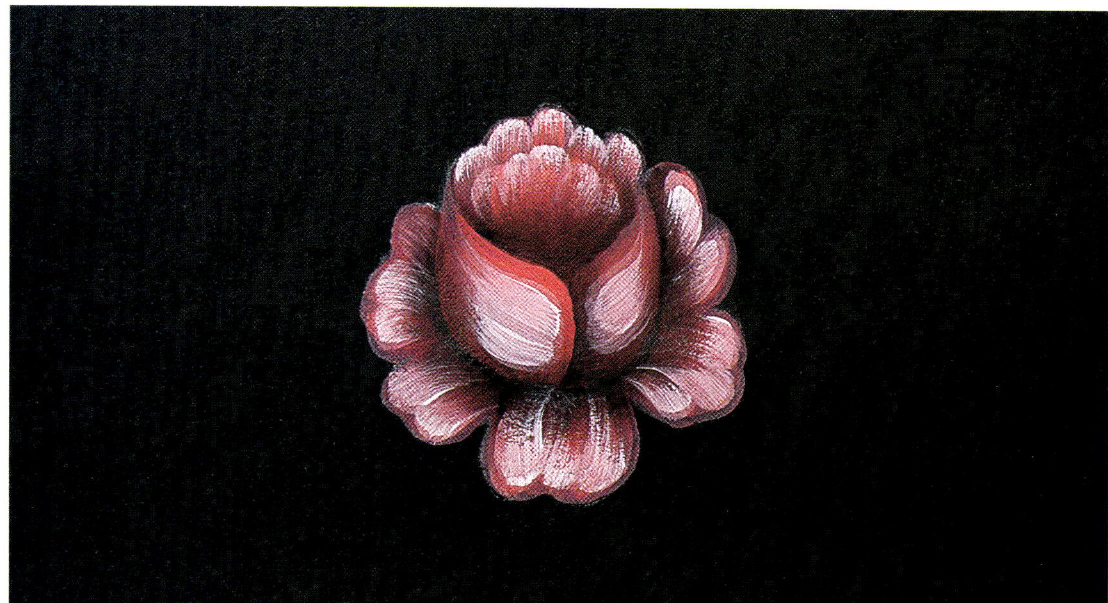

4 Brush a coat of gel retarder on the rose using the largest flat brush. While the gel is wet, begin building a series of highlights. Start with the pink mix and, using the filbert brush, re-stroke the rose as you did for the undercoat. Add more white to the brush and apply a second layer of highlights on top of the wet gel. These highlights should be slightly set back so that the edges of the first highlights show. If you feel your rose needs additional highlighting, pick up some more white on the brush and apply still another layer of highlights. Let dry.

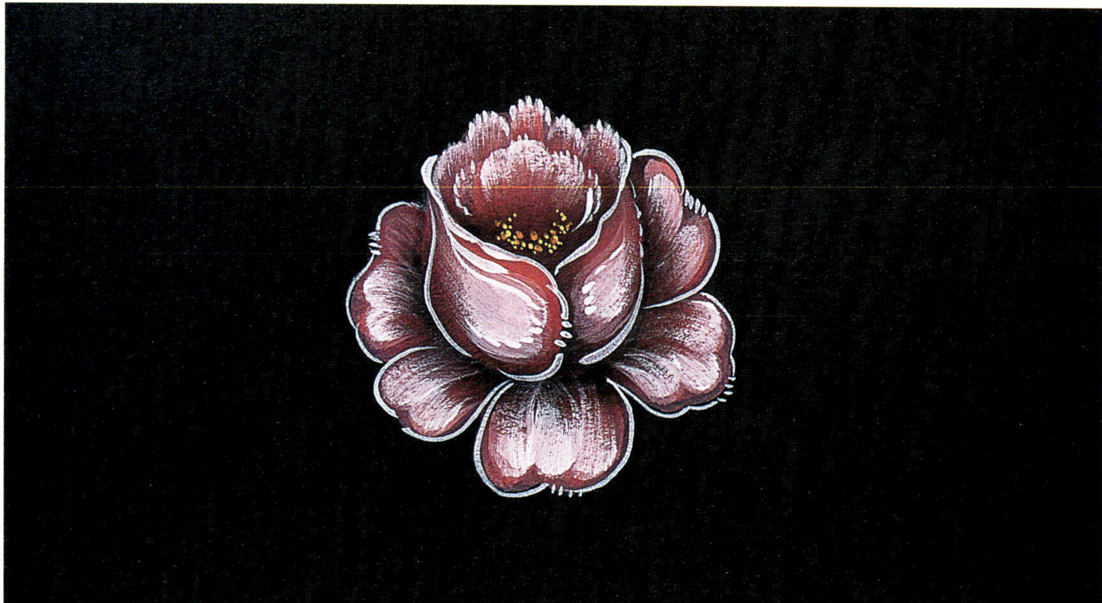

5 Finish the rose with some outlining. Use the script liner and a very light pink (almost white) made from titanium white + a tiny amount of alizarin crimson. Outline the main strokes that you applied when you undercoated the rose. Be sure to use a broken outline, not a solid continuous line. Add some small dots or dashes for variety in the outlining.

Paint the center of the rose with the script liner. Make a crescent of medium yellow dots and add a few dots of medium yellow + a touch of alizarin crimson.

FORGET-ME-NOTS

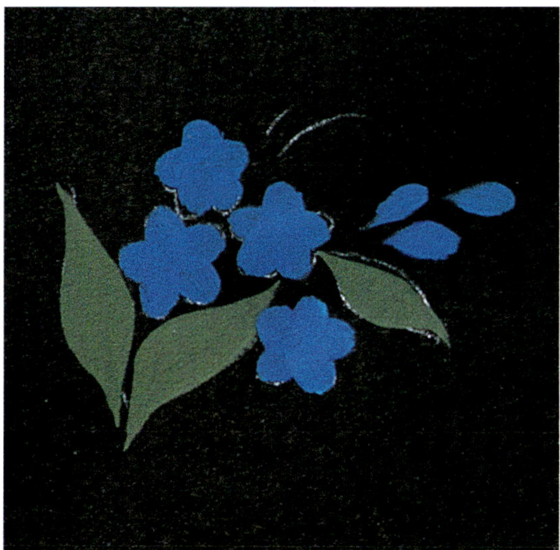

1 Undercoat the flowers with the no. 4 filbert and brilliant ultramarine + a touch of aqua. Let dry.

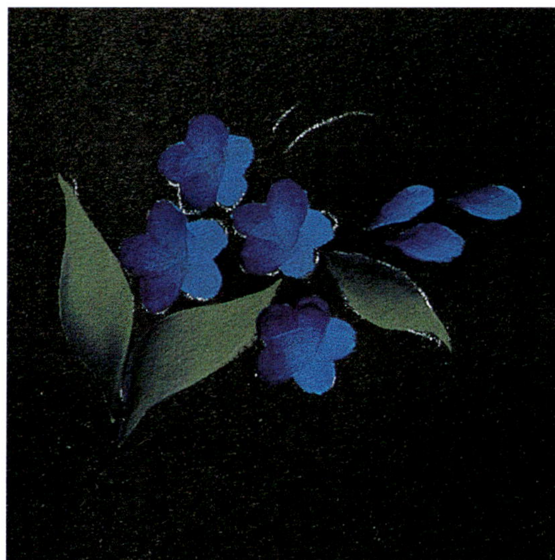

2 Sideload the no. 4 flat brush with dioxazine purple and shade three of the five petals along the outer edge. Let dry.

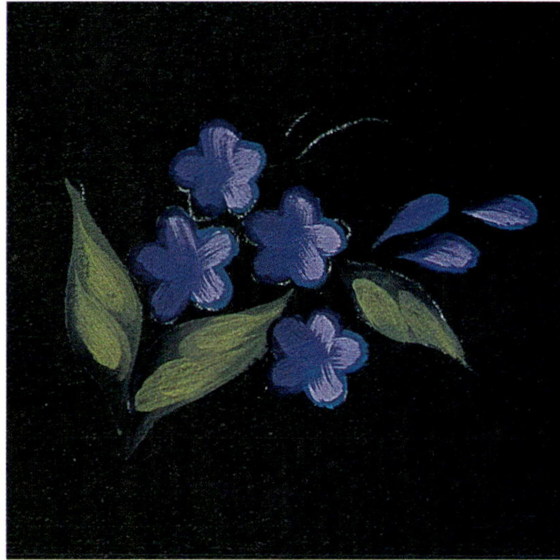

3 Pick up a little dioxazine purple + titanium white on the no. 4 filbert and stroke on highlights on three of the five petals of each flower. Be sure that the highlight stroke does not extend all the way to the edge of the petal. Let dry.

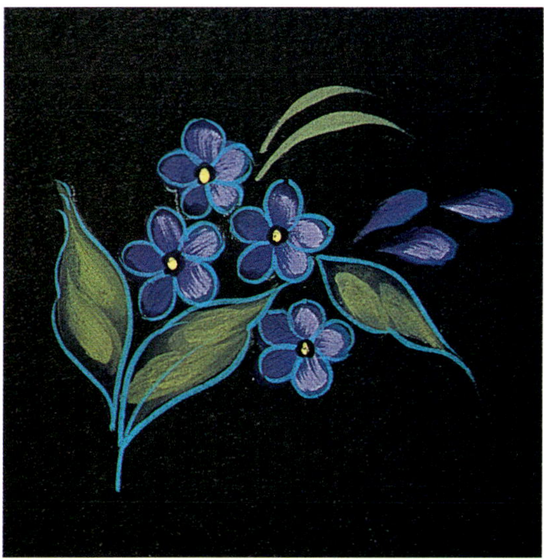

4 Outline the flower with the script liner using aqua + a touch of brilliant ultramarine. Then paint the forget-me-nots' centers with a dot of Payne's gray highlighted with a dot of medium yellow.

FINISHING

To paint the tray's border, use the script liner and metallic gold to make a series of comma strokes, lines, and dots. Paint one element all the way around the tray, then continue with the next element until the border is completed. The petals of the gold flowers at the corners should be stroked on with gold. Then paint a pure black circle to form the center of the flower and add some black linework on the petals to finish the flower form.

The Russian artists finish their trays with a lacquer to enhance their colors. I recommend that you varnish your tray with three or four coats of high-gloss spray varnish to get a lacquer-like finish.

Rogaland-Style Rosemaling

Degree of Difficulty

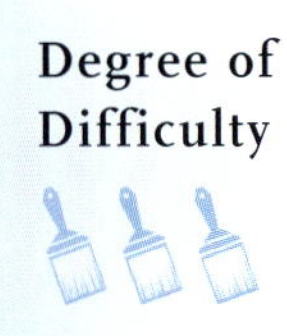

Rogaland is one of the best styles of rosemaling to begin with because of the repetition of the design elements, which helps beginners to gain proficiency. I have chosen to paint a rather simple design—with only few elements—on a tine box. The tine (pronounced tee-nah) is a typical Norwegian bentwood box used for storage. The box is constructed so that the lid slides between two wooden hinges and requires no metal hardware.

When painting in the Rogaland style, strive for symmetry in the elements you paint. I recommend that you paint from the rear toward the front of the design. Whenever you paint an element on one side of the design, paint it on the opposite side as well.

WHAT YOU'LL NEED

Pattern

Page 108

Project

Medium tine from Valhalla Designs *(see page 111 for ordering information)*

Supplies

SURFACE PREP

#400-grit sandpaper
Tack cloth
Basecoat paint: French blue (light pastel blue)

TRACING AND TRANSFERRING

Tracing paper
Fine-tip black marker
White transfer paper
Chalk
Stylus

BRUSHES

Glaze/varnish brush: 1-inch
Flats: nos. 4 and 8
Liner: no. 2
Script liner: no. 2

ARTISTS' ACRYLICS

Titanium white
Warm white
Turner's yellow
Yellow ocher
Raw umber
Prussian blue
Burnt umber

BASIC PAINTING SUPPLIES

Water container
Palette knife
Sta-wet palette
Paper towels

FINISHING

Brush-on satin-sheen or semi-gloss polyurethane varnish

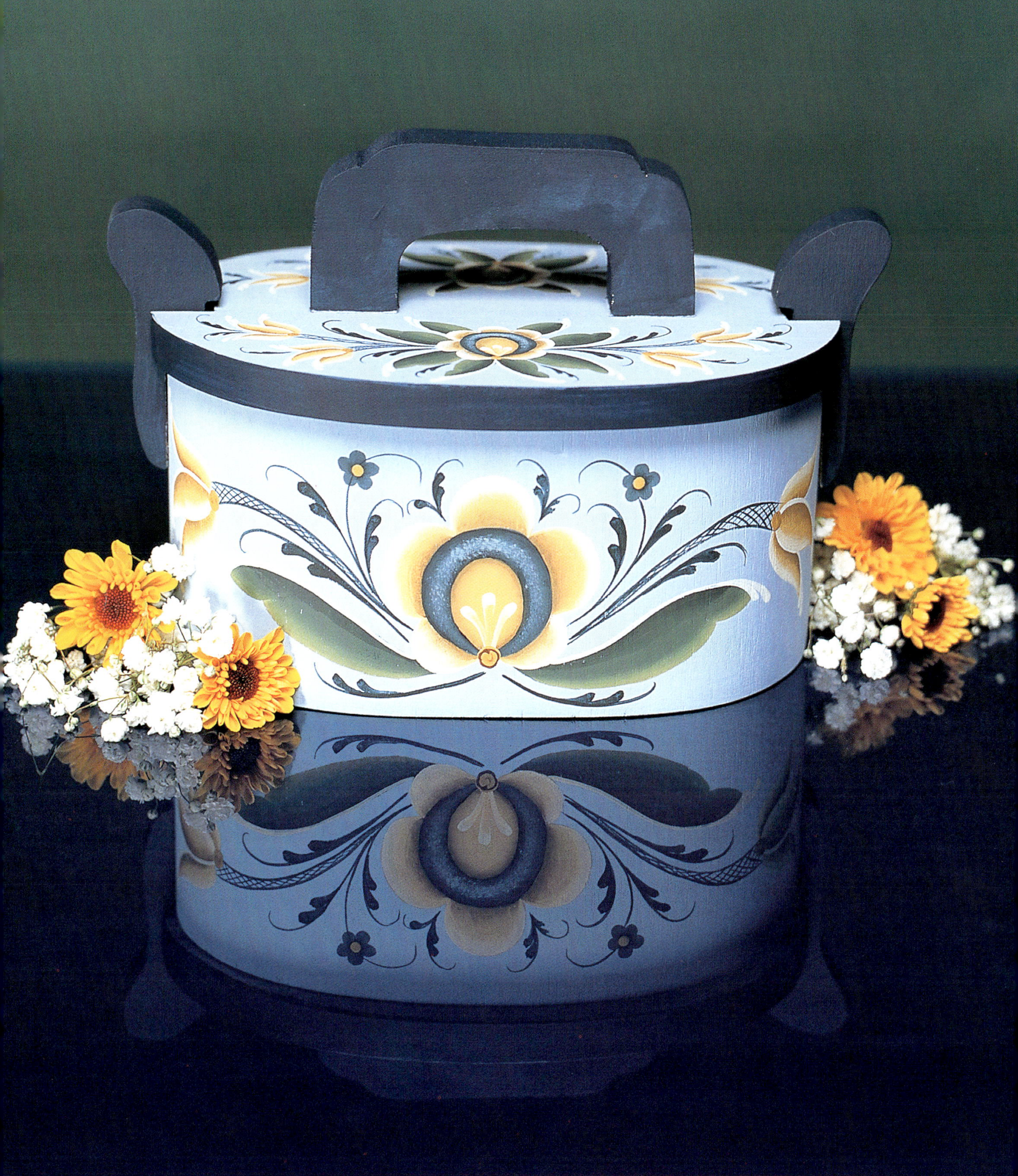

Rogaland-Style Rosemaling

GETTING READY

Using the glaze/varnish brush, paint the main part of the tine with French blue. Let dry. If necessary, lightly sand the box and apply a second coat. Paint the handles and sides of the tine's lid with Prussian blue + a touch of burnt umber. Let dry.

Following the instructions on pages 38–39, trace and transfer the main elements of the design to the tine using transfer paper. Do not transfer the small flowers and scrolls yet.

LEAVES

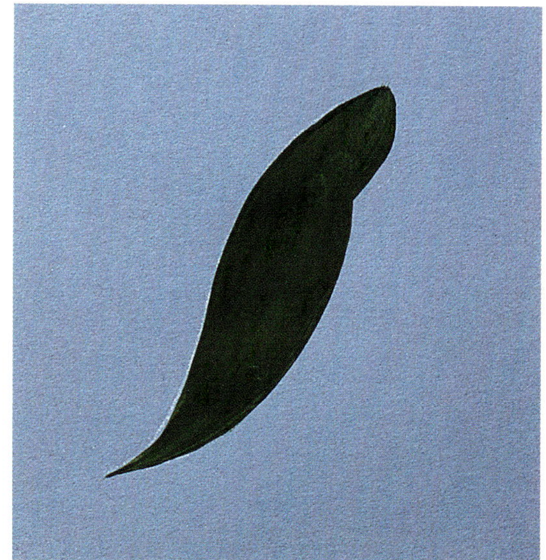

1 Using either the no. 4 or no. 8 flat brush, undercoat the leaves with Prussian blue + burnt umber + yellow ocher. This mixture should produce a fairly dark green. Let dry.

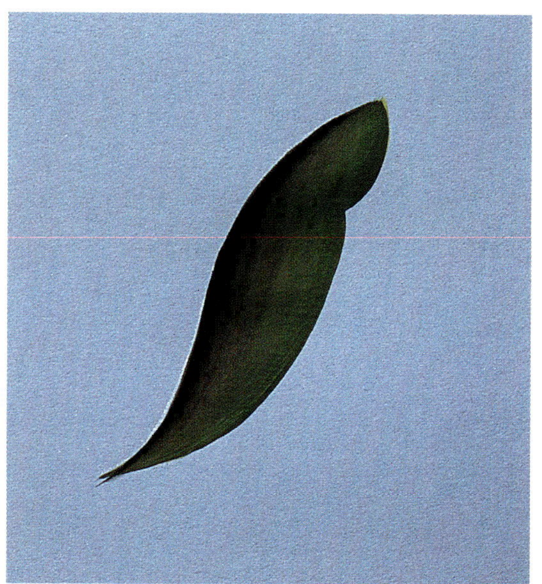

2 Shade the leaves with a brush sideloaded with burnt umber + Prussian blue. Let dry.

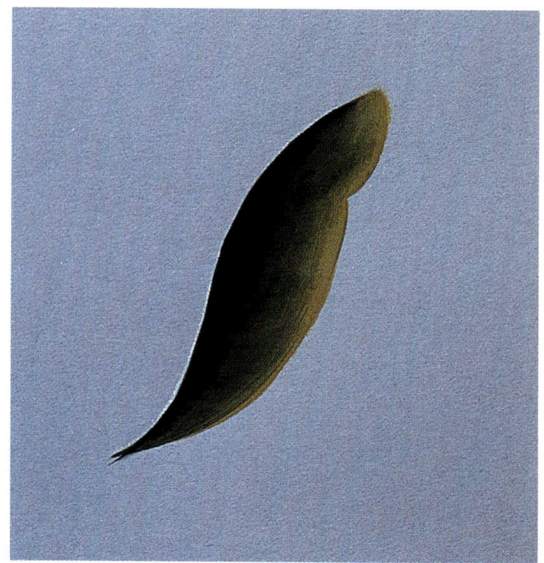

3 Highlight the leaves with a light green made from the undercoat green + more yellow ocher. Let dry.

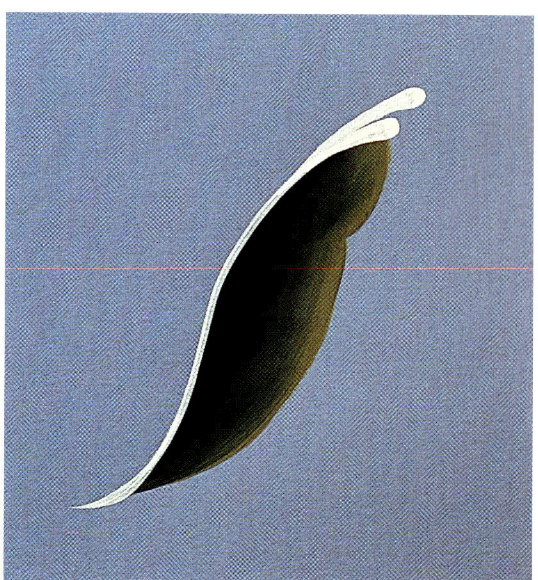

4 Using the short-haired liner, add two teardrops to the ends of the leaves with warm white + a touch of yellow ocher. Let dry.

TULIPS

1 Undercoat each part of the tulip with yellow ocher using the largest flat brush that can fit. Try to form the flowers with graceful brush-strokes. Let dry.

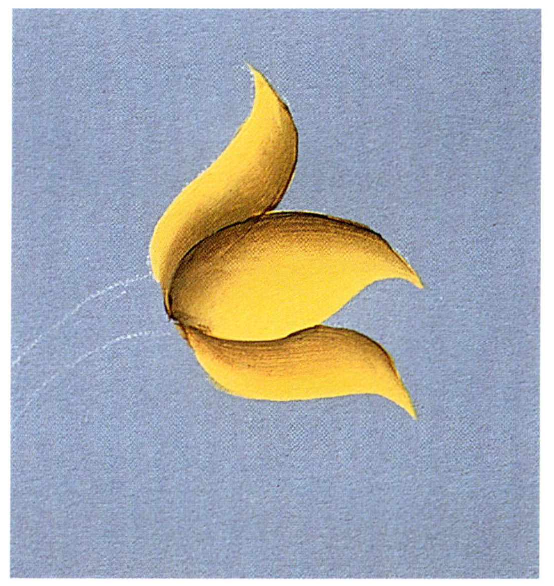

2 Add shading with a sideloaded flat brush using a small amount of raw umber. Let dry.

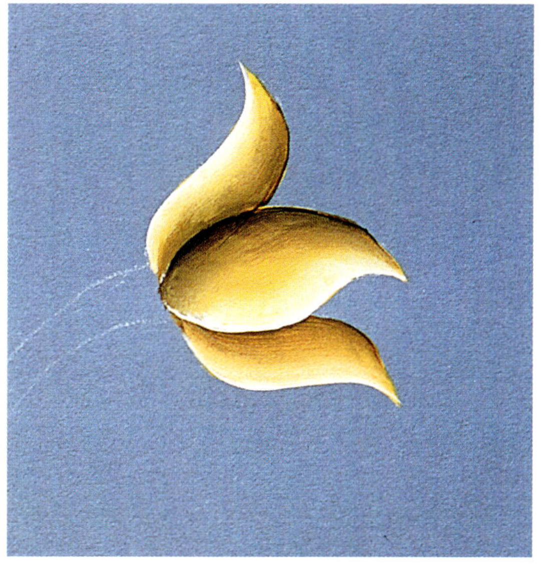

3 Highlight the tulips with the same brush sideloaded with warm white + Turner's yellow. Let dry.

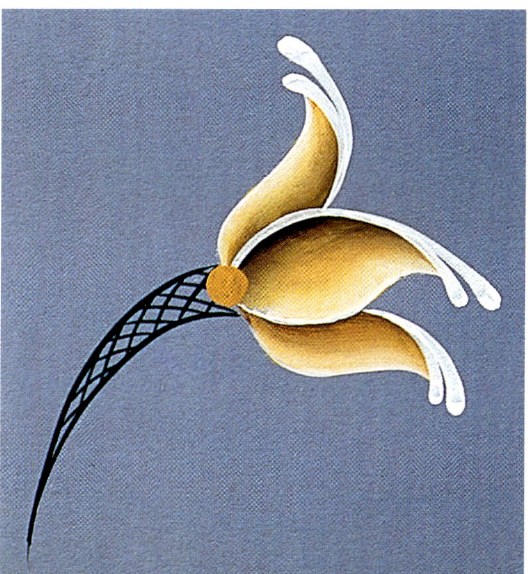

4 Add a dot of yellow ocher at the base of each tulip. The teardrops are painted using the liner and warm white + a touch of yellow ocher. Let dry. The cross-hatched stems will be added later.

BONNET LILY

1 Undercoat the center and outside petals with yellow ocher. Apply two coats if needed to get opaque coverage. Let dry.

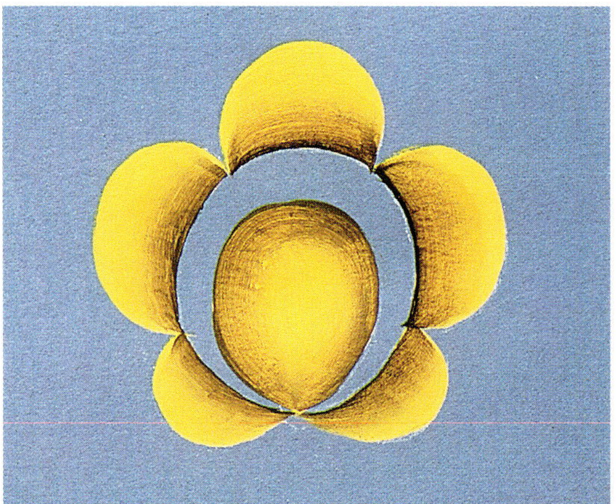

2 Sideload the small flat brush with raw umber and apply the shading on the areas of the outside petals that are closest to the center of the flower. Shade around the outside of the center at this time as well. Let dry.

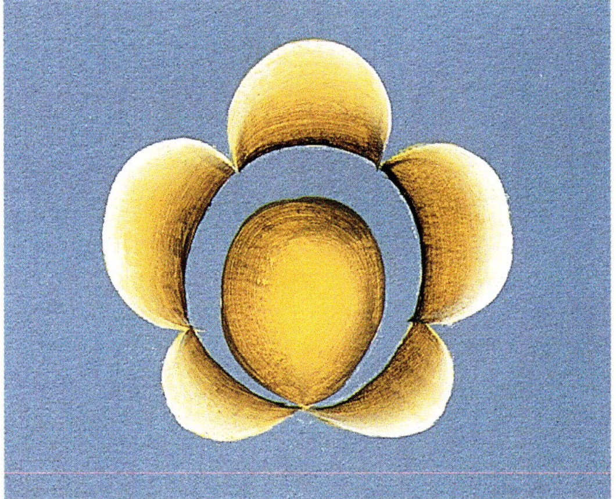

3 Sideload the same small brush with warm white and highlight the outside edges of the petals. The center should *not* be highlighted. Let dry.

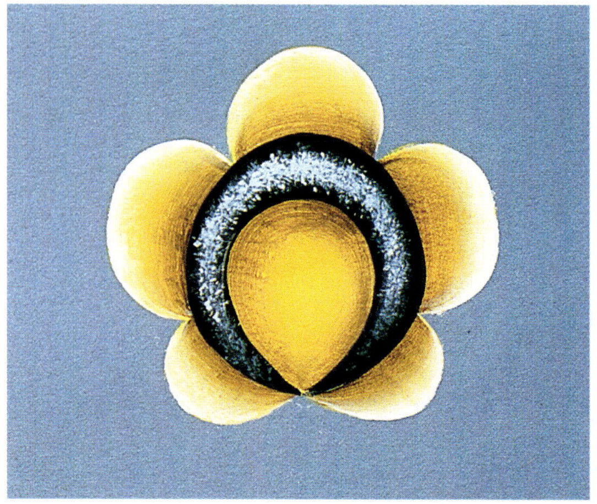

4 With the same flat brush, paint the blue band around the center with Prussian blue + burnt umber + titanium white. Let dry. To create the highlight on the blue band, use the small flat brush loaded with the undercoat blue + titanium white. Tap the brush on the palette to flare the bristles, then stipple the highlight in the center of the band. Let dry.

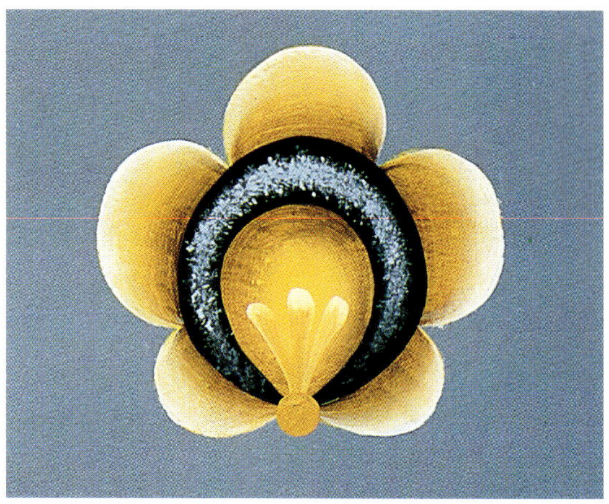

5 Place three tipped teardrop strokes in the center of the lily. Load one of the liners with warm white, wipe the tip of the brush, and pick up some yellow ocher. Form the center teardrop first, then add the strokes on either side. A dot of yellow ocher at the bottom of these three strokes finishes the flower.

SCROLLS AND FIVE-PETALLED FLOWERS

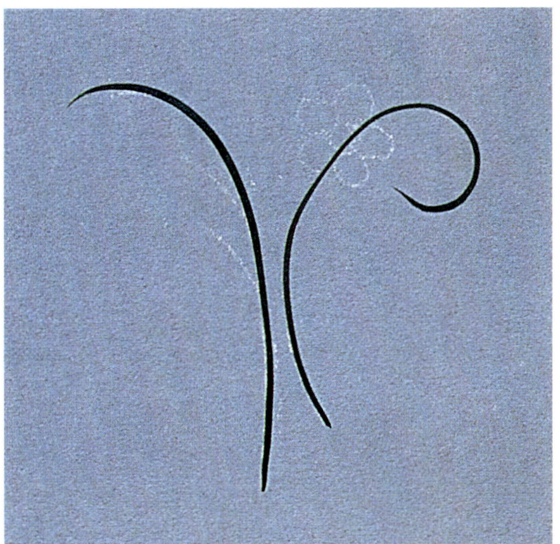

1 If you need to, transfer the design's embellishments using the chalk transfer method (see page 40). Paint the fine scroll lines using the script liner loaded with Prussian blue + burnt umber. At this time, add fine cross-hatching to form the tulip stems.

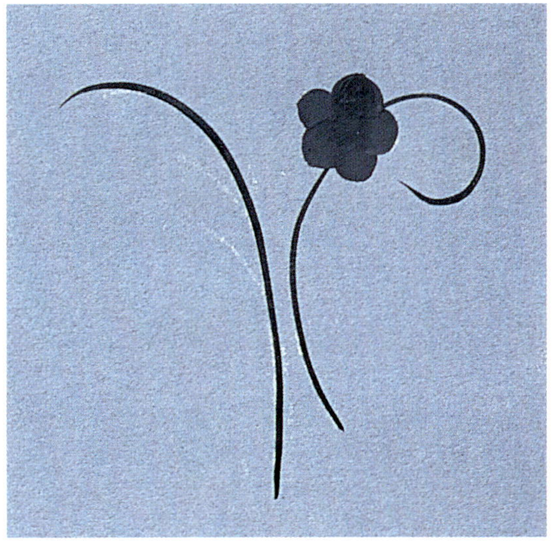

2 Add a little titanium white to the blue color and paint the five-petalled flowers.

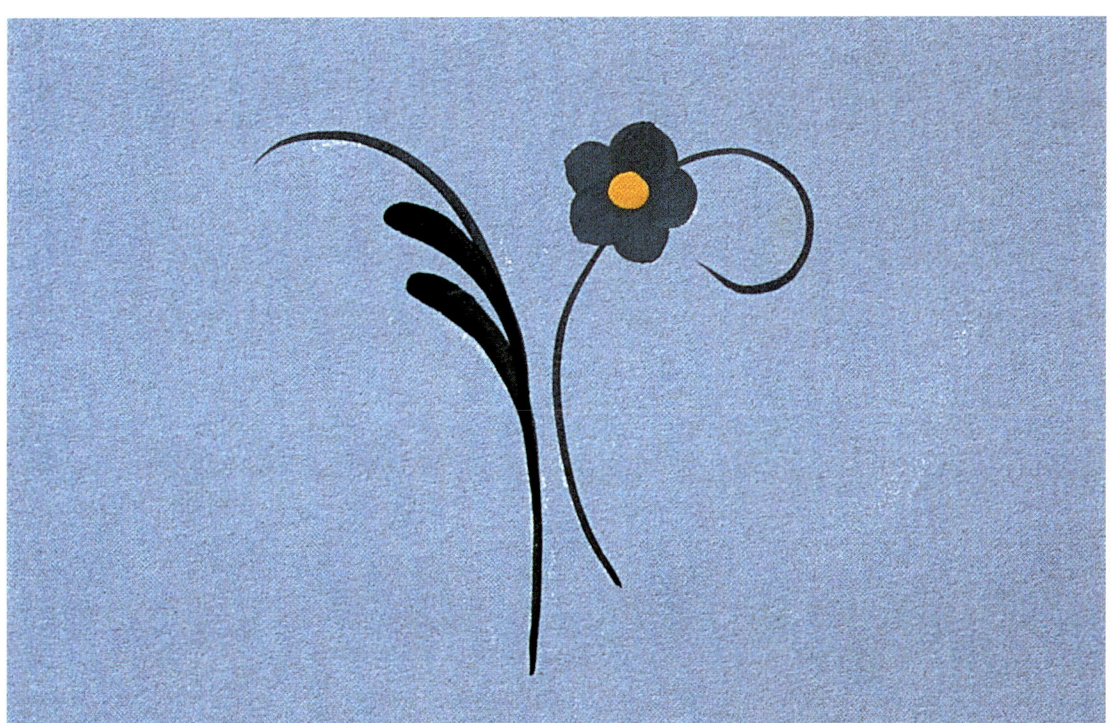

3 Paint the teardrops with the short-haired liner using the blue color from step 1. Then add a dot of yellow ocher to the center of each five-petalled flower.

FINISHING

Apply two or three coats of varnish, letting each coat dry before applying the next.

Telemark-Style Rosemaling

Degree of Difficulty

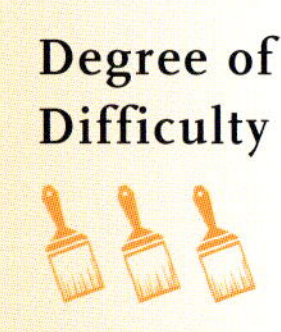

My interpretation of Telemark rosemaling is derived from studying the work of many artists and choosing what I liked best from each artist. To excel at painting pieces in the Telemark style you must have a superb mastery of brush strokes, because the style requires each element to be stroked on and left alone. There is no blending or refining of the strokes. As the saying goes, "What you see is what you get." Don't be intimidated by this; simply practice the strokes until you are comfortable painting them and then apply the strokes to your project with confidence.

While the painting required for this project may seem complex, it is simply made up of many layered strokes. You will build the design, beginning with the main scrolls, then painting the flowers, and finally adding the details. The Telemark style can incorporate a great deal of detail, but it doesn't have to. The amount of detailing added to a piece is up to the artist, but it is important to make sure that it shows some variety—the motifs should have both dark and light embellishments. When I add details to a piece of Telemark, I usually begin with the darkest color used in the design and then work with lighter colors as needed.

WHAT YOU'LL NEED

Pattern

Page 109

Project

Bentwood box by Woodcrafts *(see page 111 for ordering information)*

Supplies

SURFACE PREP

- #400-grit sandpaper
- Tack cloth
- Basecoat paints: autumn leaves *(rust-colored)*, slate blue *(dusty gray-blue)*, Prussian blue *(see list of artists' acrylics)*

TRACING AND TRANSFERRING

- Tracing paper
- Fine-tip black marker
- Chalk
- Stylus

ARTISTS' ACRYLICS

- Prussian blue
- Burnt umber
- Yellow ocher
- Warm white
- Titanium white

CRAFT ACRYLICS

- Light blue

ACRYLIC MEDIUMS

- Gel retarder

BRUSHES

- Glaze/varnish brush: 1-inch
- Wash brush: 3/4-inch
- Filbert: no. 6
- Flat: no. 8
- Script liner: no. 2

BASIC PAINTING SUPPLIES

- Water container
- Palette knife
- Sta-wet palette
- Paper towels

FINISHING

- Brush-on satin-sheen or semi-gloss polyurethane varnish

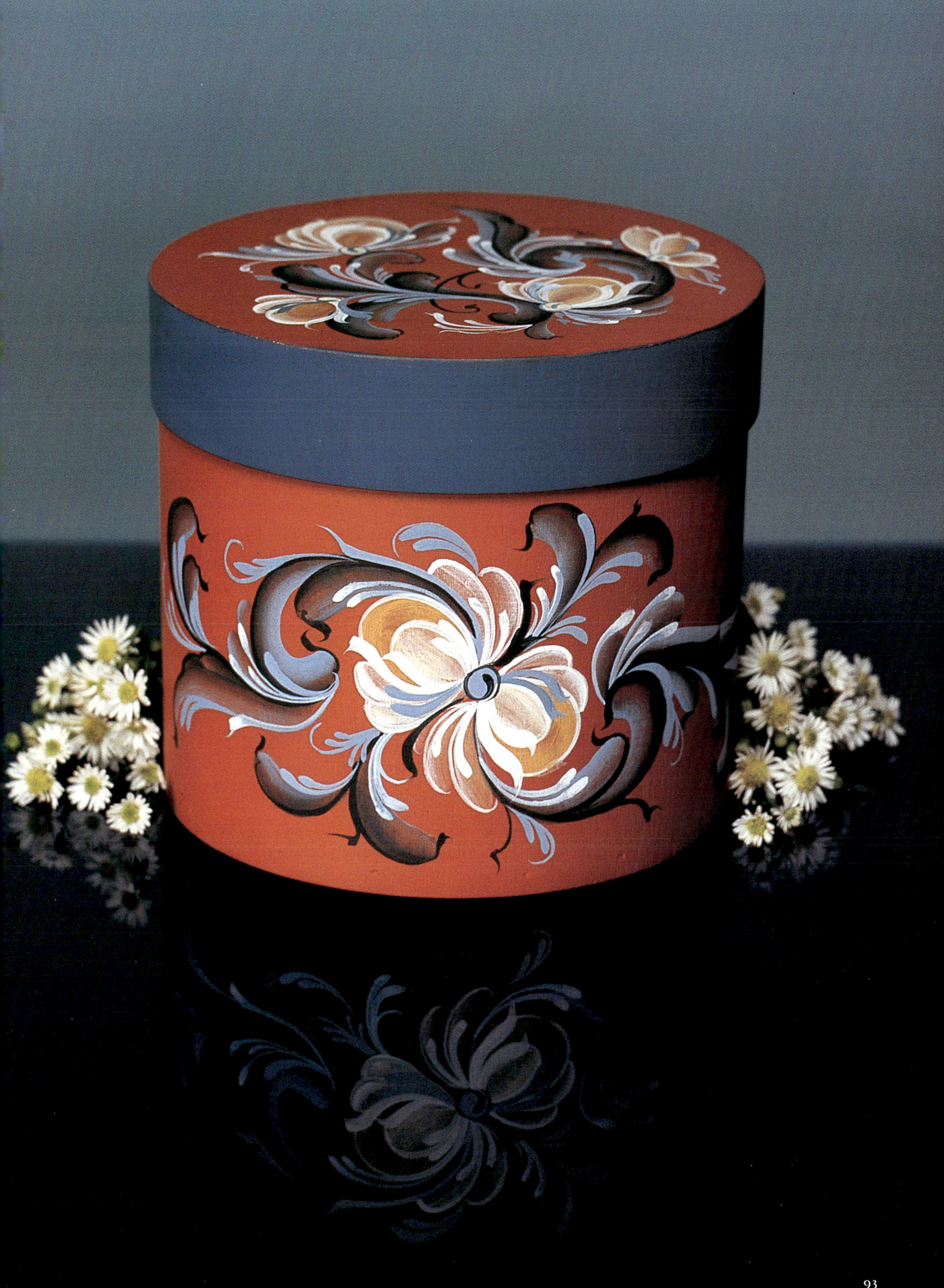

Telemark-Style Rosemaling

GETTING READY

Use the glaze/varnish brush to basecoat the box with autumn leaves. Let dry, then lightly sand the box with fine-grit sandpaper. Apply a second coat of autumn leaves and let dry. Paint the sides of the lid with the wash brush and a mixture of Prussian blue + a bit of slate blue. Let dry.

Trace the pattern following the instructions on page 38, then transfer the most basic outlines to the box using the chalk transfer method. Do not transfer any detail lines; you only want the outlines of the scrolls and the flowers. This will enable you to be freer when painting the details.

SCROLLS

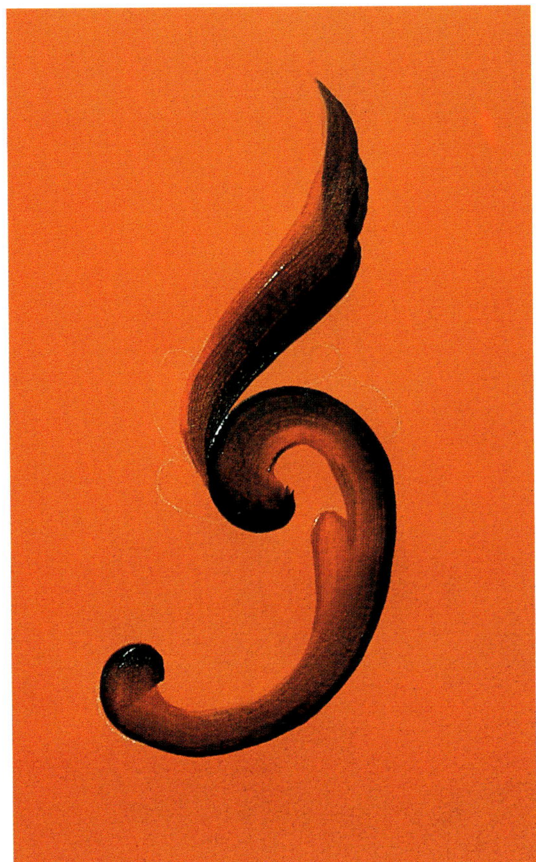

1 Mix a dark blue by combining equal parts of burnt umber + Prussian blue. If you are worried about having enough time to paint the scroll, apply a thin layer of gel retarder with the filbert brush. Then, sideload the brush with the dark blue and gel retarder. There should be a gradual transition from dark blue to a very transparent blue on the other edge of the brush.

Begin by forming the dark side of the scroll. You may start at either end of the scroll and try to paint it in one continuous motion of the brush. If you must, you can restroke the scroll to enhance its curve or make sure that the outside edge is smooth.

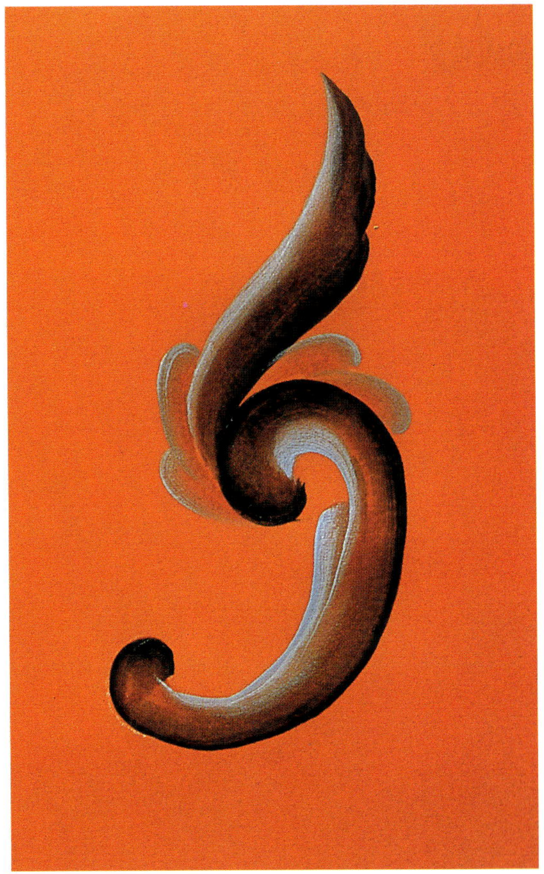

2 Wipe the brush, then reload it with gel and light blue paint. Then, stroke on the other side of the scroll. You should see some of the basecoat color showing through the scroll.

Now add any side scrolls to the design using the same procedure. Let all the scrolls dry.

FLOWERS

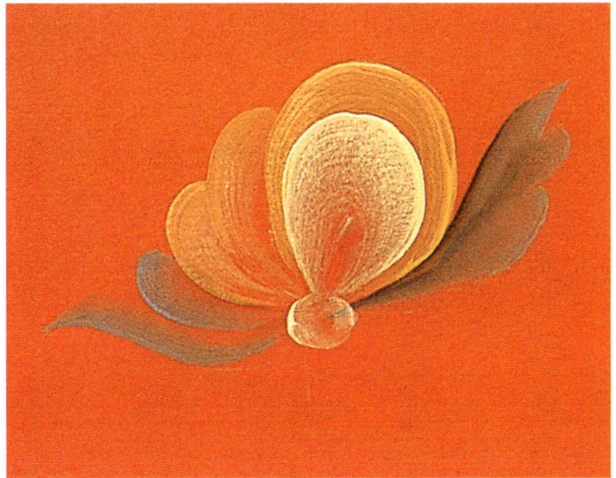

1 Sideload the flat brush with gel retarder and yellow ocher paint. Begin the motif by forming the large oval portion of the flower head. Try to make the oval shape as if you were painting a closed U stroke. The outside edge of the stroke is the most important part. It should have a graceful shape and a nice, clean edge.

Wipe the brush and load it with warm white + just a touch of yellow ocher. Place a second oval inside the first oval on the flower.

Next, paint the flower's outer petals. Use the yellow ocher for some of them and the lighter mixture for the others. It doesn't matter which flowers are which color; what is important is that you have some variety in the design. Don't paint all the flowers alike.

To add interest and variety to the flower forms, paint some blue outer petals on some of the flowers. Use light blue for the majority of these, but you may also want to paint a petal or two with a combination of the dark blue mix and light blue, like the scrolls. Let the flowers dry.

DETAILS

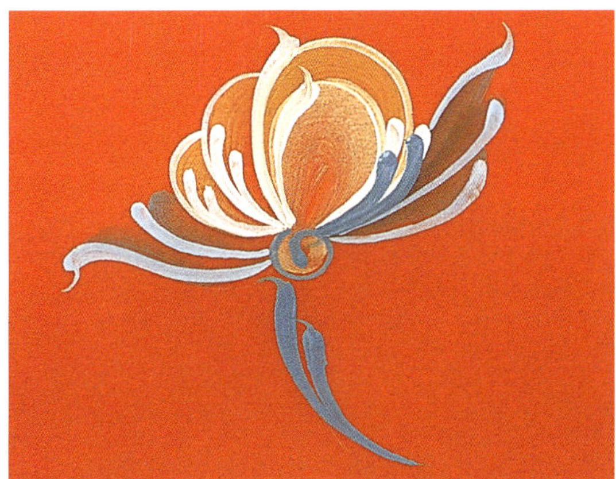

1 Outline the flowers with the script liner loaded with warm white + a touch of yellow ocher. Add teardrops of the white mixture, and then some of light blue, on the blue petals.

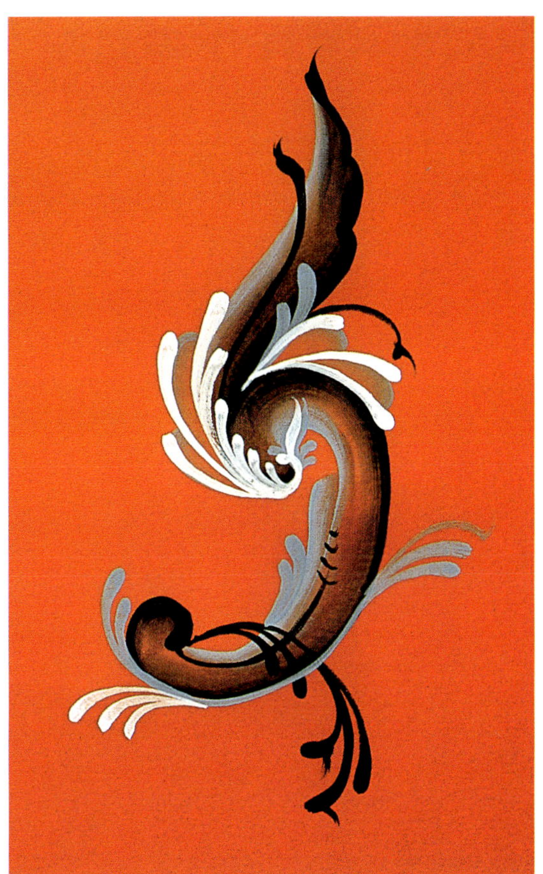

2 To detail the scrolls, use the script liner and the dark blue paint mixture. Thin the paint with water until it has a nice flowing consistency, then use it to add dark outlines. Let some of the outlines fall away from the scroll. The small "hooks" at the ends of some of the outlines are a more modern interpretation. They are made by ending the outline and lifting the brush from the surface not quite all the way at the end of the stroke and then pulling the tip of the brush out of the outline.

After the dark blue details have been added, paint teardrops of light blue, then some tipped teardrops of light blue and titanium white. To have the white show at the end of the teardrop, be sure to load the brush first with titanium white, then wipe the tip and load it with light blue. Let dry.

FINISHING

Finish the box by applying two or three coats of varnish, allowing each coat to dry before applying the next.

Valdres-Style Rosemaling

Degree of Difficulty

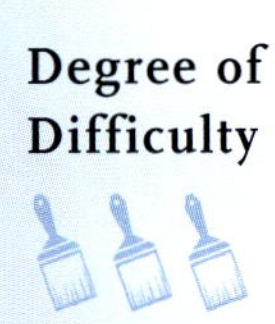

My interpretation of Valdres rosemaling is painted on a traditional Norwegian ale plate. These plates were placed under tankards of ale to protect the furniture. This project is painted using a rather simple technique combining areas of wet-on-wet painting and other areas painted with a sideloading technique. When working wet-in-wet, remember to work quickly so that the paint doesn't dry before you finish. I hope you enjoy this "free-form" design.

WHAT YOU'LL NEED

Pattern

Page 110

Project

Ale plate from Wayne's Wooden Ware *(see page 111 for ordering information)*

Supplies

SURFACE PREP

#400-grit sandpaper
Tack cloth
Basecoat paints: Prussian blue and Payne's gray *(see list of artists' acrylics)*

TRACING AND TRANSFERRING

Tracing paper
Fine-tip black marker
Chalk
Stylus

ARTISTS' ACRYLICS

Hauser green dark
Green umber
Prussian blue
Payne's gray
Light red oxide
Yellow ocher
Warm white
Burnt sienna
Raw sienna
Raw umber
Turner's yellow
Titanium white

ACRYLIC MEDIUMS

Gel retarder

BRUSHES

Glaze/varnish brush: 1-inch
Round: no. 4
Script liner: no. 2
Flats: nos. 8 and 10
Filbert: no. 6

BASIC PAINTING SUPPLIES

Water container
Palette knife
Sta-wet palette
Paper towels

FINISHING

Brush-on satin-sheen or semi-gloss polyurethane varnish

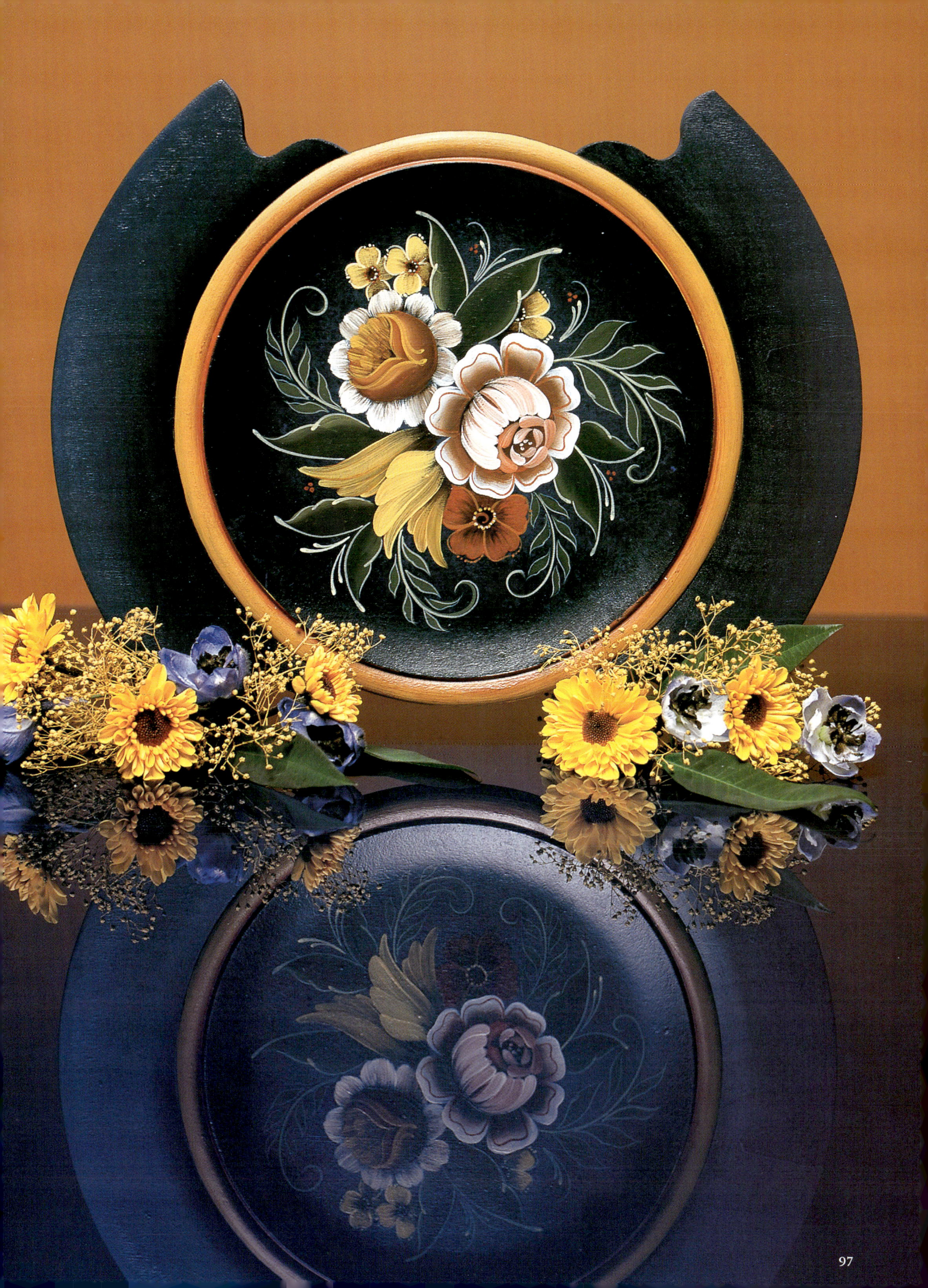

Valdres-Style Rosemaling

GETTING READY

Basecoat the ale plate using the glaze/varnish brush and a mixture of Prussian blue + a bit of Payne's gray. Let dry.

Lightly sand the plate and apply a second coat. Allow to dry completely.

Using the round brush, paint the bead with yellow ocher. You will need to apply two coats in order to achieve opaque paint coverage. Let dry.

Transfer the main design elements using the chalk method shown on page 40.

LEAVES

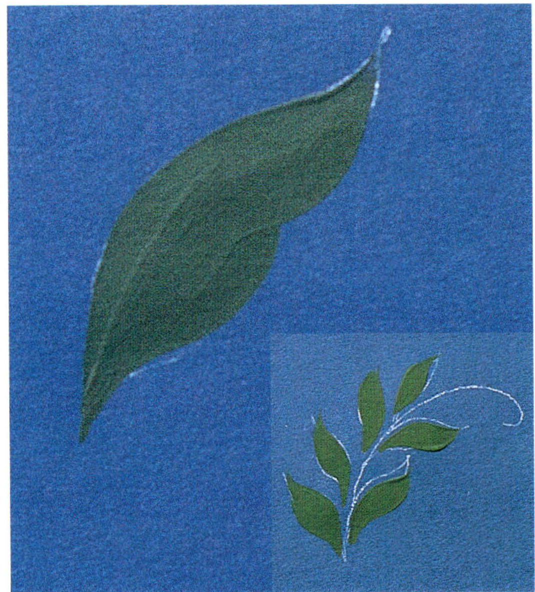

1 Use the no. 8 flat brush to undercoat the leaves with a mixture of Hauser green dark + greenish umber. Try to keep your brush strokes very smooth. Let dry.

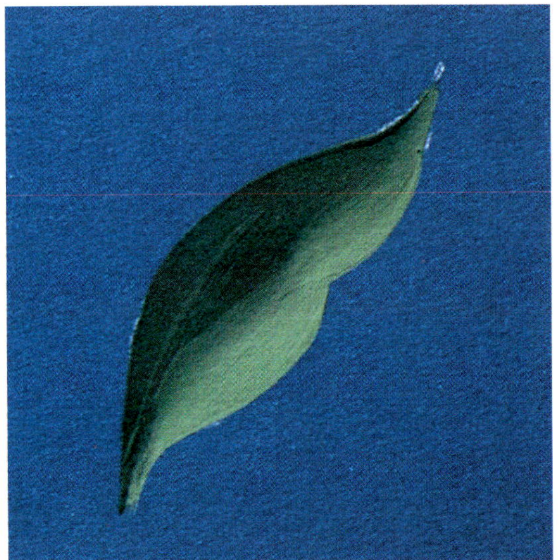

2 To highlight the leaves, begin by doubleloading the no. 8 flat with the undercoat green and Turner's yellow. The coloration of the leaves should be subtle, so make sure the yellow isn't too bright. If it is, simply touch the brush into the green and blend on the palette—the green will soften the yellow. Stroke two highlights on the side of the leaf with the bulges. Beginning at the bottom, stroke the first highlight, then move up the leaf and apply the second highlight. Do not highlight the small leaves at all. Let dry.

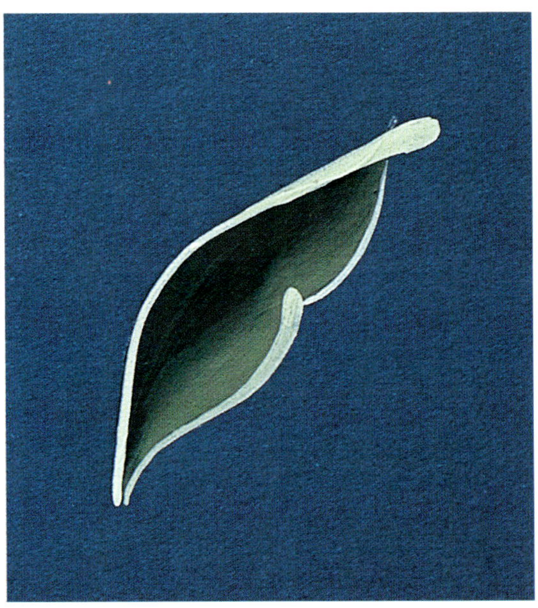

3 Outline the leaves with teardrops of a light yellow-green made by mixing titanium white + a tad of the undercoat green + a touch of yellow ocher.

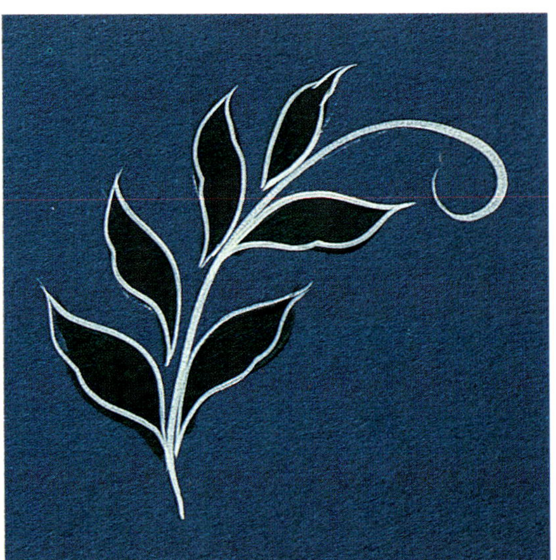

4 With this same yellow-green mixture, outline the small leaves and paint the stems.

LARGE RED AND SMALL YELLOW BLOSSOMS

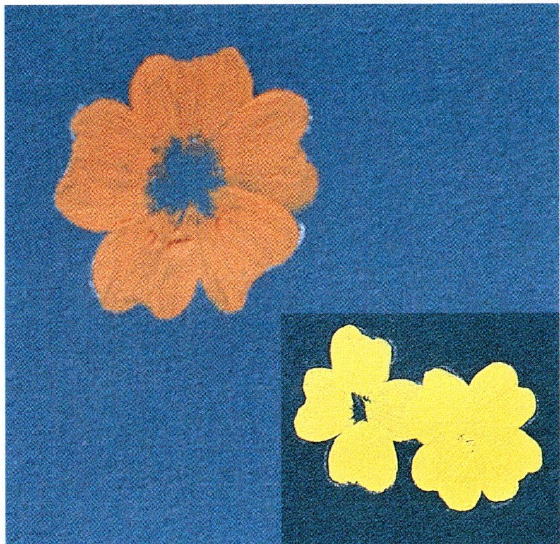

1 Undercoat the small blossoms with yellow ocher using the filbert brush. Also using the filbert, undercoat the large blossom with raw sienna. Form each petal with two strokes, and be sure that the ends of the petals have a nice ruffled look to them. You may need to apply two coats in order to achieve opaque paint coverage. Let dry.

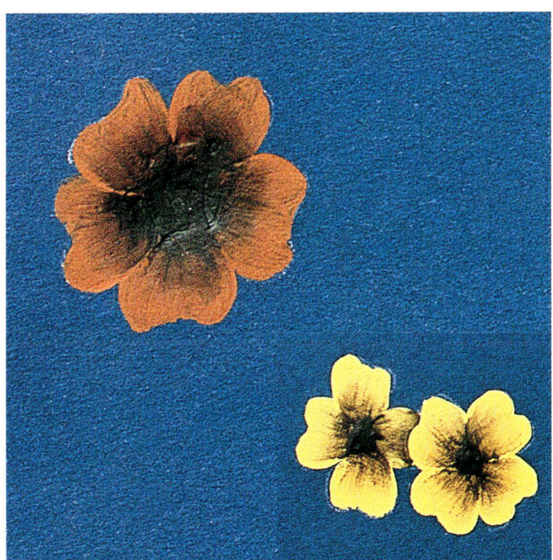

2 Shade all of the blossoms with a flat brush sideloaded with raw umber. The shading should fill in the center of the blossoms and gently be carried up into the petals. Let dry.

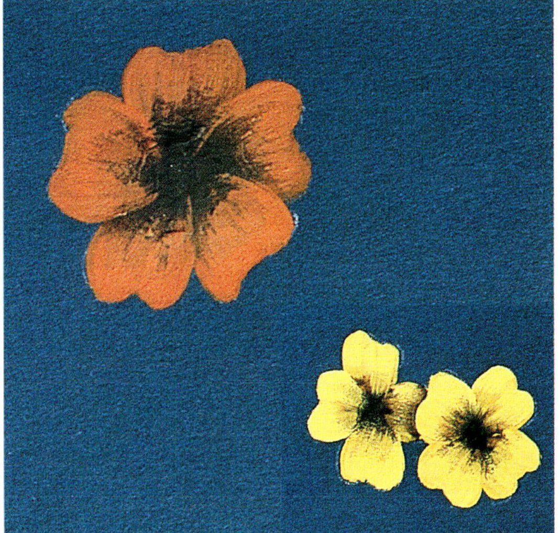

3 Apply two layers of highlights to the small blossoms. First, pick up some yellow ocher on the filbert and stroke over the original undercoat strokes. Then repeat the highlighting with yellow ocher + Turner's yellow. Let dry.

For the large blossom, use the filbert brush with light red oxide paint. Pull the highlights from the outside edge of the petal in toward the center. Do not cover the shading that you applied earlier. Let dry.

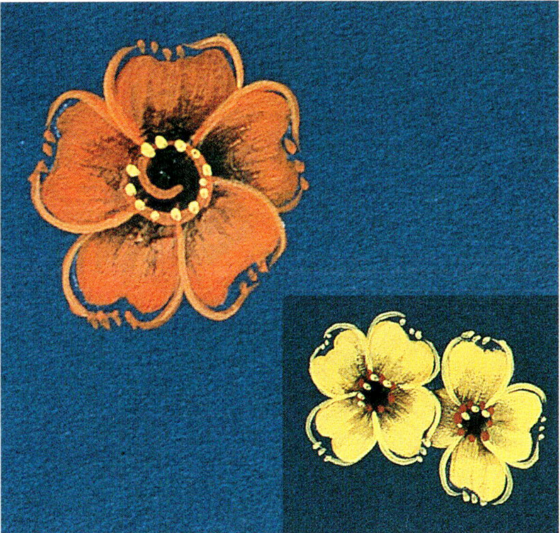

4 Use the script liner and Turner's yellow to add some detailing to the small blossoms. Make a broken outline around the petals and fill in with yellow dots. For the center of each blossom, use thinned light red oxide applied with the script liner. Then add a crescent of Turner's yellow dots.

For the red blossom, use light red oxide + yellow ocher to make the same kind of broken outline with dots. In the center of the flower, paint a spiral line of light red oxide, then add a ring of yellow ocher dots.

TULIPS

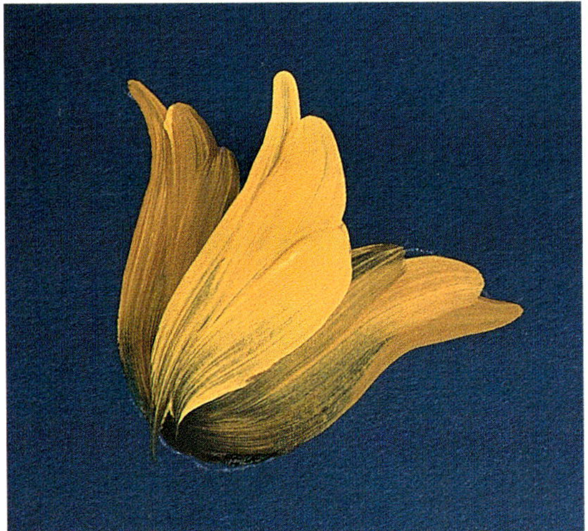

1 Using the no. 8 flat, undercoat the tulip with gel retarder. Next, sideload the brush with raw umber and apply shading across the base of the tulip about halfway up the flower's petals. Because you are using a sideloaded brush, the paint you apply to the tulip shape will automatically display a graduation of shading.

While the gel is wet, load the round brush with raw sienna and stroke on the outside petals. Do not reload the brush with each stroke. The object is to create a series of strokes that allow the umber shading to be slightly visible.

Continuing to paint into the wet gel, pick up some yellow ocher on the brush and stroke over the top petal to highlight it even more.

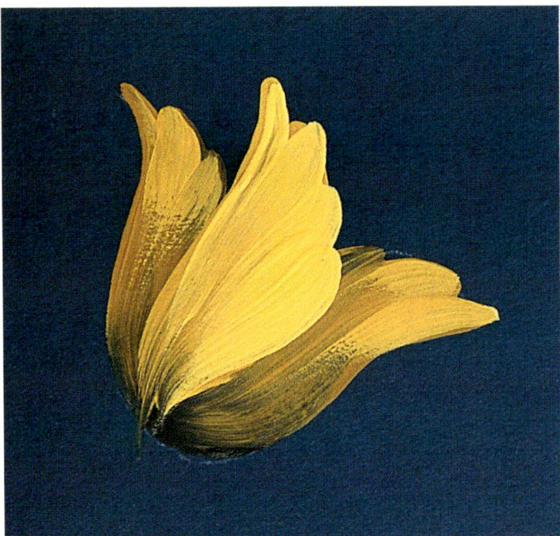

2 While the tulip is still wet, paint the final highlight. Load the round brush with yellow ocher + Turner's yellow and restroke the front petal to make it lighter and brighter. If the side petals seem a bit dark to you, you can add some fresh yellow ocher overstrokes to them. Let dry.

GOLDEN ROSE

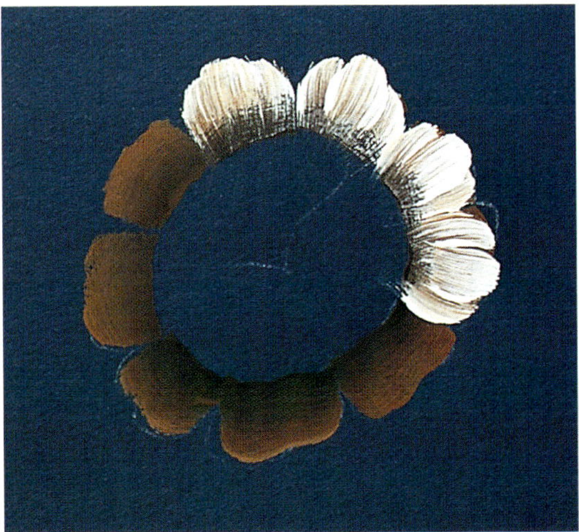

1 Begin by painting the outside petals of the rose one at a time. You will be working wet-in-wet. Doubleload the no. 8 flat with burnt sienna and raw umber and stroke on a scalloped stroke. While the scalloped stroke is wet, load the filbert with warm white and apply three strokes to the petal. Place one stroke on the right and one on the left, then reload the brush and place a third stroke in the center. Repeat the procedure for each petal. Let dry.

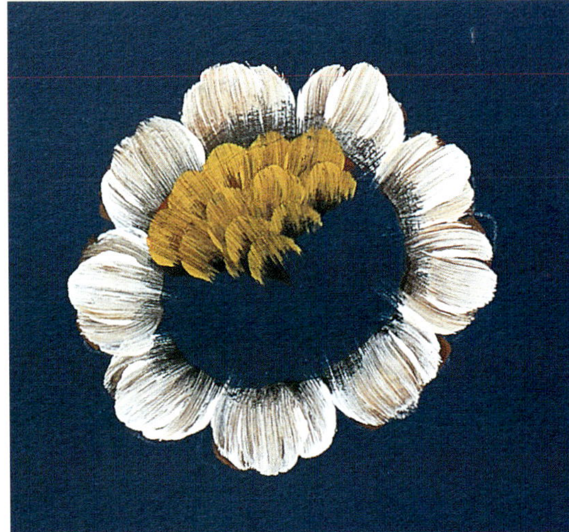

2 Next, paint the back of the rose, again working wet-in-wet. Undercoat the throat of the rose with burnt sienna. Doubleload the flat brush with burnt sienna and burnt umber and shade the throat of the rose. While the paint is wet, load the filbert with yellow ocher and form a row of pull strokes across the top of the rose. Place a second row of pull strokes directly underneath, and continue painting pull strokes until the center of the rose is filled in. Let dry.

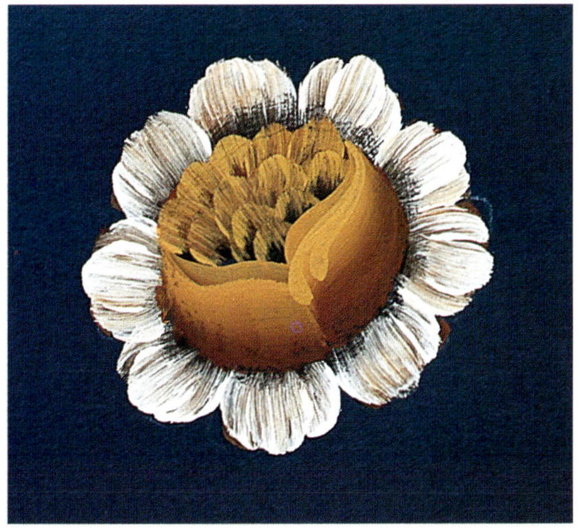

3 To paint the front of the rose, begin by doubleloading the no. 8 flat brush with yellow ocher and burnt sienna. Apply two S strokes to form the first "bowl" of the rose. Let dry. Doubleload the brush the same way and paint two more S strokes just below the first two. Wipe the brush, then doubleload it with burnt sienna and raw umber. Apply a U stroke to form the bottom of the bowl of the rose and let dry.

Finish the motif by painting two teardrops of yellow ocher across one side of the bowl of the rose. Let dry.

WHITE ROSE

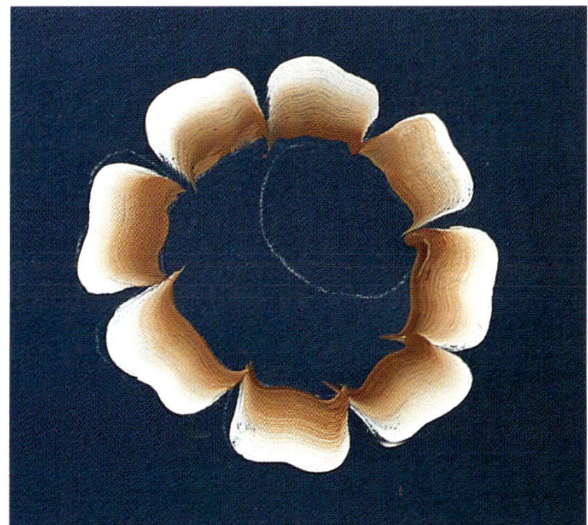

1 Doubleload the no. 8 flat brush with titanium white and burnt sienna. Then stroke the sienna side of the brush through raw umber. With the brush loaded like this, paint scalloped strokes along the outside edge of the rose. You may need to go over this stroke several times to get good coverage. If you aren't able to get complete coverage, paint all of the strokes, let them dry, then go over them a second time. Let dry.

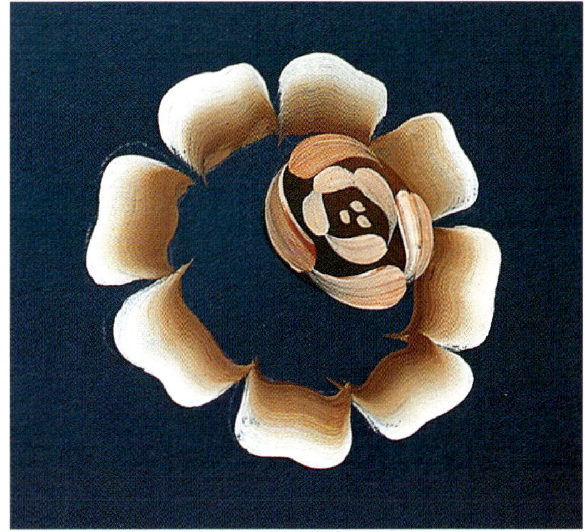

2 Paint the throat of the rose pink using the wet-in-wet technique. Undercoat it with light red oxide and shade the bottom with raw umber. While this is wet, load the round brush with titanium white and make small comma strokes in a spiral beginning at the outside edge and working inward. Finish the center by placing a few white dots in the center of the spiral. Let dry.

The front of the rose is also painted wet-in-wet. Begin by doubleloading the no. 10 flat brush with light red oxide and raw umber and forming a U stroke across the front of the rose. Make sure to paint right up to the outside petals. While this stroke is wet, load the round brush with titanium white and paint a series of vertical comma strokes from the top of the bowl toward the bottom. Be sure the strokes conform to the shape of the rose, curving to the right on the right side and to the left on the left side (they should be somewhat straight in the center). If you like, you can restroke the front of the rose with stronger titanium white. Let dry.

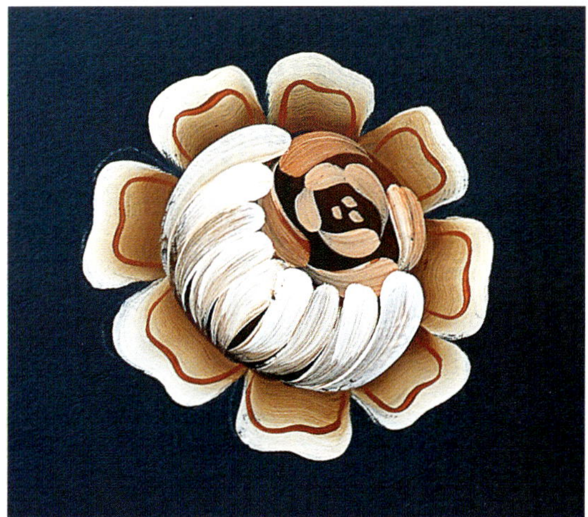

3 Load the script liner with light red oxide and paint a scalloped line on each of the outside petals.

FINISHING

Finish the design by adding a few teardrops of titanium white + the leaf undercoat green + a touch of yellow ocher near the leaves. Add a few clusters of three dots of light red oxide.

To shade the plate's bead, sideload the no. 8 flat with gel retarder and light red oxide and apply to the inner edge of the bead. Let dry.

Finish the ale plate by applying two or three coats of varnish, letting each one dry before applying the next.

Patterns

NARROW BOAT PAINTING

Project instructions are on pages 46–51. Use the tracing at same size. See pages 38–40 for detailed instructions on tracing and transferring patterns.

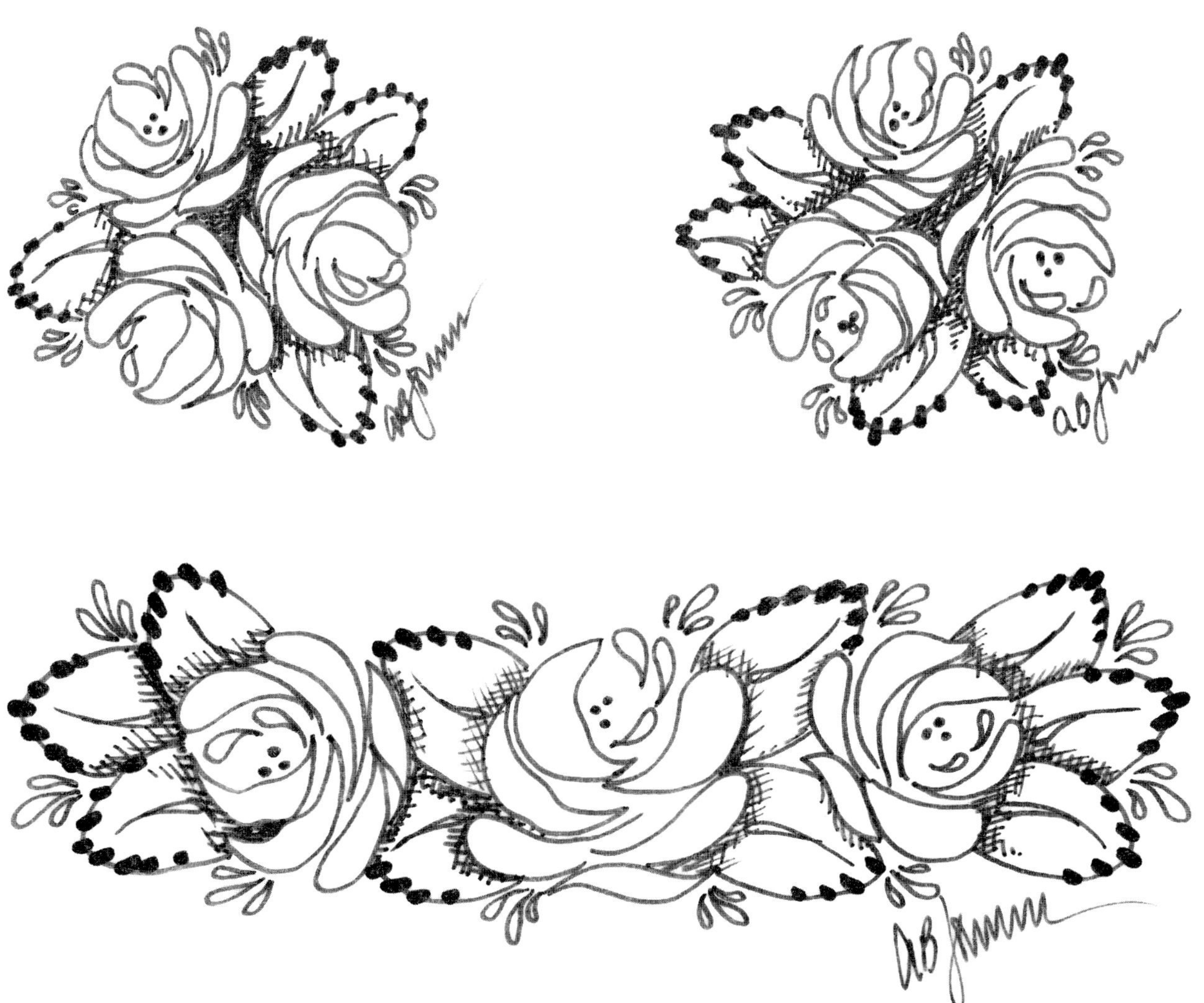

BAUERNMALEREI

Project instructions are on pages 52–57. Use the tracing at 118%. See pages 38–40 for detailed instructions on tracing and transferring patterns.

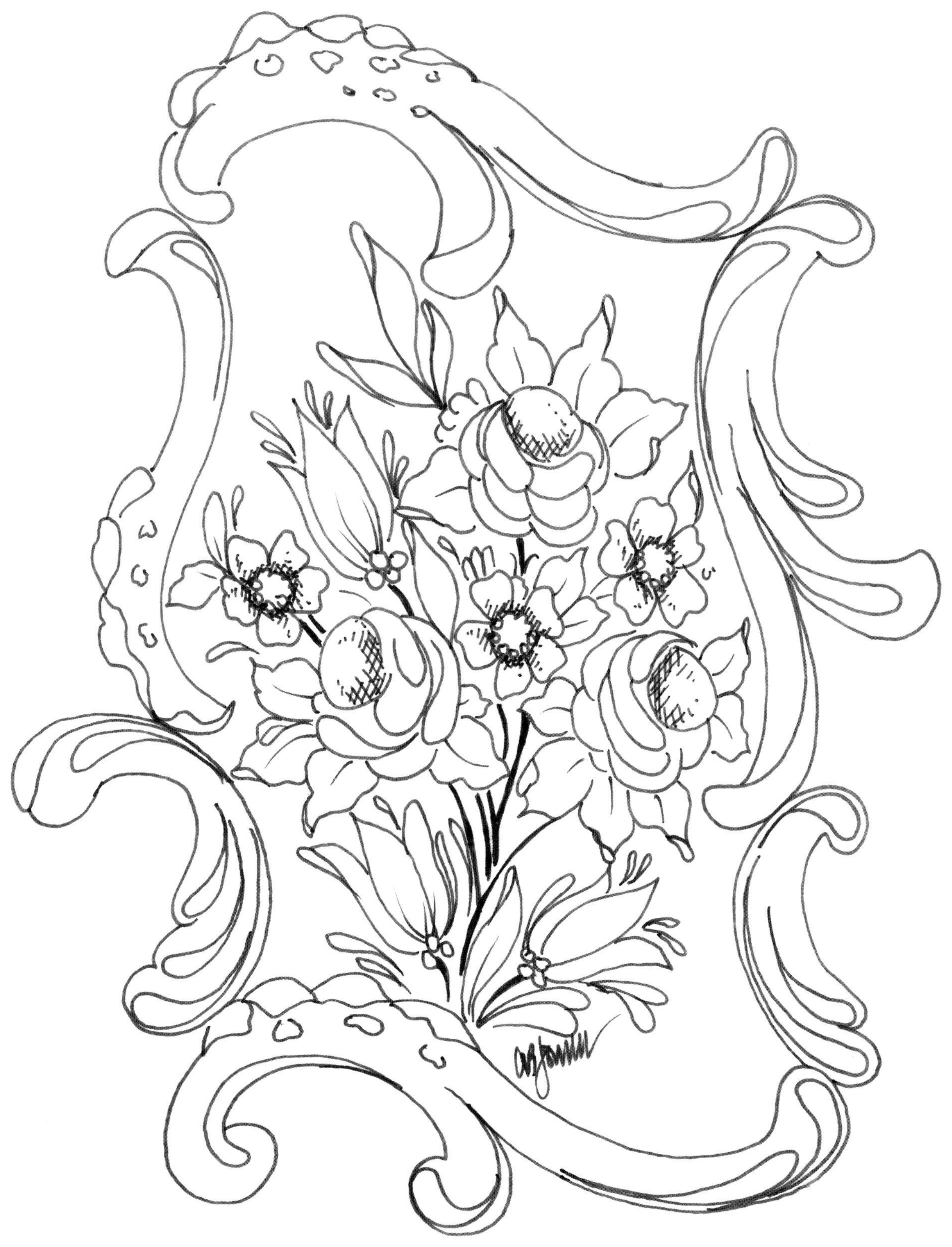

ASSENDELFTER

Project instructions are on pages 58–63. Use the tracing at same size. See pages 38–40 for detailed instructions on tracing and transferring patterns.

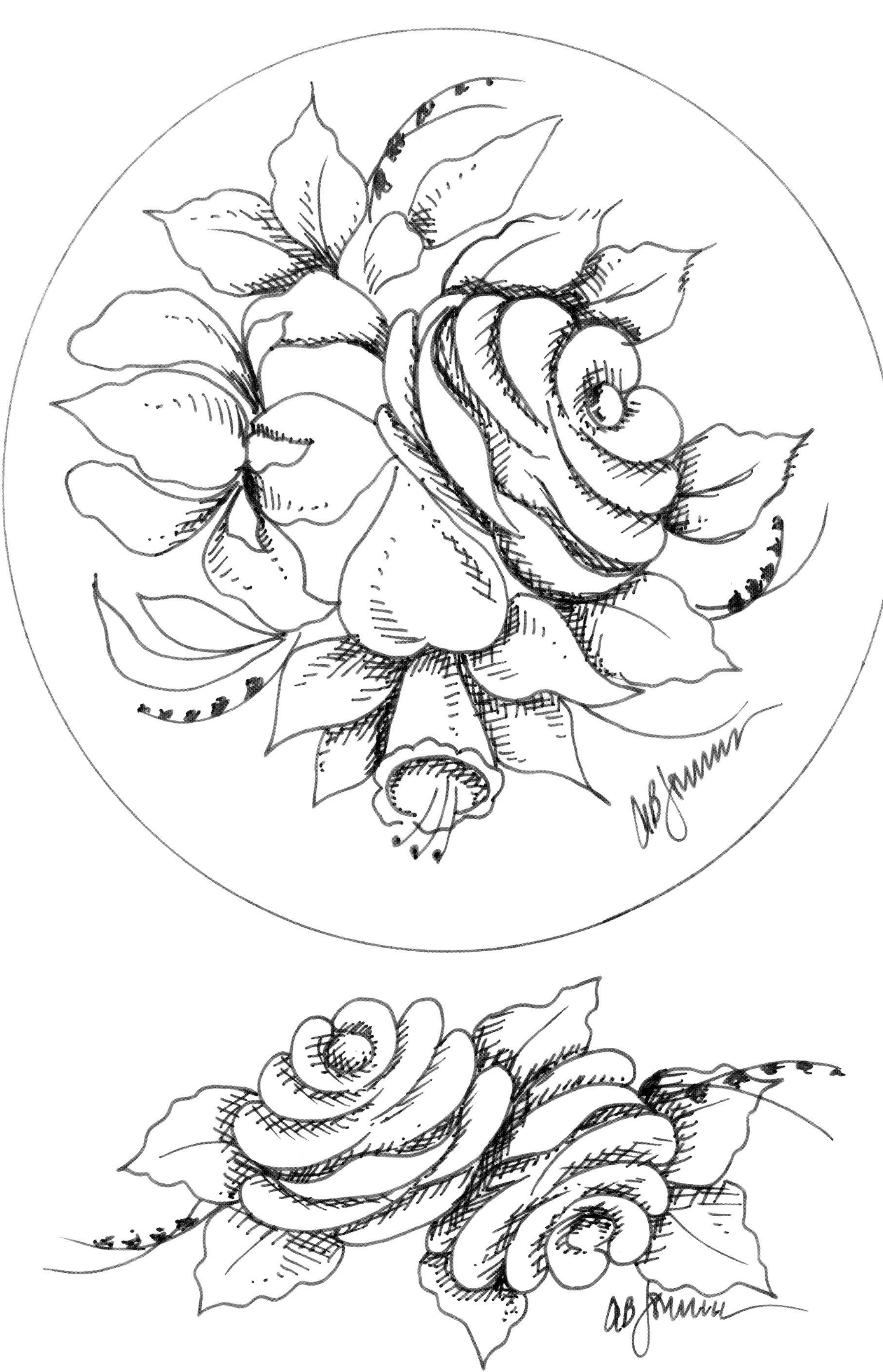

HINDELOOPEN

Project instructions are on pages 64–71. Use the tracing at 110%. See pages 38–40 for detailed instructions on tracing and transferring patterns.

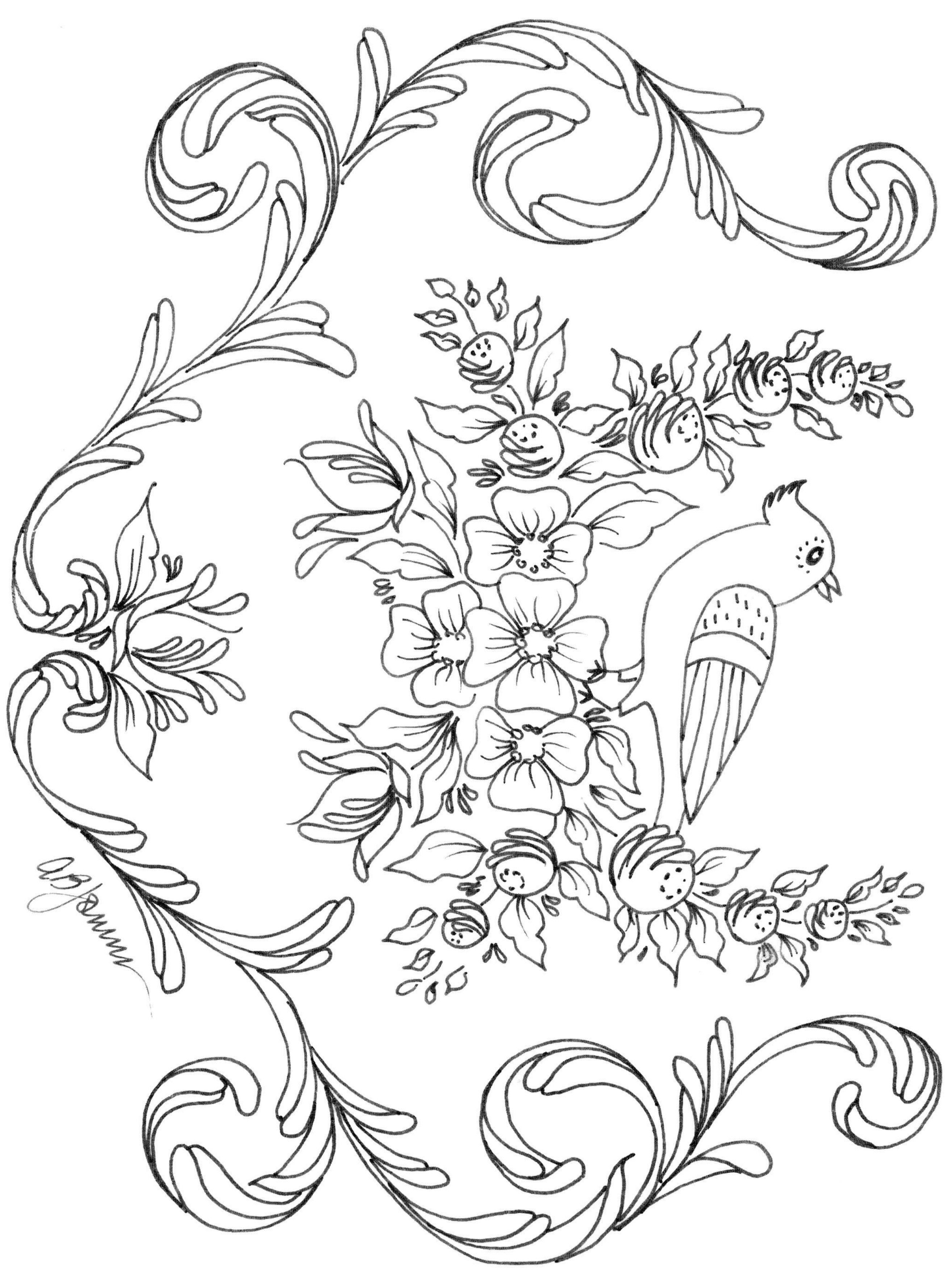

GZHEL

Project instructions are on pages 72–75. I recommend that you sketch the design freehand, but if you choose to transfer it, use the tracing at 143%. See pages 38–40 for detailed instructions on tracing and transferring patterns.

MSTERA

Project instructions are on pages 76–79. Use the tracing at same size. See pages 38–40 for detailed instructions on tracing and transferring patterns.

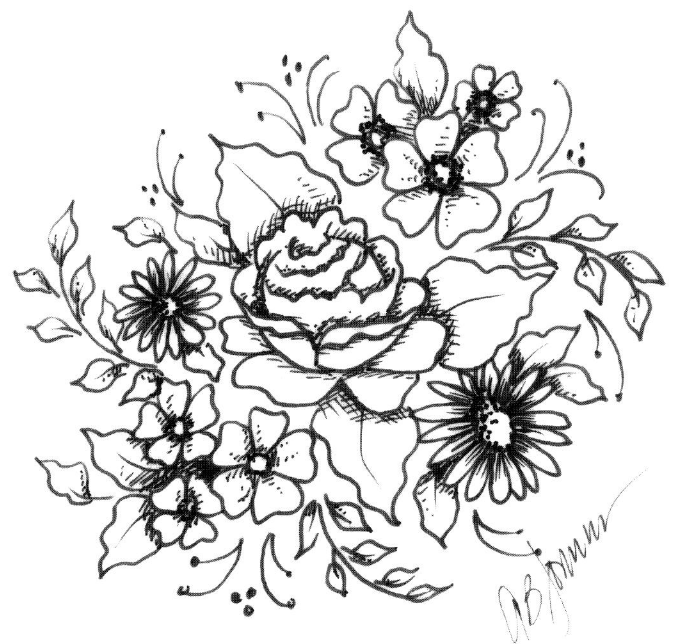

ZHOSTOVO

Project instructions are on pages 80–85. Use the tracing at 118%. See pages 38–40 for detailed instructions on tracing and transferring patterns.

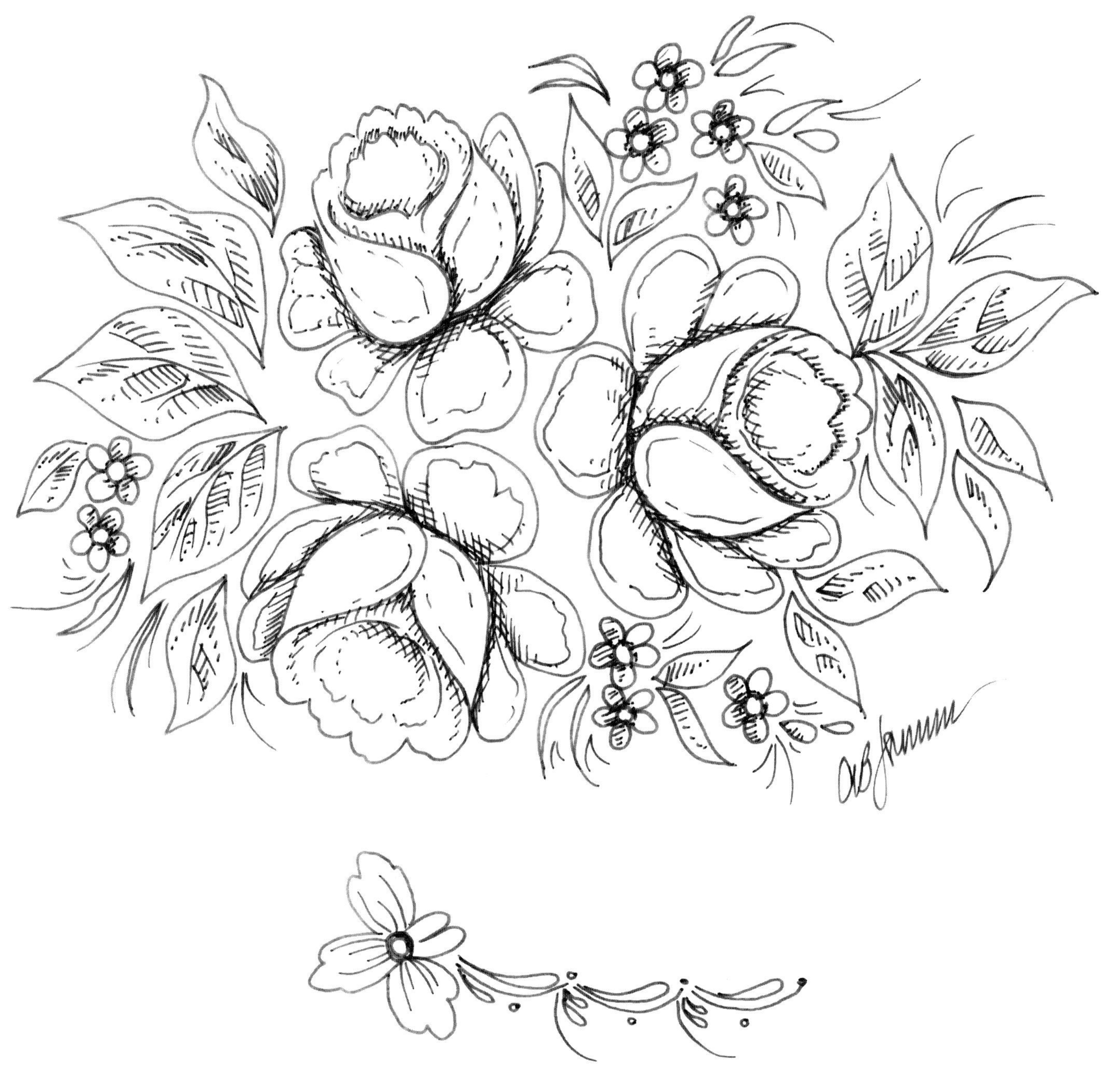

ROGALAND-STYLE ROSEMALING

Project instructions are on pages 86–91. Use the tracing at 105%. See pages 38–40 for detailed instructions on tracing and transferring patterns.

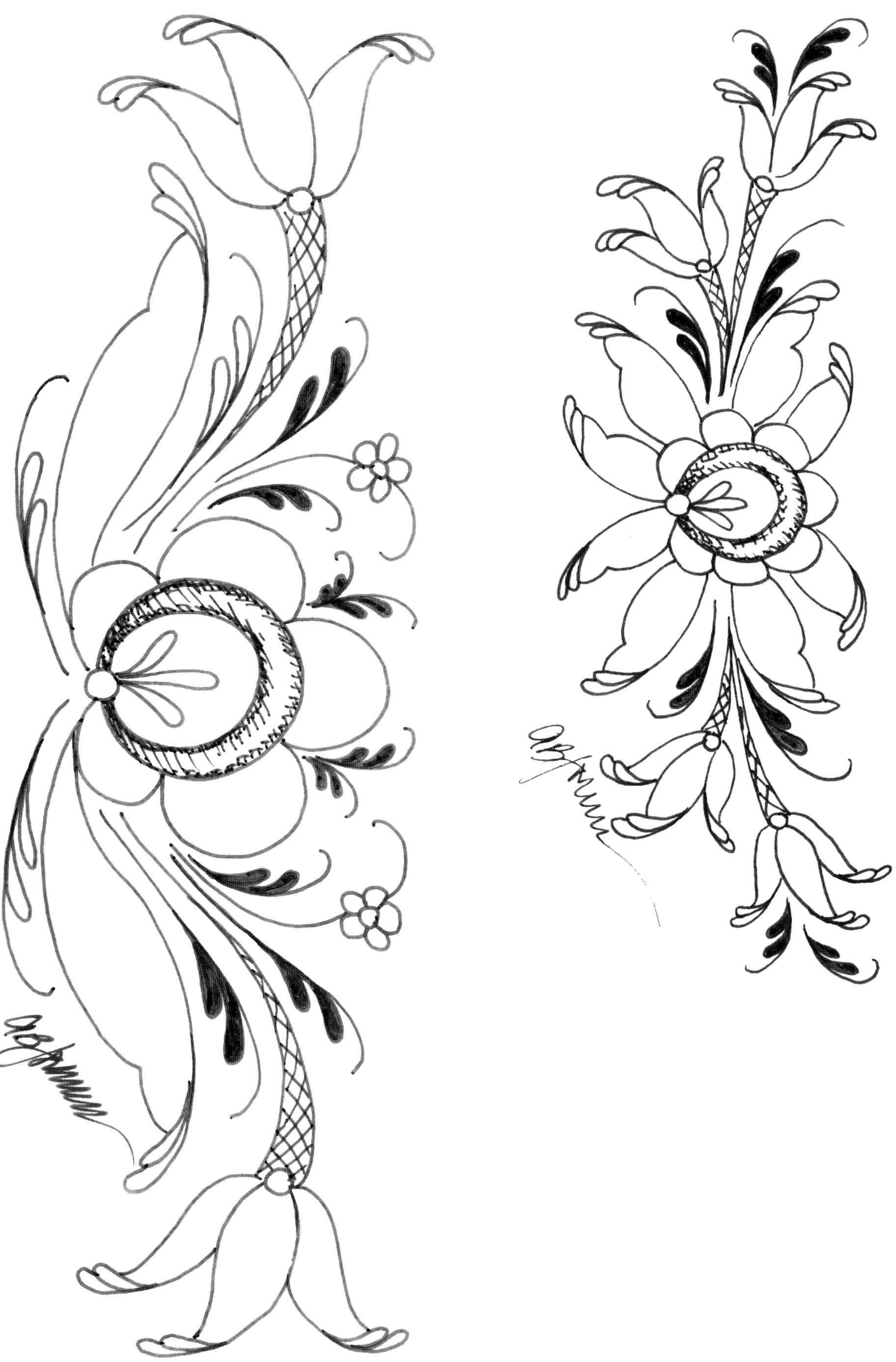

TELEMARK-STYLE ROSEMALING

Project instructions are on pages 92–95. Use the tracing at 125%. See pages 38–40 for detailed instructions on tracing and transferring patterns.

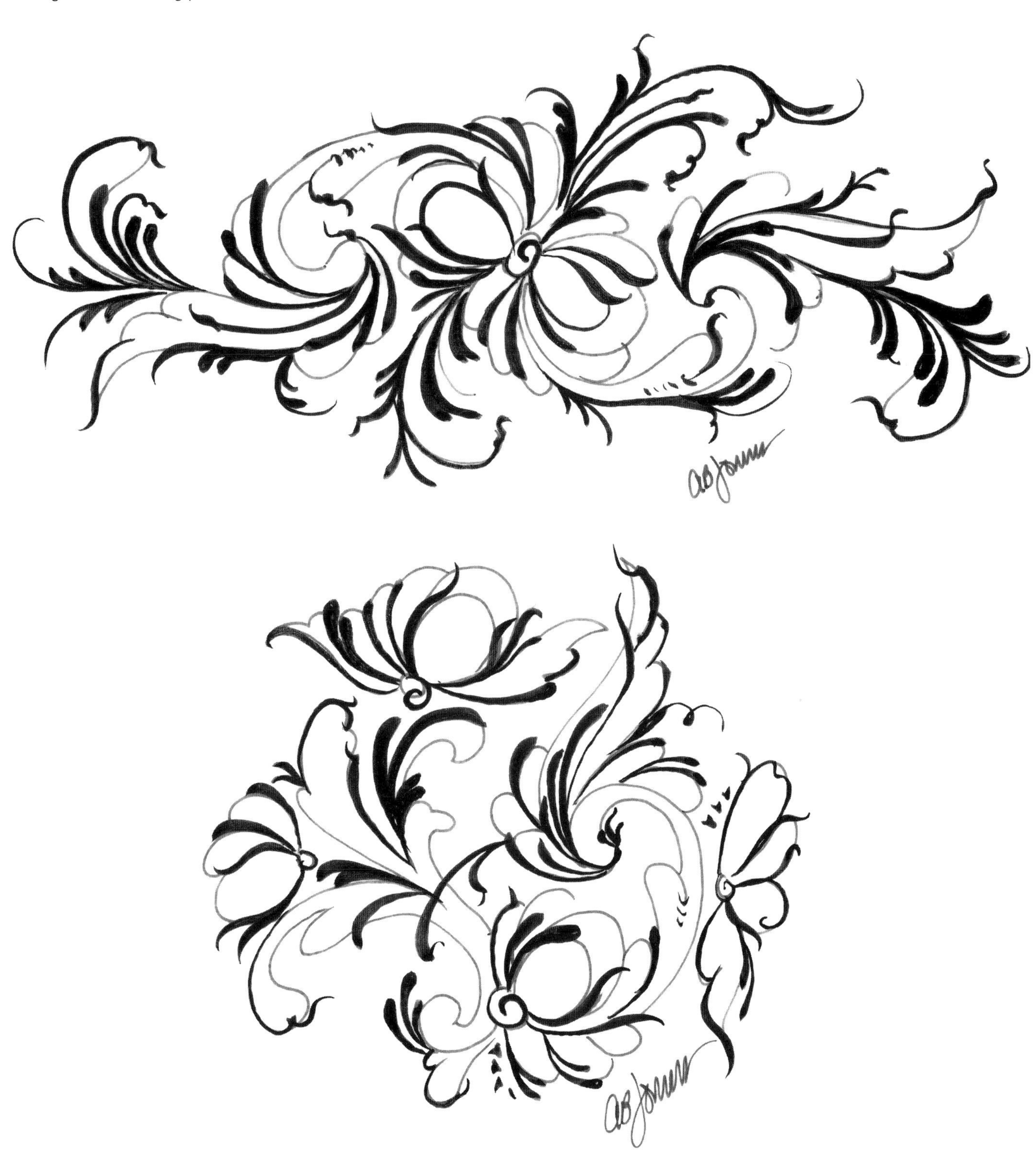

VALDRES-STYLE ROSEMALING

Project instructions are on pages 96–101. Use the tracing at 118%. See pages 38–40 for detailed instructions on tracing and transferring patterns.

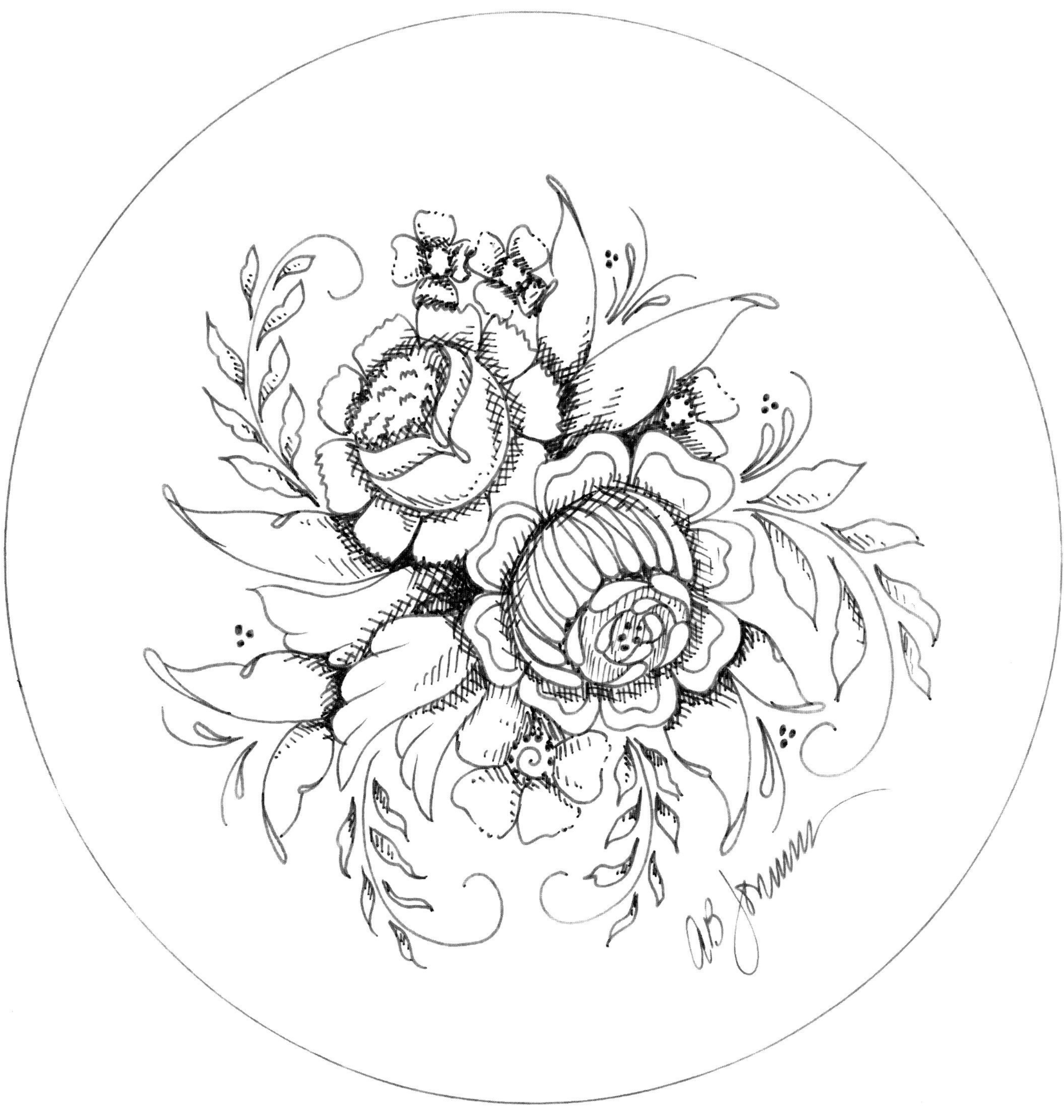

Source Directory

The following is a list of sources for the supplies and projects that are used in this book. The supplies can be purchased at most art supply and craft stores nationwide. If you're interested in purchasing any of the projects, simply contact the company at the address listed below. Note that many of the project manufacturers will send catalogs of their product lines upon request.

SUPPLIES

PLAID ENTERPRISES, INC.
Attn: Customer Service
P.O. Box 2835
Norcross, GA 30091-2835
(800) 842-4197
http://plaidonline.com/
Acrylic paints and other decorative painting materials and supplies

SILVER BRUSH LIMITED
P.O. Box 414
Windsor, New Jersey 08561-0414
http://www.silverbrush.com/
Artist-quality brushes for decorative painting, stenciling, and faux finishing

PROJECTS

BARB WATSON'S BRUSHWORKS
P.O. Box 1467
Moreno Valley, CA 92556
(909) 653-3780
http://www.barbwatson.com/
Zhostovo project: rectangular Chippendale tray (see pages 80–85)

CUSTOM WOODS BY DALLAS
2204 Martha Hulbert Drive
Lapeer, Michigan 48446
(800) 251-7154
Bauernmalerei project: herb cabinet (see pages 52–57)

LOLA GILL
Pleases Farmhouse
Stockleigh Pomeroy
Devon EX17 4AU
UK
(01363) 866369
Narrow boat painting project: miniature buckby (see pages 46–51)

J.C.'S POUR 'N MORE
407 Main
Spearville, Kansas 67876
(316) 385-2627
Gzhel project: teapot with hole (see pages 72–75)

PCM STUDIOS
731 Highland Avenue N.E. - Suite D
Atlanta, Georgia 30312
(404) 222-0348
http://creativehomepainting.com/
Mstera project: ball box (see pages 76–79)

VALHALLA DESIGNS
343 Twin Pines Drive
Glendale, Oregon 97442
(541) 832-3260
Assendelfter project: butterfly box (see pages 58–63)
Hindeloopen project: oval Hindeloopen tray (see pages 64–71)
Rogaland-style rosemaling project: medium tine (see pages 86–91)

WAYNE'S WOODENWARE
1913 State Road 150
Neenah, Wisconsin 54956
(800) 840-1497
Valdres-style rosemaling project: ale plate (see pages 96–101)

WOODCRAFTS
P.O. Box 78
Hwy 67W
Bicknell, Indiana 47512-0078
(812) 735-4829
Telemark-style rosemaling project: bentwood box (see pages 92–95)

Index